Real Barbecue

Greg Johnson and Vince Staten

REAL BARBECUE

Harper & Row, Publishers ○ New York

Cambridge, Philadelphia, San Francisco, Washington, London,

1817 Mexico City, São Paulo, Singapore, Sydney

To Chris and Kris, no relation

And to Dad

FIRST EDITION

Designer: Ruth Bornschlegel
Copyeditor: Shelly Perron
Indexer: Sayre Van Young

Library of Congress Cataloging-in-Publication Data
Johnson, Greg.
    Real barbecue.

    Includes index.
    1. Barbecue cookery.   2. Restaurants, lunchrooms,
etc.—United States—Directories.   I. Staten, Vince,
1947-   . II. Title.
TX840.B3J64   1988   641.7'6   87-46149
ISBN 0-06-096267-4 (pbk.)

88   89   90   91   92   RRD   10   9   8   7   6   5   4   3   2   1

Contents

Acknowledgments

No book is an island. If it were, you'd have to pay a lot more for it, plus closing costs and points. We had the help of a great many people in researching and writing this book. A great, great many.

We'd like to acknowledge and thank Maureen Brown, our never-tiring research assistant; Susan Johnson, one of our long-suffering wives; Judy Staten, the other one; Margie Staten, who always believed; Margaret Johnson, who really prefers roast beef; Chris Wohlwend, who introduced us to the lady who turned this project from a burnt end into a main course; Kris Dahl, that lady; and Hugh Van Dusen, our editor.

We would also like to acknowledge Will Staten for being as understanding as any four-year-old could have been when Daddy couldn't play because he had to work on his barbecue book; and Juliet Johnson, who learned to love ribs for the first time at Guy & Mae's Tavern.

Our thanks also to Carla Thomas, Adam Guenther, Dawn Dawson, Bruce and Rosie Haney, J.B. and Nona Brown, Herb and Walter Shankel, Gary Burbank, Bob and Karen Moody, John Raven, Carolyn Wells, Judy Wimberly, John "Ribs and Wrigley Field" Hughes, Ardie Davis, "Daddy-O" John Sharpe and Jaime, Michael Coers, Marty Bass, Ann Kellan, Bob and Bev Jones, Matt Mirapaul, David McGinty (who is just another name in a list), Luther and Esther Shanks, Sara Tucker and Patrick Husted, Tom and Marsha McNeer, Tom Jester, Grady Clay, Johnny Maupin, Tom and Judy Poe, Robin Beard (America's number one barbecue lover), Rusty Brashear (we knew him when he was Russ), Jay and Lois Hunt, Edith Huffman, Bill and Margaret Huffman, Andy and Charlotte Smith, Wilson Browning, Kevin and Dana Browning, Jim and Carrie Shanks, Elaine Shanks, Herb and Linda Shanks, Bic and Melanie Berney, Rodney Irvin for the surf, Sarah Fritschner, Margy Clark for keeping the barbecue chain letter going, Becky Masters, Rick Patterson, John Hitt, Bob Edwards, and Verta Mae Grovenor.

And to Tom Atkinson, George and Janice Gillis, Roger and Judy Carter, Nancy Pridemore, David Inman, Jena Monahan, Tommy O'Brien, Michael O'Brien, Elizabeth Owen, Dennis Sigman, Beth Polson, George Larrimore, Paul Skolnik, Jim Dodson, Barry Farber, Mildred Flack, Kathy Flack, Lewis and Debbie Flack, Dan and Leslie Pomeroy, Frank and Kathy Gibson, Mike and Cindy Toth, Sherman Toth, Matt and Debbie Toth, Powell and Caryl Toth, Paul and Elsie Toth, Amy and Eddie Booth, Carrie Toth, Jerry and Carol Toner, Dick

Kaukas for Big Bubba, Arlene Jacobson, Glen Kenny, Deborah Bowditch for a complete report from Denver, Valerie Marks, Ken Arendt, Jim Morgan, Bobby and Pat Stallard, Pam Sprague, Bill Kight, Tom Wiseman, Ernie Slone for wire-watching, Bobby Rowan, and Richard Zacks.

And to Les Whitely, Deni Hamilton, Leonard Pardue, Don Seaver, Don Delaurin, Jim Reed, Milly Lemajich of the Restaurant Consulting Group, Dan Rubin, Scottie Martin, Bob Harris, Dennis Rogers, Mike Jones, Smoky Hale, Joe Peterson, Chip Nold, Raymond Gibson, Valerie Elmore, Ed McClanahan, Bob Hill, Jeff Puckett, Shane Best, Donnie Welch, Thelma Tabler, Carol Burch, Al Futtrell, Charlie Willard, Walter Chapin, Erica Rauzin, Matt Fisher, Keith Williams, Pat McDonogh and Jeri McDonogh, Mr. and Mrs. Lawson Safley, Charles and Charyl Safley, Sheriff Bev McClendon, and the helpful folks at the *Tompkinsville News.*

And to the barbecue taste-test crew: Maureen McNerney, Elmer Hall, Cindy Inskeep, Warren Payne, Martha Elson, Bill Norton, Linda Watkins, Mike Haralson, Leslie Ellis, Linda Stahl, Angie Partee, Ellie Brecher, C. Ray Hall, Marc Norton, Steve Sebree, Charitey Simmons, Diane Heilenman, Andy Adler, Ira Simmons, Jane Fleischaker and Alice Colombo. Each week for four months they unselfishly gave of their lunch hours to taste sauces and sandwiches we brought back from all over the country.

And to Dr. Steve Wheeler who kept us in the healthful zone, Ronni Lundy who kept the beat, Karen Smith, Donnie Boggs, Steve and Julie Hensley, Zack and Brenda Binkley, Paul Echols, Dorothy Dee of the National Restaurant Association, David and Carole Jean Goldberg, Beth Anne Mercurio, Linda Bybee, Pat Chapman, Kay Stewart, James H. Heady, John Kirkham, Ruth Ann Messner, Ray Martin, Robert B. Smith of *Ohio* magazine, Joann Hall, Emily Drabanski, Lonnie Falk, Holly Greenhagen, Paul L. Hayden, A.D. Hopkins of the *Las Vegas Review-Journal,* Whitney Drake of *Arizona Living,* M.J. Van Deventer, Sheryl Howell of *Tallahassee* magazine, and Suzie D. Nolen of *Nashville* magazine.

And Mary Caldwell, who doesn't know anything about barbecue but wanted her name in the book anyway.

We'll stop here, before this acknowledgments gets longer than the Academy Awards show. But we can't end without thanking all the barbecue pitmen and owners who cooked barbecue that is as good as we've ever eaten.

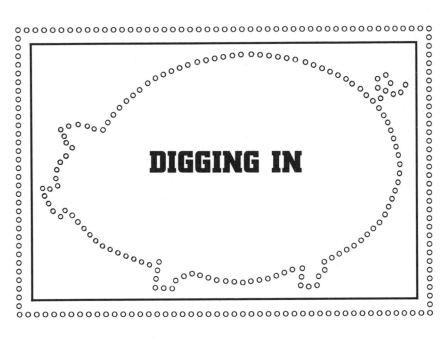

DIGGING IN

INTRODUCTION

The best thing to do with a book about barbecue is wipe your hands on it. No matter how brilliant the prose (and some of it is darned brilliant), reading about barbecue is like hearing about a hot date: It's interesting, but it's nothing like being there. The whole point of *Real Barbecue* is to bounce you out of your Barcalounger and into the delicious world of great eating, from America's best BBQ joints to your own backyard.

There are those who will tell you that real, slow-smoked, pit-cooked, fall-off-the-bone barbecue is a lost art. Don't you believe it. Finding the real thing isn't always easy and preparing it yourself requires a little effort, but it's there to be had. And it is truly the pinnacle of culinary creations, the most coddled and cared-for food in the world. Eating it is the goal; reading about it just gets you there.

Luckily, your loyal and hard-working authors are on hand to assist you. We have logged almost 40,000 miles, visited nearly 700 barbecue joints, and burned the hair off a couple of knuckles in rounding up the very best this country has to offer. We estimate we swallowed about 200 pounds of barbecue, which is somewhere in the neighborhood of 629,200 calories—enough to power a Buick up Pike's Peak. And that's not counting the beer. It was a lot of eating, but it was worth it. We found sauces so rich and luxurious that we wanted to climb in the pot and bask in them. We found sauces with more snap than a set of new suspenders. There were ribs that had people speaking in tongues and sandwiches that had businessmen sneaking them home in briefcases.

Besides the barbecue itself, there were the barbecue chefs—a friendly, entertaining, and colorful bunch of folks who have dedicated their lives to a food that gets them up at four in the morning to stand in a sweltering room. Their determination to produce a product they can be proud of, no matter how demanding the effort, is evident in every steaming bite. It is what elevates barbecue joints, despite their modest means, above restaurants staffed with cordon bleu chefs decked out in designer finery.

Barbecue is more than a meal; it's a way of life.

THE HISTORY OF BARBECUE
Or As Much of It As You'll Ever Need to Know

About 27,000 years ago, according to paleontologists, man discovered fire. Later that same day, along about suppertime, it's very likely that he invented barbecue.

Like all great ideas, barbecue came out close to perfect from the start. And unlike the wheel, which was another good idea, man has had the sense to leave barbecue pretty much alone. In the intervening eons, civilization has taken the wheel and frittered it away on inertial guidance systems, roulette tables, and fertilizer spreaders that take up both lanes on Sunday afternoon. Barbecue, on the other hand, is still the same mystic communion among fire, smoke, and meat familiar to *Australopithecus afarensis* as he knelt over a smoldering stump with his chef's hat on.

For your average twentieth-century American guy or gal, barbecue is a ticket back to simpler times, when men were men and women had hair on their knees. Surely it's not necessary to detail the animal attraction of gnawing at a slab of shortbacks, and the subject of lasciviously licking sauce-drenched fingers would bring a blush to any maiden's cheeks. So let discretion rule. Let us just say that there are primal pleasures involved in enjoying barbecue the likes of which aren't legal, except maybe in Nevada. Good barbecue now is like good barbecue always: simple and slightly sinful. After all, that whole man-woman thing can be traced back to a spare rib in the Garden of Eden.

In its early days, the saga of barbecue is a bit hard to trace, partly because the chefs were just as likely to be the main course on any given prehistoric evening. The ancient history of barbecue is mostly made up of old wives' tales, the most famous of which is the oft-told story of barbecue's origins set down in 1822 by the cockney Charles Lamb in "A Dissertation upon Roast Pig." According to Lamb's flowery account, partaking of porkers was unknown in the world until accidentally discovered by Bo-bo, a "great lubberly boy" and eldest son of Ho-Ti, who was a swineherd in ancient China. Left in charge of the swineherd's humble cottage, Bo-bo took to playing with fire and set ablaze the "sorry antediluvian makeshift of a building" and the pigs within. Fearing his father's wrath, Bo-bo poked a hot porker to try to revive it, burnt his finger, then popped it into his mouth to cool it. Well, Bo-bo may have been lubberly, but he was no dope. "O father, the pig, the pig! Do come and taste how nice the burnt pig eats," he shouted, simultaneously discovering roast pork and restaurant criticism. Soon it seemed that Ho-Ti and Bo-bo's little shack was burning down fairly frequently, once or twice a week, even. Called to trial at Peking for such misdeeds, the pair saw their secret get out among the judge and jury and the population at large, and soon "there was nothing to be seen but fire in every direction." Humanity moved on into the Age of Barbecue, and the Chinese stopped fooling around with gunpowder and got busy inventing Wet-Naps.

Unfortunately, the march of progress led mankind away from the simple pleasures of cooking out. Across Europe, cooking was done in fireplaces hung with cast-iron griddles and pots. Thus started the whole process of moving food away from fire, an insidious historical movement that continues to this day and can be seen at its most soulless during feeding time on a wide-body jet. Eventually, after too many years away from a hot fire, a good meal came to mean a couple of suitably "ripe" fowl simmered in the depths of a dank inn and served in a dim room full of guys who hadn't rinsed out their leathers lately. It might have stayed that way, too, with unenlightened modern man blithely wolfing down centuries of truly terrible food, if it hadn't been for one fortunate accident: America.

Despite its origins in the misty dawn of man, barbecue never really hit its stride until it was rediscovered along the shores of what turned out to be the You Ess of Ay. In fact, reliable sources (as reliable as sources get on the subject of barbecue) tie the name itself to a portable frame of green sticks used by the Arawak Indians to smoke and roast game and fish over an open fire—an early form of barbecue pit discovered in the West Indies by the first Spanish explorers. In their version of the native inhabitants' Taino language, *barbacoa* referred to that frame of green sticks. To the explorers, it translated as "Oh, boy! Takeout!"

In classic conquering-hero fashion, the Europeans ended up claiming the invention of barbecue—or at least the word—for their own. A common shaggy pig story gives the French credit for coming up with the idea, based on the phrase *barbe à queue,* which translates roughly as beard-to-tail, referring to whole hog (or goat, as the case may be) cooking. Most serious scholars, including the barbecue-loving *Oxford English Dictionary,* allow themselves a discreet snicker at that one, the dictionary pooh-poohing the story as "absurd conjecture." Europeans can claim credit for one thing, though: They brought the domesticated pig to North America.

With a combination of steamy climate, Spanish explorers selling secret recipes, and lots of easy labor, the South got a head start on the new American art of barbecue. Southerners settled on a common technique of digging pits in the earth, filling them with aromatic hardwood, and then tending a slow fire of hot coals beneath a pampered but uncomfortable guest of honor.

The first European settlers in Virginia, pretty much a salt-pork-and-scurvy bunch of sailors, probably adopted the Indians' techniques over the decades, adapting them to hogs and other creatures of choice. Outdoor barbecues reportedly were common along the James River in Virginia. The rediscovered thrill of the barbecue was adapted by colonists in their kitchens as well. Pieces of meat sometimes were hung by twine in the fireplace and twisted so they'd unwind slowly, slowly in the smoke. Spits were common fireplace accessories, often with pans underneath to catch juices for basting.

Spanish settlers who encountered the barbecue stands of the Creeks and Cherokees in the Carolinas and the Gulf Coast area were taking notes, too. Eventually they became a barbecue migration, which followed the establishment of herds and ranches farther west into strange lands like Mexico and *real* strange lands like Texas. As time passed, such carriers of the barbecue flame added their own variations, like tomatoes, garlic, and hot peppers. Tomatoes, called "love apples," had been shunned by early barbecuers along the East Coast because they were thought to be poisonous aphrodisiacs. It was not until Sept. 26, 1830, when Col. Robert Gibbon Johnson publicly bit into a basket of tomatoes on the courthouse steps in Salem, N.J., that many Easterners believed they were safe to eat. That may seem hopelessly dense to present-day barbecuers, but the road to rib tips has been littered with less-than-brilliant thinking. In the 1700s and 1800s, for instance, New York had its chance to go down in the history books with a regional style all its own. What did the bead-and-trinket sharpies of Manhattan Island come up with? Turtle barbecues.

At some point in here, barbecue more or less stopped having a national history and broke into an interrelated mess of local and regional histories. In many rural areas of the South and Midwest, big outdoor barbecues became associated with political get-togethers and church meetings. Catholic churches, short on members in many areas of the South, used the tempting smoke of an all-day barbecue wafting across the countryside to attract scores of sniffing Protestants eager to make a small contribution in exchange for some prime pig. By the turn of the century, barbecue in Texas had become a common feature out behind butcher shops, as a way to make less highfalutin' cuts of beef more salable.

From such backwoods roots, barbecue hitched a ride across America. It followed various migrations to various cities, moving up the Mississippi to Kansas City, for instance, where the beef-and-spicy-ketchup traditions of Texas mingled with the vinegar-hot pork of the Carolinas and a multitude of other variations. Barbecue moseyed into

Chicago and Cleveland and Los Angeles. Even if anyone had been trying to keep track of all this, it would have been pretty near impossible. Tradition and invention became mixed in a delicious confusion.

Sometimes, powerful interests tried to harness barbecue to their own ends. Giant barbecues were one technique Boss Tweed used to wrangle votes for Tammany Hall. More recently, Lyndon Baines Johnson and Jimmy Carter tried the same thing. But all the while, barbecue kept its essential character. After the occasional vote-getter blowout, it would return to its natural state, smoldering away in relative obscurity, tucked into country crossroads and big-city street-corners, generally ignored by the nice folks of America, who were busy developing gelatin molds and meat loaf.

In recent times, there have been a couple of barbecue booms, one associated with the nation's first flirtation with automobiles and highways (and hence roadside stands) in the twenties and thirties, and another in the postwar suburban fifties, when backyard barbecuers by the millions rediscovered the thrills of pyrotechnic hamburger patties, if not exactly traditional barbecue.

Now Americans are surrounded by multinational corporations and sophisticated image manipulators, many of which are more than passingly interested in parting the Average Man from his hard-earned dining dollar. The twentieth-century image-and-eating machine has coughed out fast-food franchises at such a rate that it is becoming mathematically impossible to build more, for fear that there will be more people working in them than eating in them. Convenience stores, with their microwaves, battle against chicken joints that buy birds raised in fowl factories where the lights are on all night long.

And yet, the chuffing, ramshackle barbecue joint endures.

Like crabgrass, it pops up through the cracks of corporate America. The Mom and Pop grocery is dead; the little roadside motel is staggering. Mystery Spots and Indian Caves gather cobwebs while people seek out theme parks. So why does the barbecue joint, boisterous and boastful, remain while all the rest vanish? The answer lies in its very nature. Even though you can walk into a rib joint and walk

○○

PORKLORE ○ First Family Barbecue

In George Washington's diary for the year 1769 is this entry. "Went up to Alexandria to a barbicue. Back in three nights."

○○

right out with a slab of ribs, barbecue is not "fast food"; it is the very opposite. Barbecue is *slow* food, laboriously smoked even when prepared in the most "modern" electric ovens, and it's a cuisine that looks to the past. The care and craftsmanship of the pitman recall a simpler time when pride meant more than profit. You can see it in the names of America's barbecue joints themselves, always harking back to their individual histories for the touchstone of better days, for the purest style and the ultimate taste: "Texas barbecue" in New York City and "Oklahoma-style barbecue" in Los Angeles, "Southern-style" in Kansas City and in Fort Collins, Colo.

At such outposts of good eating, and in backyards and parking lots across the nation, there is a vast flickering ritual, a shadow play of flame and smoke that can envelop a modern cook lost in the simple satisfactions of the evening's meal and whisk him for a moment back to the *barbacoa.* At such times, the history of barbecue is present in every pit, with thousands of years of human history flavoring the meat. No twentieth-century corporation can hope to fake a flame like that.

BARBECUE ARCHITECTURE
From Bauhaus to Sowhaus

How different things might be if Frank Lloyd Wright had taken the road less traveled, the one with the barbecue joint on the right, just past the trailer court. Wright's fondness for concrete would have suited fire-conscious barbecue men just fine because he came along at the right time, when health departments were forcing sidewalk barbecue stands to clean up their acts and put up buildings. But Wright and other architects didn't take an interest in barbecue places. So the Memphis style has nothing to do with the debate over wet or dry ribs. The Chicago School isn't where Leon and Lem learned to cook barbecue. And Art Deco isn't the guy who owns Art's Bar-B-Que out on the bypass. Barbecue men were left to their own designs, and they have created an architectural style all their own. Believe us.

In the beginning there was no barbecue-joint architecture. Barbecue was an outdoor food served at political rallies and picnics, sold in pastures and backyards. Around the turn of the century barbecue moved to the street corners and, in rural areas, to roadside stands. "These locations they picked, particularly the streetcorner locations, were crucial," says Grady Clay, urban environmental expert and author of *Close-Up: How to Read the American City*. "They had visibility; they could be seen from four directions. The smell attracted from four directions. Smoke signals were very important to success. There was always a little commotion. Commotion is an absolute necessity for success in this kind of business."

Then came the health department inspector. He had more to do with creating barbecue architecture than all the design firms combined. He required tin sides. Then he wanted the sawdust floors replaced with concrete. The barbecue men pondered the health requirements and saw that the only thing left of the old days was the tent top. So they added a tin roof, and the barbecue joint was born.

That was the original barbecue joint: corrugated tin sides, bare concrete floors, and a tin roof. We call the first wave of barbecue-joint architecture the Greasian style. The focus of the place was the grease-caked pit. For a number of years that was all there was to barbecue architecture: a shack built around a pit. But that great American business force, competition, entered. Just as lawyers find that when there is only one in town, there isn't enough work, but when there are two there is more than either can handle, so too did barbecue men discover that competition created more barbecue eaters. And soon that little six-stool shack wasn't big enough. So the first barbecue man expanded. He built a wing on the side. As business continued to increase, the building took on a life of its own, a new wing on the other side, a take-out window out back, a picnic area, indoor restrooms. And thus was born the Sowhaus style: the place has grown in all directions, like a sow fattened up.

When Fred, the grocer down the road, saw how well Jim Bob and his new competitor Joe Frank were doing selling barbecue, he built a little pit out back of his store and started selling sandwiches. And people started buying them. That old competitive machine was at work again. Pretty soon Fred was selling more sandwiches than soap. So he cut out the soap section and set up a dining table there. And before he knew it, he was out of the grocery business and into the barbecue business. He still had the little one-pump country store building, but he was a full-fledged barbecue joint. This kind of evolution was happening everywhere. In one town it might be a service station; in another a meat market. But all began as one business and then shifted. The old building remained, and maybe even remnants of the old business. George Hooks in Milledgeville, Ga., still sells a few groceries. Owens Barbecue in Lake City, S.C., started out as a grocery store, but five years after opening the store, Mellon Owens decided to start cooking barbecue. Soon the barbecue just took over. The building still has the basic characteristics of a country store, but with a screened pit out back. It is the Re-Modeling School, an architectural style characterized by minor changes to major structures.

As competition heated up, a new guy moved into town. When the laundromat closed, he took over the lease, built a counter, set up booths where the washers used to be, and began cooking out back. On the outside it still looked like a laundromat. On the inside it was a barbecue joint. Scholars of architecture call this "adaptive reuse," taking old structures and using them for new purposes instead of abandoning them. We call it the Bizarrantine style because the results are bizarre: barbecue joints in former residences, where they probably burn stacks of zoning and fire regulations instead of hickory; barbecue joints in former gas stations, where one can only hope they washed out the underground tanks a bit before they started lighting fires. Pratt's Barn, which serves one of the best barbecue pork sandwiches in east Tennessee, is housed in a barn-shaped building. But out front, standing guard over the door, is a twenty-foot-tall cement Indian. Don't ask what Honest John (that's the Indian's name) has to do with barbecue. He has nothing to do with barbecue. But he used to draw a lot of gawks from tourists back in the days when Pratt's was Honest John's, a gift shop.

Probably the most common Bizarrantine barbecue joints are in former fast-food restaurants where an old marketing concept has died and where barbecue men now scurry like hermit crabs. When a Super Burger franchise goes out of business, hungry citizens dreaming of barbecue will gather, drawn by still-unexplained forces, and stand in the parking lot surrounding the place until a pit opens there; it is the central process of Darwinian dining, the survival of the fittest cuisine.

With its proud history of succeeding in those places that have mismanaged money and ended up hopelessly in debt, the barbecue joint may yet play a larger role in American architecture—at the Pentagon, for instance. That hole in the middle would make a terrific place to roast a few pigs, and you could sell from all five sides. And trying a little "adaptive reuse" on the items in the Pentagon's final yard sale might be nice. Subs, with a good length of stovepipe welded to one end, would make great grills. A fellow could smoke a lot of brisket in a missile silo if he left the lid shut. And burning post oak instead of alcohol and liquid oxygen would save money, too.

Actually, the great forces of history make the direction of all this quite clear: Left unattended, structures will tend to experience the rapture, becoming born-again barbecue joints almost overnight, sprouting rusty smokestacks and misspelled mottoes where once an architect trod. Eventually absolutely everything in America will be a barbecue joint.

What a wonderful world that will be.

BARBECUE IS WHERE YOU FIND IT
Heres How . . .

The problem: It is a dark and stormy night. You have been all day on the road. You're tired. The wife's tired. The kids are irritable. And you are all starved.

The solution: Barbecue.

Nothing can turn a day around like hot barbecue and a cold drink. But how do you find a good barbecue joint in a strange town? It's for sure you won't find it by calling the AAA. They can plan your journey and pick your motel and get your car towed. But they are not the Rand McNally of the rotisserie.

Begin by asking (but never ask a man in a leisure suit about barbecue). It helps if you know someone. Even people who can't stand barbecue invariably know someone who loves it. Get an introduction, call the barbecue fanatic, and ask for a guided tour. That's the ideal situation. But even if you only remotely know someone in the strange town, give him or her a call. Vince knew someone who knew Bill Powell, a retired newspaperman living in Paducah, Ky. He called Powell up, explained that he was looking for a good barbecue place, and spent a delightful twenty minutes talking barbecue. And his recommendation, Starnes, turned out to be so good that it made our top 100 list.

But what if you don't know anyone in town? "Ask at the grocery store or the filling station," advises former Tennessee congressman Robin Beard, a barbecue fanatic if there ever was one. Beard admits to having eaten barbecue for breakfast. On more than one occasion. His former press secretary, Rusty Brashear, says that they had to arrange their campaign stops to coincide with barbecue joints. We've taken Beard's advice and found it right on target. The boys who pump gas may not know French cuisine, but they know pig sandwiches. A dusty-faced fellow at a Gulf station on U.S. 60 steered us to the Marion Pit Barbecue in Marion, Ky., and we still thank him for it. Marion Pit is so good that restaurants from all over the country order Bill Marion's sauce.

And when we asked a filling-station attendant in Jackson, Tenn., for directions to a nearby joint, he gave us a dissertation on the local barbecue scene. "What do you want to go there for?" he challenged, pulling himself upright. We told him we'd heard they had good barbecue. He shook his head and allowed, "Oh, they've got good barbecue. But they don't want to give you any of it. They're tight with it, give you these little old sandwiches. You want some good barbecue, you go back up this road to the bank and then look over to the left. You'll see this little trailer. That's Bill Case. Now, he's got good barbecue, and he's not so tight with it, either." We followed his advice, and Bill Case had good barbecue.

If you can't get a recommendation anywhere, head for a phone booth. Don't just look under "Barbecue" in the Yellow Pages. Some of the best barbecue joints don't know there is a separate listing. Check under "Restaurants," too. Check the names. You can tell a lot from a barbecue joint's name. If the owner is sure enough of his product to lend his last name to the place—such as Allman's Barbecue in Fredericksburg, Va., or Dorsey's Tasty Barbecue in Orlando, Fla.,—that's a good sign.

"There are some fairly good places in the cities that are institutional-type barbecue places that will have some kind of fancier names," says Beard. "But in the country, it's good to have that guy's name on it. It means he takes pride in his barbecue." If he is sure enough of his product to use his first name, then you can almost bet on a winner: Brady and Lil's in Memphis. Daddy Bruce's in Denver. Emmett's in Gadsden, Ala. Angelo's in Fort Worth. And surest of all is the barbecue man who will lend his name to something stupid-sounding. Take Maurice's Piggie Park in West Columbia, S.C. Can you imagine the ribbing Maurice would have to take if his Piggie Park were to serve inferior sandwiches? Fortunately for Maurice, and for you, Maurice serves barbecue that is real good. Given a choice between a joint named Fred's Barbecue and a joint named Swiss Chalet Barbecue, go for the first name every time.

Sometimes the phone book listing will tell how long a place has been in business. Generally, the longer the better. There are exceptions to this rule, towns with such poor taste that they have kept a mediocre barbecue joint going. And sometimes a place may have been in business too long. The original owner, the one who created the sauce and built the reputation, may have died or sold out. It is rare indeed for the new owner to be as careful and good as the original. For a rule of thumb, use this tip from Wayne Monk, owner of Lexington Barbecue No. 1 in Lexington, N.C. He says, "The lifespan of a barbecue place seems to be twenty to forty years."

Now get out your change and get on the phone. Ask for directions. A really good barbecue joint usually is slightly, if not impossibly, difficult to find when you're a stranger in town. If giving directions comes second nature to the person who answers the phone, good. It means they've done it before. And if that person answers, "Yeah?" instead of "Good evening. How may I help you?" start driving.

Now comes the real test: the drive-by. How does the joint look? Don't be leery of a rundown exterior. As the saying goes: "It's not much on the outside but . . ." The "but" is usually followed by a testimonial to the quality of the meat, the heat of the sauce, the freshness of the bun, the gusto of the beans. Beard says, "If it looks too slick, then I'm worried. I don't want them spending a whole lot of time cleaning tables and shining windows. If it's a small operation, I want that guy spending time with his barbecue."

Beard says the reason many rural barbecue joints are nothing more than shacks is because the owner didn't start out with the intention of opening a barbecue restaurant. "It usually started out with a farmer raising pigs, and when he had too many he'd pull out a few and put 'em on a spit. It would be too many for the family to eat, but if he had the right touch and his wife could come up with a tangy sauce, the neighbors would drop over—and, first thing you know, he'd dig a pit, build a shack for the smoker, and start cooking them by the batch, as a side business. He wouldn't have any overhead. He had the property, he had all the raw products right there. Then when the crop went bad, there was always the sandwich trade to fall back on. When the farmer found he was making more money out of barbecue than farming, he knew he'd found his true calling."

The parking lot can tell you a lot, too. Is there a bizarre mixture of cars, say a Mercedes, a Chevy with a flame paint job, and an animal-control dump truck? That's good; it means that the cooking crosses cultural lines. Do you realize how good barbecue has to be to get a Mercedes owner to park next to a dump truck? Also, look for mail delivery vans. Mail carriers can stop anywhere on their routes; if the food wasn't good, they'd be tired of it already.

Now it's time to give the place a closer look. Check the front window. Is the owner advertising other products? "Anybody that's looking for barbecue who stops at a place that has barbecue on the sign, but hamburgers and hot dogs advertised in the window, is going to be disappointed," says Beard. "That's not a very good place, and you're not going to get very good barbecue. I just want to see a place that does nothing but barbecue." Jack Sweat of Sweat's Barbecue in Soperton, Ga., laughs when he recalls the time a family of Yankees returning from a vacation at Hilton Head stopped by his place and ordered fried shrimp.

Next, look around back. It is a serious mistake to walk directly in the front door of a barbecue joint without making a lap of the place. The front is show biz; the back is where the truth hangs out. What should you look for?

o **Wood.** "Always look for that stack of wood," emphasizes Beard. "And if it's a real neat stack of wood, you'd better watch out. Some people will put wood out there for aesthetics. If they are really using it, the stacks are going to be a little messy, a piece lying here and there. Because if they are really cooking barbecue, they are going to be going out in the middle of night to grab some wood, and they aren't going to be taking time to stack it back neatly."

o **Backup smokers.** Out behind many good barbecue joints it will look like a used-car lot—a real *bad* used-car lot—with piles of rusting iron parts, barrels, sheet metal, and mobile smokers with or without flat tires. These are experimental models, and a pretty good sign the place isn't experimenting on you.

o **A guy leaning against a wall.** At barbecue joints, guys leaning against walls aren't goofing off; they're working. Tending a good pit takes years of experience, boundless patience, expert knowledge, and the ability to lean against a wall. Leaning against a wall in a cloud of hickory smoke and puffing on a cigarette is worth style points.

o **Flies.** If it's summertime and there are no flies hanging around, you should ask yourself, "What do they know that I don't?" Actual flies aren't required, however, if you can spot a flyswatter on a windowsill somewhere.

If the joint has passed the drive-by and the closer-look tests, you are ready to park and get out. Time for one last test. Robin Beard again: "Look for the smokestack and sniff the air for the smell of hickory or whatever wood they're using. If it's a weak, almost nonexistent smell, then they're not cooking it right. If there's a good heavy smell, then that's just another indication you've stopped at a good place."

If the joint has passed all these tests, then go on in. Don't be alarmed by a plain interior. Remember, any barbecue joint with a pit on-site probably has had its share of fire problems. No point in complicating matters with a lot of wooden shelves and seats or tacky plastic doodads that will just fuel the flame.

Jim Dodson, a North Carolina barbecue fanatic who now lives in Maine, says, "I prefer a place with cheap plastic tablecloths and mismatched utensils and hard plastic section plates that are the color of an old schoolhouse bathroom wall. It helps if there is no printed menu. It helps if there is a sink located right in the dining room and there is a friendly but bored gum-chewing waitress with her name scripted in frilly pink letters above her left, ample breast. It helps if her name is Wanda. Or Trixie."

Look around. Lewis Grizzard, the Georgia humorist, believes, "If there are any religious posters on the walls, you can usually count on the barbecue being good." We could make a list of barbecue places that fit that description: Maurice's Piggy Park, Otto's in Houston, Ollie's in Birmingham, Ala. The Old Plantation House in Birmingham has a genealogical chart tracing Jesus' lineage all the way back to Adam and Eve. If there aren't posters, look for calendars—the local ones, from slaughterhouses and farm-implement dealers. The more calendars, the better the barbecue. Louie Mueller's in Taylor, Texas, has a nine-calendar wall, and the brisket backs it up.

What should you order in a strange barbecue joint? For starters, order something small. A half-slab instead of a slab of ribs, a sandwich instead of a dinner plate—and even a small sandwich at that. Barbecue aficionado Beard: "What I'll usually do is get the smallest sandwich they've got, and then if I like it, I go in for the kill." If the clerk asks you a question, like "Do you want it hot?" answer in the affirmative. If they ask, that probably means most customers get it that way. If most get it that way, that's the way you want it, too. Another tactic: If there's something on the menu that you've never heard of, order it. It doesn't matter if it's "soaks," "pit-cut," a "C-B Joe," "burnt ends," or even "snoots." The fact that it's there means the locals demand it, even if the tourists don't have a clue. Nine times out of ten, whatever it is, you'll love it—and you'll get a smidgen of respect for having given it a try.

We could give you other barbecue rules. Over the years we've heard them all. But these are the ones that seem to be most important. And remember: These are only guidelines. We have found exceptions to every one. "You can take all these things that I have said and still get blasted out of the water," says Beard. "Barbecue just defies rules."

PIG PICKIN'
How We Selected the Hundred Hot Barbecue Joints

We don't use the star system to rate barbecue places. We're not even sure we understand the star system. What is the difference between a three-and-a-half-star place and a four-star place? Nothing else in life is rated on stars. When you go in for a salary review, your boss doesn't tell you that you have had a three-and-a-half-star year. And he doesn't rate you on a 1-to-10 scale, either. He just tells you how you did. So that's the way we're going to rate barbecue joints, the way the people who eat there rate them. No stars, no grades, no 1-to-10 scale.

Our ratings scale is derived from hours and hours of conversations with barbecue connoisseurs, people who drive 100 miles out of their way to try a new barbecue joint. To begin with, there is no low end of the scale, no barbecue equivalent of a one-star restaurant. They just don't survive. A barbecue joint that is fair to middling is called "Pretty Good," by barbecue connoisseurs. One step up the ratings ladder is the joint that does a respectable job, that might get you back again if you want some barbecue and the better places are closed. It is rated "Good" by barbecue connoisseurs. Now we arrive at the exalted plateaus, where the barbecue is considered special, worth a far drive, a long wait. These are the places that are packed every noon and supper hour. They receive the next-to-the-highest rating: "Real Good."

Now comes the top, the pinnacle of barbecue knowledge, where secret sauces deserve to be secret. Barbecue places that are worth a special trip. These are the places that are packed at three in the afternoon. Barbecue connoisseurs have a special term for them: "As Good As I've Ever Had." In barbecue conversation, that is the ultimate compliment. Why won't a true barbecue connoisseur just come out and call a place "The Best"? We wondered about that for a long time. And after much conversation and much thought, we have arrived at the answer. The barbecue purist, the true connoisseur, knows that out there right now, at this very minute, some barbecue cook is building a pit, hand-lettering a shingle BAR-B-Q, and hanging it out. And the connoisseur thinks maybe, just maybe, this one may be a little better than the place up the road or across the county line. So his barbecue fanaticism becomes an eternal quest, an unending search for the best barbecue joint in America.

WHAT WE LOOKED FOR

Here is how we judged the hundreds of barbecue joints we tried on our barbecue quest. First and foremost was the meat. Was it tender? Was it flavorful? The bottom line in barbecue is meat. Second was the preparation. Did the cook know what he or she was doing? The third was the sauce. We recognize the broad range of sauces used in American barbecue; in fact, we enjoy most all of them. But the sauce must form a perfect union with the meat. Next we noted the service. Was it cheerful? Was it fast? Was it service at all? And finally we checked the atmosphere. Would we want to return? Would we want to bring our mother? (Sometimes a place can score extra points if you wouldn't want to bring your mother.)

We used much the same testing methodology as regular restaurant critics use. We arrived at each barbecue place unannounced, ate unattended, and if the barbecue didn't stack up, left unnoticed. We didn't want special attention, we wanted to test each place under normal conditions. In short, we wanted the same kind of sandwich, the same kind of service, that you would receive if you stopped in after a long day on the road. Any cook can wow you with a special meal. We were looking for the places that can wow you day in and day out, eat-in or take-out.

(By the way, we give you phone numbers in this book so you can call ahead and make sure the owners aren't closed for vacation or something, not so you can call for reservations. No one calls for reservations at a barbecue joint.)

WHERE WE WENT

We didn't eat at every barbecue joint in America. That would be an impossible task considering all the barbecue places there are and all that modern medicine has discovered about the link between cholesterol and good health.

There are 6,412 barbecue restaurants in the United States, according to the Restaurant Consulting Group, an Evanston, Ill., company that makes it its business to know such things. That's not very many in the scheme of what consulting groups like to call "restaurant concepts." There are twice as many Mexican restaurants and five times as many hamburger places. It's less than two percent of the 353,536 restaurants in business in 1986, just a drop in the sop bucket. It's also a number that would probably not be accepted by any except the guy who owns the consulting company. A Texan would look at that number, rub his chin and say, "Texas is a big state, but it's not that big." A Tennessean would ask, "Does that include places in Texas?" and when the answer was yes, reply, "Then that number's too high." And a barbecue purist of any origin would sniff, "I bet 90 percent of them cook with gas or electric. And that's not barbecue."

So what is barbecue? That question will start an argument in most any bar in the country. Finding an answer was our dilemma when we began this book. We toyed with the idea of "when in Rome." If the locals call it barbecue, then we would call it barbecue, too. Then we mentioned that idea to our friend Bill Schuetze, a Wisconsin native. "In Wisconsin they think a Sloppy Joe is barbecue," he said. His answer convinced us that "when in Rome" was not the right way to go. In the end we adopted the U.S. Department of Agriculture's definition, even though it applies to packaged foods and not restaurants. The USDA says barbecue is "[meat that] shall be cooked by the direct action of heat resulting from the burning of hard wood or the hot coals therefrom for a sufficient period to assume the usual characteristics . . . which include the formation of a brown crust. . . . The weight of barbecued meat shall not exceed 70 percent of the weight of the fresh uncooked meat."

The definition has several appeals for us. It's been in use since the turn of the century. It conforms pretty closely to what purists think of as barbecue. And it guarantees that whatever goes on the grill, be it hog or heifer, will come off as barbecue, no matter what kind of baste has been mopped on during the cooking and no matter what kind of sauce has been slathered on afterward. With that definition we also could eliminate many of the Restaurant Consulting Group's 6,412 so-called barbecue restaurants.

We still didn't make it to every wood-burning pit in the country. But we did eat at almost 700 (689 to be approximately exact). Most had been recommended to us by at least one barbecue connoisseur. Some had been recommended over and over again. We have confidence that if you try any of our top-rated places, you'll have barbecue as good as you've ever had.

If your favorite barbecue choice isn't on our list, don't despair. It could have been having a bad day when we passed through. A good barbecue joint can have a bad day. But we have confidence in our selections because we don't think the converse is true: a good place can have a bad day, but a bad place can never have a good day. If you think there is a barbecue joint that is as good as you've ever had that we might have missed, write us at the address at the end of the book. We'll stop by the next time we're in the neighborhood. We might even take you along.

We don't claim our selections for the Hot 100 as the absolute last word. Close, but we like to think that somewhere out there at this very moment, some young barbecue cook is hanging out his first hand-lettered shingle, BAR-B-Q, and that his barbecue is a little bit better than the fellow's down the road that we said was "as good as we've ever had." So our quest for the best barbecue joints isn't over. It has just begun.

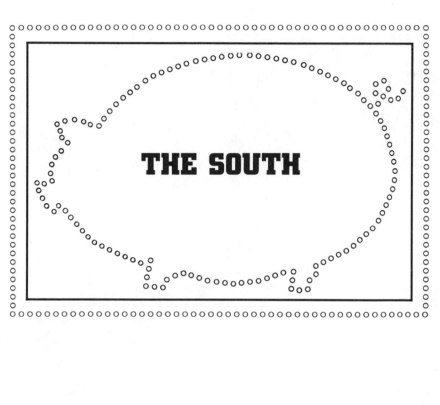

THE SOUTH

ALABAMA

Birmingham

THE OLD PLANTATION BARBEQUE

o 830 1st Ave. N. o (205) 252-0443
o Mon.–Thurs., 11 A.M.–6:30 P.M.; Fri.–Sat., 11 A.M.–8 P.M.
o Closed Sunday

Barbecue lovers love to make barbecue rules: Never go in a barbecue joint that has a gas pump outside. Never go in a barbecue joint that sells hamburgers. Never go in a barbecue joint that's nicer looking than your house. But for every rule there is an exception.

Take the rule: Never eat at a barbecue joint that has its own T-shirts. The Old Plantation Barbeque shoots that rule all to hell, an appropriate place to shoot it to since The Old Plantation is decorated in early Sunday School: Biblical posters, religious tracts lying around, a religious radio station playing over the speakers, and a hand-lettered wall chart tracing the complete Christian bloodline, from Jesus all the way back to Adam and Eve. The tracing of the Jesus family tree was a monumental task, performed several years ago by Jim Shaner, a former owner of the Old Plantation. And it is Shaner who was responsible for the Old Plantation T-shirt, which combines the two great obsessions of the South: religion and race. On the front, right under the name The Old Plantation House, was an outline of three figures, one of whom was supposed to be saying, in a dialect so thick you don't have to be a racist to figure it out: "Yas Suh! It's cooked in de pit." Then on the back of the shirt was the simple legend: JESUS IS LORD.

The new owners no longer have the T-shirts, but they still use the "Yas Suh! It's cooked in de pit" as their slogan. Apparently the racist dialect doesn't bother the locals, because they flock to the Old Plantation. And we agree with their assessment of the barbecue. We think the Old Plantation surpasses both old-line Birmingham barbecue joints: Ollie's and The Golden Rule. Its meat is moist without being mushy and with enough brown pieces to give it an interesting texture. The sauce, a buttery blend of tomato puree, pepper, and vinegar, doesn't bowl you over, but it is a nice complement to the meat. But the good food doesn't stop there. The fried pies are exceptional, with that authentic pressed-down look; and after eating some of the craklin (that's how they spell it) muffins, made from the crunchy part of the hogmeat, plain old cornbread will never taste as good again.

The Old Plantation is now on its fourth owner, but the quality of the food has remained high because the people who cook it are the same. Imajean Rogers has been working in the kitchen for thirty-five years. When Shaner was co-owner, he used to kid her: "I can't replace you because no one else can do it your way." She's left-handed.

The best recommendation for the Old Plantation may come from Shaner himself. "When I started there, I weighed 165 pounds. Then every day when I came in I'd have me a fried pie and a buttermilk and then a little later a sandwich. Pretty soon I was up to 210."

Rating: As good as we've ever had.

Directions: First Ave. N. is downtown; go downtown and ask how to get there. It would be too confusing for us to write it down. Birmingham numbers both its North-South streets and its East-West streets, and makes some of them one way and some of them both ways and cuts some of them in half with expressways. Just ask. Or call. And it's closed Sunday, of course.

PORKLORE ○ Lamb on pig

"There is no flavour comparable, I will contend, to that of the crisp, tawny, well-watched, not over-roasted, *crackling,* as it is well called—the very teeth are invited to their share of the pleasure at this banquet in overcoming the coy, brittle resistance—with the adhesive oleaginous—O call it not fat! but an indefinable sweetness growing up to it—the tender blossoming of fat—fat cropped in the bud—taken in the shoot—in the first innocence—the cream and quintessence of the child-pig's yet pure food—the lean, no lean, but a kind of animal manna—or, rather, fat and lean (if it must be so) so blended and running into each other, that both together make but one ambrosian result or common substance."

—Charles Lamb,
"A Dissertation upon Roast Pig,"
London Magazine, 1822.

OLLIE'S BARBECUE

o 515 University Blvd. o (205) 324-9485
o Mon.–Sat., 10 A.M.–8 P.M. o Closed Sunday

Ollie's is the only barbecue joint in the history books. In 1964 Ollie's became a test case for the newly enacted Civil Rights Act. It was a simple lawsuit: Ollie said he would allow blacks in the kitchen and at the take-out window but not in the dining room. The attorney general of the United States said: If you employ them in the kitchen and sell to them at the take-out window, then you will serve them in the dining room. So Ollie McClung, Sr., and Ollie McClung, Jr., co-owners of Ollie's, filed suit against the United States government, claiming that the public accommodations section of the 1964 Civil Rights Act was unconstitutional. Ollie and Ollie said their restaurant grossed $350,000 annually, and if they served blacks they would stand to lose $200,000. They said their decision to segregate was strictly a business one. "I would refuse to serve a Negro as well as a drunken man or a profane man or anyone else who would affect my business," said Ollie, Sr. And thus began *Katzenbach* v. *McClung,* or, as we prefer to call it, *United States* v. *Ollie and Ollie.*

As is usual in the courtroom, the thrust of the lawsuit had little to do with the original intent of the law. The Civil Rights Act was designed to integrate public motels and restaurants. But when the case went to court, integration took a backseat. The case turned on whether or not Ollie's Barbecue was a part of interstate commerce. Ollie and Ollie claimed they were not a part of interstate commerce, that they used $150,000 worth of food a year, all of it purchased locally in Birmingham. They further claimed they were eleven blocks from an interstate highway and even farther from a bus or railroad station. The U.S. said that $69,783, or 46 percent of their food, was meat bought from a local supplier who had procured it out of state. That made Ollie's a part of interstate commerce, the government said, and rested its case.

Ollie and Ollie won the first round of the fight. On Sept. 17, 1964, a three-judge federal court in Birmingham ruled that the public accommodations section of the Civil Rights Act was unconstitutional. "No case has been called to our attention, we have found none, which has held that the National Government has the power to control the conduct of people on the local level because they may happen to trade sporadically with persons who may be traveling in interstate commerce," the court said. But three months later the U.S. Supreme Court reversed the lower court's ruling by saying that Ollie's was a part of interstate commerce and ordering Ollie's to comply with the law. And on Dec. 16, 1964, after six months and a large legal bill, Ollie and Ollie gave up the fight. They agreed to abide by the Supreme Court ruling and "serve Negroes inside if they enter."

The whole affair must have looked strange to anyone outside the South, where segregation was a practiced art. This was an odd way to be a racist. Here was Ollie operating a restaurant in the heart of a black neighborhood, employing a predominantly black staff, and selling barbecue to blacks out his take-out window. But he wouldn't let the neighborhood crowd inside to sit down and eat. Ollie said at the time it had nothing to do with racism and he stands by that statement today. "This was not a racially motivated thing at all. Three-fourths of our employees were black. No, this was about the government trying to tell someone how to run their business. They really twisted the Constitution around on that one."

We've always found it ironic that one of the two things bringing blacks and whites together in the pre–civil rights era was barbecue (the other was jazz), and that it was a lawsuit by a barbecue joint aimed at preventing integration that made integration the law of the land. Ironic and perhaps fitting.

If you want to see Ollie's historic barbecue joint, you can't. The old joint, the one Ollie and Ollie fought to keep segregated, is gone—a victim of interstate commerce: the interstate highway system. But Ollie's is still around, still in the same area, a black residential neighborhood on Birmingham's south side. The staff is still predominantly black. Only now blacks and whites eat side-by-side in sparkling clean dining rooms that jut out from the kitchen like spokes on a wheel. There are three wedge-shaped dining rooms, and individual ones can be closed off. But they weren't designed that way because of integration. Now, during slow periods, Ollie can close sections and keep cleaning costs down.

The focus of the new Ollie's, the hub of the restaurant, is the barbecue pit. "We put the pit in the middle of the building so people can look at the cooking while they eat," says Ollie, Sr. "Out-of-towners really like that." Integration doesn't seem to have kept customers away. Ollie, Sr., says he has some regulars who have eaten there every day for fifty years. "They like how the restaurant and the food hasn't changed." Oh, there has been a menu addition. "We have frozen yogurt for the health nuts." Otherwise it's still the same barbecue sandwich that Ollie's has been serving since it opened in 1926. It's juicy pork meat, with a few crunchies for texture, and a tingly ketchup-based sauce, which Ollie says isn't mild or hot, but in between. "Medium" he calls it. It's one of the spiciest table sauces we came across. It is a sauce that talks to you.

It talks to everybody. "Rich folks and poor folks alike love it," says Ollie. "The laboring man'll come in and eat right beside a millionaire. Every time George Bush comes through, he eats a pile of it. Billy Graham eats here every time he's through. Gomer Pyle [Jim Nabors] is crazy about this stuff. He takes it back to Hollywood and makes tacos with it."

Ollie credits his many years of success to two things: the sauce and the Lord. In the center of his place, high above the dining room, for all to read, is a giant hand-lettered sign:

O TASTE AND SEE THAT THE LORD IS GOOD:
BLESSED IS THE MAN THAT TRUSTETH HIM.

And to that we might add: "And has a good sauce."

Rating: Real good.

Directions: If you are going south on Interstate 65, you can't miss it. It is off to the right, just past downtown Birmingham. It butts up against the interstate fence. When you see the Ollie's sign, get off at the next exit, the Sixth Ave. exit, and turn right on University Blvd. If you are going north, do everything in reverse.

Decatur

BIG BOB GIBSON BAR-B-Q

o 1713 Sixth Ave. S.E. o (205) 353-9935
o Open daily, 6:30 A.M.–9 P.M.

In north Alabama one name is synonymous with barbecue: Gibson. There's David Gibson's Bar-B-Q, and just plain Gibson's Bar-B-Q in Huntsville, David Gibson's No. 2 in Huntsville, Little Bob Gibson's in Courtland, and Big Bob Gibson's in Decatur—five barbecue places that trace their lineage back to the north Alabama barbecue giant, Big Bob Gibson.

Big Bob started cooking in a dug pit back in 1925. "Back in those days, they killed their own hogs and used the bones for stew," recalled his daughter Catherine McLemore, who took over his Decatur restaurant when he died in 1972. "On Saturdays, people would come from miles around to eat. And he would have tables built from tree to tree." Soon there weren't enough trees to shade all of Big Bob's hungry customers. That's when he decided to open a restaurant. As his business grew, so did his dining room. He kept jumping to bigger places, finally settling into the Sixth Avenue location in 1952. A year later Catherine joined the company. And in 1975 her son Don quit the computer business and returned to the family business. This continuity from generation to generation is important at Big Bob's. Catherine said, "Just a few weeks ago, we had a guy come in and tell his waitress, 'I haven't been here for twenty years, and you're the same girl who waited on me then!' Sure enough, the waitress had been with Big Bob's for thirty-two years!"

What keeps the employees is the family atmosphere; what keeps the customers is Big Bob's barbecue. The pork sandwich is a mound of shredded meat bathed in a flimsy tomato sauce that bites but doesn't sting. Big Bob's uses only pork shoulders and only hickory wood.

Big Bob would be proud of Catherine and Little Don. Business is booming again, forcing Big Bob's to move across the parking lot to larger quarters. In fact, Big Bob would be proud of all his heirs. "He had five children, and every one of them went into barbecue," said Don. "And now all of those places have passed down to the grand-kids."

Rating: Real good.

Directions: If you're coming on I-65 from the south, take Exit 334 (U.S. 67) west to Hwy. 31. Turn right (north), and Big Bob's is up the road on the left. If you're coming from the north, take Exit 340 (U.S. 72A) west across the Tennessee River and into town. It becomes Hwy. 31. Big Bob's is on the right, between Copy Boy and Quik Print.

Dora

GREEN TOP CAFE

o 530 Hwy. 78 o (205) 648-9838
o Mon.–Sat., 8:30 A.M.–midnight o Closed Sunday

George Gillis remembers well his boyhood visits to the Green Top. "It was the only decent barbecue you could find in Alabama." Gillis grew up in Memphis, a town that considered Alabama a poor relation when it came to barbecue. And it was his poor relations that took Gillis to Alabama. "We'd visit my cousins in Sumiton, which is right across the street from Dora. They're sort of twin cities. They were big rivals, Sumiton and Dora, but they were both crummy towns. We used to say they ought to combine them into one and they could call it Dumb-iton. The Green Top was on the Jefferson-Walker county line. And in Walker County, which at that time was dry, the bootlegger would take a check. That's the kind of place Dumb-iton was."

But the thing Gillis remembers most about the Green Top is Leo,

Leo Headrick. "Leo and Susie ran the Green Top. They lived in a trailer out back. And if you hung around the Green Top long enough, Leo would bring out his guitar and sing without any encouragement at all." Leo and Susie still own the Green Top. They've altered the name of the place slightly. It is now known as Leo & Susie's Famous Green Top Bar-B-Q, to reflect its elevated status in the barbecue world. But if you hang around long enough you might get to hear Leo sing.

The name may have changed, but it's still the same old Green Top it was when it opened in 1951. The top is still green. "Every time we re-roof we have to get green shingles," says Preston Headrick, Leo & Susie's Famous Son, who manages the Green Top for his parents. It still looks like a fifties roadhouse. The main dining area is stucco with fifties-style booths. "These booths were made in the fifties, though, not made to look like they were made in the fifties." Leo & Susie's Famous Oil-Tinted Portrait still hangs on the wall, alongside those of celebrities who have frequented the Green Top over the years: Auburn football star Bo Jackson; boxer Marvelous Marvin Hagler; politician George Wallace; astronaut Gene Cernan. ("We told him he'd been everywhere now—the moon and the Green Top," says Preston.) And, best of all, there is still Leo & Susie's Famous Barbecue Sandwich, a peerless pork production with crunchies in the middle and a tart, medium-hot vinegar-and-tomato-based sauce with a jolt that doesn't hit you until it is too late to turn back. If you want even more kick, you'll have to get it from a store-bought hot sauce they keep on every table.

The only things that have changed at the Green Top have changed for the better. "Prior to '78 the bathrooms were outside," says Preston. "We're a lot more popular with the women now that we have indoor restrooms." And there is a new portrait of Big Jim Fulson, two-time governor of Alabama and a frequent customer at the Green Top. Preston recalls, "Whenever Big Jim would come in, him and Daddy would sing together and one of them would use a bottle of hot sauce as a microphone."

Singing governors, a spot on a Birmingham TV station's list of the best barbecue restaurants in Alabama, and now selection as one of the top barbecue joints in America for this book. Leo & Susie's Green Top really is Famous. But Preston Headrick says he still has one more dream. "I've always wanted to be interviewed by *Playboy*. Maybe this is as close as I get."

Rating: Real good.

Directions: It's 20 miles west of Birmingham on Hwy. 78. If you're heading west, it's the roadhouse on the left with the green roof.

It's just past Wesley's Boobie Trap—Go Go Girls, which is on the right. If you're coming from the west, which we figure few people will be doing, then go to Wesley's Boobie Trap and turn around. See the chapter on Side Dishes at the back of the book for Leo & Susie's Famous Baked Bean Recipe.

Phenix City

CHICKEN COMER'S BAR-B-QUE

o 1222 10th Ave. o (205) 297-9889
o Mon., 11 A.M.–4 P.M.; Tues.–Wed., 11 A.M.–6 P.M.;
    Thurs.–Sat., 11 A.M.–7 P.M. o Closed Sunday

Somewhere in one of the many articles we have read about barbecue, there is this Barbecue Rule: Never eat in a barbecue joint with red-checked tablecloths. If we could find that reference again, we'd like to take the author to Chicken Comer's. It has red-checked tablecloths and the best bright yellow barbecue we found outside of South Carolina. You'd never know Chicken Comer's had red-checked tableclothes by looking at it from the outside. From the road it looks as if it could pass all the barbecue rules. It's a plain white storefront sitting in a dreary neighborhood of auto repair shops and low-rent duplex houses.

But don't judge the cook by the restaurant's cover. Owner Mary Ann Screws keeps the inside of Comer's spotless: tidy tables, gleaming red Formica counter, polished red asphalt tile. "We're not a traveler's luxury rest stop by any means," Screws said modestly. "We're a mostly down-home type place. But we try." So how did a woman named Mary Ann Screws come to run a place called Chicken Comer's? "My uncle started the business many years ago. He was a butcher by trade, and he just wanted to try a barbecue restaurant. I started working for him when I was in the tenth grade." Her uncle's real name was Anderson Comer. "But people called him Chicken from the time he was a kid because he used to kill chickens." Comer's was Phenix City's barbecue joint of choice for years. When Comer died, his cook, Mrs. Cromwell, took over, rechristened the place in her own name, and continued until her retirement in 1985. That's when Mary Ann Screws decided she wanted to revive her uncle's business and his name.

It has been Comer's and then Cromwell's and is now back to Comer's, but one thing hasn't changed: the product. It's still Chicken Comer's recipe. The meat is cooked in an open pit out back, fired with hickory and pecan wood. Comer's smokes Boston butts four to five hours, slices them by hand, chops the meat, and then pours on Uncle Chicken's heirloom sauce, a yellow lava made from mustard and a healthy spice cabinet. "Most people credit the sauce for why they like our place so much," says Screws. "The meat is good and everything, but the sauce is *it*. It's not really bitter; it just has a good taste. You can eat it with anything. In fact, just the other day this lady came up to me and said, 'Do you know what I did with the last sauce I bought from you? I just crumbled up crackers in it and ate it like that!' "

Rating: Real good.

Directions: Turn at the corner of 10th Ave. and 13th St. There's a Kentucky Fried Chicken on the corner. Comer's is a half block up on the left, slightly recessed from the adjoining rent-house. "On the outside of the place there's a little old sign with a cartoon character on it," says Screws. "It's a chicken with an apron and a comb." A Chicken Comb-er.

Tuscaloosa

DREAMLAND BAR-B-Q DRIVE INN

o Jerusalem Heights o (205) 758-8135
o Mon.–Thurs., 10 A.M.–9 P.M.; Fri.–Sat., 10 A.M.–10 P.M.
o Closed Sunday

What a wonderful name for a barbecue joint: Dreamland Bar-B-Q Drive Inn. It stirs images of puffy clouds with pig faces hidden in them, of '55 Chevies with hula-skirted pigs dancing in the back window, of old men napping to barbecue dreams. The Dreamland is located in idyllic surroundings (if you don't glance across the road at the trailer park). Nestled off the road in a stand of pine trees, it looks like an Elks Club that has gone to heaven.

For a barbecue lover it is heaven.

John Bishop, Sr., known as Big Daddy, opened Dreamland in 1958. He has turned over some of the daily operations to his son, John, Jr., but he's still there every day doing the important stuff, like cooking ribs.

We were at Dreamland on a Saturday night, where it seemed as if a party were going on. Customers were arriving in twos and fours— it was obvious that nothing had been planned—but each new arrival seemed to be welcomed spontaneously into the circle. It was one of the noisiest barbecue places we were in, but it wasn't irritating noise. It was the sound of a good time. Bishop and his wife were settled into rocking chairs in the back corner, next to the open brick pit, tending to the cooking. Occasionally Bishop would lift himself, move some coffee-brown ribs off to the serving plate, and lay a new rack down on the grate.

Dreamland is a simple place. The menu is so simple that they don't even have a printed version: All you can get is beer, white bread, and ribs. It's what Bishop, Jr., calls an "inside picnic." The ribs are served hot off the grill, just asking to be devoured. The meat doesn't fall off the bone, it just oozes off. Bishop, Jr., says, "You can pull your dentures out and eat my ribs."

Dreamland's sauce has a unique taste, a nip that is hard to pin down. What is his secret ingredient? Turnip greens? Bishop shakes his head. He won't say. There is a theory, first explained to us by some of the newsroom staff at WVMT-TV in Birmingham, that Big Daddy puts moonshine in his sauce. We decided not to ask. If the answer was yes, he couldn't tell us. And if the answer was no, we didn't want to know.

Rating: As good as we've ever had.

Directions: From I-20-59, take Exit 72 (U.S. Hwy. 82 south). Go through the intersection, and just past the McDonald's, turn left on Jug Factory Rd. Go to the fifth right turn (about three miles). When you see that fifth road branching off to the right, slow down. You should see the Dreamland's sign pointing right. The restaurant is just down the road on the left, across from the trailer park.

P.S.: As long as you're in the neighborhood, stop by **Archibald's** for a pork sandwich. This little grocery story on the outskirts of Tuscaloosa has been a favorite barbecue haunt of famous Alabamans from governors to football coaches. Archibald's is even harder to find than Dreamland. The address is 2602 Fosters Ferry Rd. Call 758-9219, tell them where you are, and ask for directions. We'd try to tell you ourselves but we got lost three times on the way. Count on at least twice yourself.

PORKLORE ○ Coming Soon!

Urban Classics, a Hollywood film and video production company, announced it will release the movie *Barbeque Bimbos* on March 7, 1989.

ARKANSAS

Blytheville

THE DIXIE PIG

o 701 N. Sixth St. o (501) 763-4632
o Mon.–Thurs., 7 A.M.–9 P.M.; Fri.–Sat., 7 A.M.–9:30 P.M.;
  Sun., 11 A.M.–9 P.M.

There's no sense dwelling on looks. The Dixie Pig looks numbingly
ordinary, like any of an army of little family restaurants stamped out
of bricks and paneling and muted floral carpeting. But the sandwich,
well, that's something else—a mountain of pork with a volcano of
sauce. It proves, among other things, that you can walk into a place
about as exotic as a TraveLodge lobby and still end up with a tantalizing bunful of barbecue.

Actually, the Dixie Pig and its cookie-cutter decor started out in
1923 as the Rustic Inn, a log cabin that had to stretch to earn the word
"rustic." Buddy Halsell's dad, Ernest, started it, and, as Buddy says,
"It if it wasn't the oldest place in Arkansas, it was close to." They
figure it was up and running before Memphis's legendary Pig and
Whistle, for instance. Ernest moved it to a rock building for a while
and then sold it in 1946 to try farming. In 1950 he came to his senses
and opened the Dixie Pig at its present location. "We used to have a
curb business," Buddy says, "but we stopped that when people got
crazy." Besides not selling to crazy people in cars, Buddy also doesn't
sell ribs. "People eat ribs about one night a week," he figures, "but if
you try to serve 'em a second or third night, you just messed up your
business." Instead he serves 'em sandwiches, great heaping sandwiches of pork flecked with bits so singed they taste like bacon, all
nestled beneath a layer of mild vinegar slaw. It's the sort of sandwich
where your second bite is apt to be bigger than your first, and so on,
until you can begin to appreciate the motto: "Feeling Piggish? See
Buddy." The sandwich also serves as a perfect canvas for some artistic
splashes of the spicy vinegar sauce that reposes in converted Heinz
ketchup bottles at each table.

The credit for the sandwich's crunchy come-on goes to Buddy's
hickory-pit technique: Cook it hot and cook it fast. "I don't believe in
smoking the meat," he says. "I don't understand people who put their
meat on a rack and leave it until the next day; I don't see how they

keep from making people sick." Credit for another of Buddy's specialties, the Pig Salad, goes to Miss Lucy Q., Lucile Quellmalz, a teacher at Blytheville High School who ordered barbecue piled on her tossed salad so often that other customers began wanting it, too. A Pig Salad in its full glory, with lettuce and tomatoes and crunchy pork underneath a glob of oddball "blue cheese" dressing, is the sort of life experience one is not likely to find outside of Blytheville. Especially not at the two Dixie Pigs in the Little Rock area, run by Buddy's brothers. "They try," Buddy allows, "but they don't do it as good as I do."

Rating: Good.

Directions: To get to the Dixie Pig, get off I-55 onto State Rd. 18 and follow Main St. west to Laclede. Take that north until the T intersection with E. Moultrie Dr. Follow that over to Sixth St., and if you're not completely lost, you should find the Dixie Pig a little ways down Sixth St. to your left.

Hot Springs

MCCLARD'S BAR-B-Q

o 505 Albert Pike o (501) 624-9586
o Tues.–Sat., 11 A.M.–8 P.M. o Closed Sunday and Monday

It's like this: Back in 1928, Alex McClard and his wife were running a tourist court out on Albert Pike near Hot Springs when a roomer couldn't lay his hands on the ten dollars he needed to pay his monthly bill. But he made them a proposition that if they'd cancel his debt, he'd give them the recipe for "the best barbecue hot sauce in the world." It was a tempting offer (not to mention a tempting sauce). The deal was closed, and soon the little motel sported a barbecue pit.

McClard's moved into its current whitewashed, neon-bedecked building in 1942, operating for a time as a drive-in, with carhops and a special jukebox that beamed tunes out to the car radios. Now it's a cheerful little sit-down/carry-out place run by Alex McClard's son, J. D., who's been in the business sixty years and keeps that ten dollar recipe locked in a safety deposit box at the bank. He has his sons, son-in-law, daughter-in-law, and grandchildren working there, too.

The sauce is still basically the same, a flavorful and sizzling creation that captures a pleasant freshness by building on tomato puree instead of a ketchup base. There's vinegar and lemon in there, too, for an aggressive tartness, and enough pepper of various varieties to make your lips feel like Mick Jagger's. The sauce is cooked by J. D. and his wife, beginning at three-thirty in the morning, in thirty-gallon batches that are reduced by half to get the proper thickness. It's a masterfully balanced amalgam of flavor and fire, the sort of thing that could lead people to pack a place and spill out into the parking lot at lunchtime, which is exactly where customers willingly stand, waiting for a booth or a stool at the long counter.

And McClard's doesn't quit with a great sauce. Or even great barbecue. The chili-accented beans are Great Northerns, washed and cooked from scratch. The long, crisp french fries are cut from real potatoes. "We don't have no frozen ingredients," says J. D.—except maybe for the ice cream in the milk shakes, which are mixed on the spot. And the place even makes its own hand-rolled hot tamales fresh daily; they're meaty, crumbly, and close to addictive.

The barbecue itself is at least that good, and almost two tons of it are smoked every week—sirloin butt for beef, fresh hams for pork and ribs with meat that is plentiful and smoky pink. The ribs are cooked over "nothing but hickory wood," like the rest of the meat, but their flavor isn't overpowered by too much smoke. And the beef is fall-apart tender after languishing in the two big brick pits on double-decker grills. All this stuff comes in typical combinations, from a beef or pork sandwich to an order of ribs with fries. But there are also meals only McClard's offers, such as the Hot Tamale Spread, which includes Fritos, two hot tamales, beans, chopped meat, and barbecue sauce. It's the kind of order that can make you glad that beer's available, along with the milk shakes and pop. But there's one specialty that's no longer on the menu.

"Back when we first got started," J. D. says, "we did goat. It cost fifty cents for a front quarter and sixty cents for a hind quarter, and we furnished the hot sauce. We had a customer at the hotel where we'd deliver the goat; it was Alvin Karpis, Public Enemy No. 1 at the time. He gave me a fifty-cent tip, the first I ever made." Despite his criminal record, Karpis couldn't have been all bad: "He liked that barbecued goat."

The official McClard's motto is "Best in the State Since '28," a rhyme obviously composed by someone who hadn't gotten around much. It's an okay motto as far as it goes, but it aims a little low. McClard's is one of the best in the nation.

Rating: As good as we've ever had.

Directions: To get to McClard's, follow U.S. 70 to where it makes a Y with Albert Pike in town, and just veer left along Albert Pike. McClard's will be on your left.

Little Rock

LINDSEY'S

o 203 E. 14th St. o (501) 372-9947
o Mon.–Thurs., 9 A.M.–10 P.M.; Fri.–Sat., 9 A.M.–midnight
o Closed Sunday

"We only have one peach pie left," the counter girl said with a sly look. "And I was sort of saving that for myself." It's true: The only problem with Lindsey's selling first-rate barbecue is that it gets in the way of a headlong rush to dessert—one of those mystically flaky fried pies with its waves of intense peach and cinnamon. The peach pies (and the apple ones, which are almost as good) are part of a thirty-three-year tradition at Lindsey's. They are made from dried fruit, which gives them a concentrated dose of flavor, and the fruit is packed inside a crust as crisp and light as the breath of an angel.

Begun in 1956 by Church of God in Christ Bishop D. L. Lindsey, this downtown barbecue joint has been specializing in the heavenly ever since. Other Little Rock BBQ legends, like Fisher's, for instance, have changed owners and given up consistency, but Lindsey's (owned since 1972 by the founder's nephew, Richard Lindsey) still produces barbecue that's practically preordained to be delicious. "It's not easy mixing religion and barbecue," says Lindsey, "because religion is a twenty-four-hour-a-day job, and so is barbecue."

With its orange walls, the eat-in half of the restaurant is clean and neat, down to the forks that arrive in fork-sized plastic bags. A fork sinks easily into the restaurant's rich, thin-sliced beef, which is cooked for fourteen to sixteen hours. It's complemented nicely by a distinctive, watery sauce that combines a sharp tanginess with meaty undertones. The pork ribs are even better with the sauce; they are at that state of tenderness where a sharp look is sufficient to make them slide off the bone. Small ribs that have been specially trimmed, they are pushed into the pit about eight in the morning. After six hours or so, they are dunked in a thin dipping sauce and cooked for a couple more hours. "I remember the first bite of barbecue I ever put in my mouth," Richard says, "and I want to be the one to put that first bite in somebody else's mouth."

Rating: Good.

Directions: Lindsey's is in North Little Rock, which is across the Arkansas River from Little Rock proper. To get to Lindsey's, take the 15th Street Exit off I-40 and head right a couple of blocks to Poplar, and then left a block to 14th St.

FLORIDA

Boca Raton

TOM'S PLACE

- 7251 N. Federal Hwy. ○ (305) 997-0920
- Tues.–Sat., 11:30 A.M.–10 P.M. ○ Closed Sunday and Monday, and for two weeks in the summer

There is a saying in Florida that the farther south you go, the farther north you are. What Floridians are trying to tell you is that south Florida is the home of many transplanted Northerners. Not fertile ground for a barbecue pilgrim? To the contrary. The best barbecue joints in Florida are located a bone's throw from each other on the so-called Gold Coast, the ritzy strip from Palm Beach to Miami. Okay, you'd have to have a mighty strong arm to throw a bone from Boca Raton to Fort Lauderdale. But they are close in the scope of things in Florida: It is 813 miles from the tip of Key West to Pensacola whereas Ft. Lauderdale to Boca is only 38 miles.

Boca Raton is the home of Tom's Place. Tom Wright had cooked for the rich folks in Boca for twenty years when he decided he wanted to go out on his own. In 1979 he opened up a soul food shack in some lend-lease–leftover Army barracks that he rented for thirty dollars a month. To call it a barbecue "joint" would have been charitable. It was located in Pearl City, one of Boca's poorest neighborhoods. Wright says it was a full year before he had his first white customer, a newspaper reporter who ate some ribs, went back to the office, and drooled in print. That's how the rich people rediscovered Wright. It wasn't long before his lunch lines were longer than a New York City block. He made enough money to buy the barracks, tear it down, and erect a large modern place. Recently, he moved again—to an even bigger place—which seats 270 people instead of 80.

But success hasn't spoiled Tom Wright. He still comes in bright and early each morning. He still oversees all the kitchen work. And he hasn't forgotten who he is or where he came from. He insists that his employees start each day with a prayer. Some days he stands by the cash register at lunchtime and randomly pulls checks and rips them up, giving the customer a free lunch. Matt Toth, a regular customer who lives in nearby Coral Springs, says, "I've been there when he's torn up one in every twenty checks."

But it isn't Wright's philanthropy that keeps those lines long. It's his barbecue: baby back ribs spooned with a delicately sweet sauce. David Pinter, a fellow from Tappan, New York, was so taken with Wright's sauce that he offered $100,000 for the recipe. When Wright declined, Pinter tried paying a chemist $10,000 to duplicate it. He took the cloned sauce and opened a barbecue restaurant in Tappan. It closed soon. There's a moral there, and we don't think we have to enunciate it.

Rating: Real good.

Directions: From I-95 take the Yamato Rd. exit east to U.S. 1 (Federal Hwy.). Go north about a mile and a half. Tom's Place is sandwiched between Capital Lighting and the Peter Pan Hotel. If you're planning a summer visit, call ahead. Tom's closes for about two weeks during the low tourist season (usually in July). And he doesn't accept credit cards or checks, so come prepared with cash.

Fort Lauderdale

HOUSE OF PRAYER BAR-B-QUE

o In the 800 block of West Sunrise Blvd. o (305) 583-5056
o Fri.–Sat., 11:30 A.M.–dusk

The Reverend Noble Harris was hunched over his backyard pit, anointing his ribs with some of his special sauce, when he spotted an ominous thunderhead cracking out over the Everglades. He dropped his head and offered a silent prayer that a stationary front would move in. And within minutes the clouds had lightened, the rumble had died off and the Reverend Harris was smiling. "He's always helped us. He helped when I started the barbecue. I'd never even cooked ribs before. But God gave me the talent."

Rev. Harris has been an ordained preacher since the age of nine, but it wasn't until 1974 that he started his barbecue ministry. "It helps our church. It funds our outreach program, our Sunday School." When Rev. Harris says, "Barbecue has been good to this church, and this church has been good to barbecue," he's not just whistling Winn-Dixie. The barbecue has provided the church with two choir vans, a station wagon, a laundromat, and a new sanctuary over on 27th Street. Reverend Harris himself has a Cadillac and a pickup truck.

It isn't just the saved who worship the House of Prayer's ribs, but barbecue lovers of all persuasions. Eating them is a religious experience. Rev. Harris marinates his spareribs overnight. He barbecues them on his barrel cooker and, if you want, he'll baptize them in his/His sauce, a molten orange dip that reminded us of the sweet, rich sauce favored in south Georgia. (He also has a hot sauce that is hotter than the Sinai desert.)

The House of Prayer Bar-B-Que is open (for takeout only) two days a week, Friday and Saturday. Rev. Harris is too busy to cook ribs more often than that. In addition to his rib mission and his House of Prayer ministry, he is a notary public, runs the House of Prayer's laundromat, and tapes a radio preaching show for a Jacksonville station. And he is always on the lookout for ways to expand his ministry. "Let me ask you this," he began, when we went for our second visit, "is there any way I can get some royalties off this book?"

That's when we wished we had the wisdom of Solomon.

Rating: Real good.

Directions: Take the Sunrise Blvd. exit from I-95 and head east. The barbecue is on the south side in the 800 block of West Sunrise, on a dot of grass between the Shell station and the House of Prayer's offices.

Orlando

RED'S BBQ

o 2516 W. Washington St. o (305) 299-0700
o Mon.–Thurs., 10:30 A.M.–9 P.M.; Fri., 10:30 A.M.–midnight;
    Sat., 10:30 A.M.–11 P.M. o Closed Sunday

Florida is the only state that has "Native" novelty license plates. Or needs to. Maybe that's why Sonny's and Fat Boy's, two barbecue chains, have done so well there. Too few natives to build up a strong barbecue tradition.

That doesn't mean you can't find good barbecue in the Sunshine State. We enjoyed Bob Foster's in Tallahassee (he uses homemade peach brandy as his sauce base) and Dave's in Ocala. But our favorite stop north of the Gold Coast was in Orlando, home of Disney World, Epcot Center, and Red's BBQ. Red's is to authentic barbecue what Disney World is to manufactured fun.

Red is Vernell Birden, a Georgia native—of course—who got into the barbecue business twenty-six years ago, washing dishes at an Orlando barbecue place. "I didn't even know how to flip a hamburger without tearing it up. But after a year I decided I wanted to learn how to cook." She started as a short-order cook. "I started observing the barbecue. And after three years I was promoted to barbecue helpmate. I did that for two years. Then one day the main cook just disappeared so I took over. And after two years they made me manager."

By then she had been working at the barbecue place for six years. "I started looking around and I said to myself, 'God, I'm making a lot of money for this guy.' I had a dream that someday I would own my own place." And for the next fifteen years she worked toward that dream. "We were very poor. In the sixties Orlando was very depressed." In 1981, twenty years after she got into the barbecue business, she decided she should strike out on her own. She mortgaged her house and opened up Red's BBQ. "When I first started, I had six little tables and twenty chairs. And only two hundred dollars in the bank. I had no customers and a lot of debt." But the customers soon discovered Red's, and in a year and a half she expanded. As we go to press she is getting ready to expand again.

Red's cooks Boston butts over an oak wood fire. Birden says she uses no marinade or rub, but a mustard-paprika-and-sugar basting sauce. She has two sauces, a mild one with ketchup, vinegar, and spices. The hot one she calls "radioactive." "It'll definitely burn you. I had one man come in with a head cold and it cleared him right up," Birden says. "The secret to good cooking is not to overcook the meat or undercook it. You can't use too hot of a fire either." What's the right temperature? Birden says she doesn't know. "I just know when I open the door to the pit, I can tell if it's too hot for what I have in there. It's just my instinct." Red's sliced pork is super tender, with brown crunchies mixed in for texture. Red's covers the meat with a slightly tangy sauce. And yes, it's a red sauce.

Rating: Real good.

Directions: From I-4 take the Colonial Blvd exit. Go west to Orange Blossom Trail (U.S. Hwy. 17-92). Then head south to Washington St. Red's is on the left, just outside the Orlando city limits, on the corner past Tom's Used Cars. It's a white run-on building with red and blue awnings. You can also take Tampa Ave. west past the Citrus Bowl, then south on Washington St. Just look for the smoke. Red is usually putting out a mess of it.

GEORGIA

Atlanta

A Drive with Dr. LaFong: For some, barbecue is an occasional indulgence, a foolish pleasure. For Dr. LaFong, it is a mission.

"There is simple truth in barbecue," he said and then lowered his eyes as if he had found a simple truth in that statement. Dr. LaFong has been on a never-ending search for Cosmic Barbecue since we met him twenty years ago. At that time he was a copy editor on a minor metropolitan newspaper. It was a low-paying, late-night, long-hours job, and his sole joy at work was taking press releases from the Mobile Home Dealers' Association and everywhere the phrase "mobile home" was used, marking it out and replacing it with "trailer." His joy outside work was barbecue. He made pilgrimages to Texas and Tennessee, to Charlie Nickens' in Nashville and the Pig and Whistle in Memphis, Sonny Bryan's in Dallas and Arthur Bryant's in Kansas City. Once he left a fellow barbecue traveler asleep in a Birmingham bar with a note pinned on him that read PUT ME ON A GREYHOUND BUS FOR LITTLE ROCK.

For the past five years, Dr. LaFong has been living in Atlanta. And still searching. So when we took our Traveling Barbecue Show to Atlanta, we asked him to give us a guided tour. "There's no such thing as bad barbecue in Atlanta," said Dr. LaFong, summing up the tour route he had mapped out. "Of course, there's no such thing as bad barbecue."

In one weekend Dr. LaFong introduced us to twenty Atlanta barbecue places, fourteen of them in one day. That's not just popping in, taking a nibble off a sandwich, and then popping out. That's Eating with a capital *E*, giving a place a fair shake. If it happened not to measure up to our standards, then pitching the rest. No sense in wasting a good appetite on inferior barbecue.

MELEAR'S

o In Fayetteville on Ga. 85 o (404) 461-7180
o Mon.–Fri., 5 A.M.–9 P.M.; Sat., 5 A.M.–10 P.M.;
    Sun., 10 A.M.–10 P.M.

We started our Atlanta pilgrimage with a barbecue breakfast at Melear's. Dr. LaFong and former Congressman Robin Beard are the only people of our acquaintance who not only accept the necessity of a barbecue breakfast when on a barbecue safari but also actually like it.

We found Melear's to our liking. Owner and founder A. Kenneth Melear is the third generation of Melears to open stands on the south side of Atlanta. His grandfather John opened up a place in LaGrange in 1927. His father, John Virgil, started a joint in Union City in 1938. "I wasn't born with blood in my veins; I was born with barbecue sauce in them," he said. Melear's sells a finely cooked, finely chopped pork sandwich, served on white-bread toast with a temperate ketchup-and-vinegar sauce. He has a hot sauce, but be warned it is hot enough to melt fillings. In 1987, Melear celebrated his thirtieth year in the barbecue business, all in the same homely block building. He said it suits him fine; he has no designs on a fancy new place. "Barbecue don't go high class."

"Oh, you've seen my car," said Dr. LaFong as he steered us out the door.

Rating: Real good.

Directions: Fayetteville is 20 miles south of Atlanta. Melear's is just south of the courthouse on Ga. 85.

HAROLD'S

o 171 McDonough Blvd. SE. o (404) 627-9268
o Mon.–Sat., 10:30 A.M.–9 P.M. o Closed Sunday

Our next stop, not counting the ones we don't count, was Harold's, the old-line barbecue place in Atlanta. Harold's is in a low-slung pink brick building with bars on the windows, a nod to the nearby penitentiary. Dr. LaFong led the way to the first two seats at the back bar. "Look in there," he pointed. "Just inside that first door to the pit." There was a shotgun leaning up against the wall. "What's that for?" we asked. "Just in case," he answered.

We ate at the bar, but not that kind of bar. Harold's doesn't serve alcohol in any form. "Mama won't allow it," Harold Hembree, *the* Harold has said. Dr. LaFong tried to explain why Deep South barbecue joints seldom sell beer. "These places grew up as family restaurants. This was where you took the wife and kids after church. In Texas it's different. In Texas everything is different, of course. All the barbecue places there have beer. But in the Deep South, where the Barbecue Belt and the Bible Belt share a buckle, you just don't see it."

Harold served a sliced pork sandwich that any barbecue lover would kill for, thereby offering one possible explanation for the shotgun. He loaded the meat on white bread, then toasted it over charcoal. It went real well with the religious bumper stickers all over the walls.

Rating: As good as we've ever had.

Directions: They're always working on the roads in Atlanta so any directions are contingent on the roads still being there. Just south of Atlanta Fulton County Stadium (home of America's team) from I-75-85 take Exit 89 east on University Ave. When it bangs head first into Ridge Ave.-McDonough Blvd., go right. It's just down the street on the right. If you pass the penitentiary, you've gone too far. Unless you're not going to Harold's.

ALECK'S BARBECUE HEAVEN

o 783 Martin Luther King Dr. NW. o (404) 525-2062
o Mon.–Sat., 10 A.M.–2 A.M.; Sun. 11 A.M.–8 P.M.

It was on to Aleck's Barbecue Heaven, a downtown place that was a haven for civil rights activists in the sixties. "You may be sitting on the same stool where Martin Luther King, Jr., once sat," said LaFong. "Or Julian Bond. Or Andrew Young." We looked around. There were only eight stools, so the odds were pretty good. LaFong continued. "Or Roberta Flack. Or Miles Davis. Or Cecily Tyson. Or even Flip Wilson."

Aleck's, which was started by Ernest Alexander back in 1942, has had more than its share of celebrities over the years, but they weren't there to rub elbows. Rather to lick up some of the tart "com-back sauce" Aleck's sops on its ribs and sandwiches. Dr. LaFong said it was aptly named: It would keep him coming back.

Rating: As good as we've ever had.

Directions: "I think it was the Cherokees who started the highway construction here," said LaFong. "It's been going on continuously ever since." From I-75-85 get off at the Martin Luther King Memorial Dr. exit, assuming it's open. Head west and watch the house numbers.

THE ACE TAXI AND BAR-B-QUE BARN

o 30 Bell St. NE. o (404) 659-6630
o Open 24 hrs. every day

We wound up our Atlanta barbecue safari at Ace Taxi and Bar-B-Que Barn, a cab stand and barbecue restaurant located on Bell Street in Atlanta's Sweet Auburn district. "They're talking about tearing this neighborhood down to build a slum," Dr. LaFong said, explaining why he would guard the car from the inside while we went into Ace's place. We heard the door lock click as we walked away. The barbecue part of Ace's is a tavern and restaurant. It was early afternoon when we visited, but already several neighbors were getting a head start on

Saturday night. We ordered a rib sandwich and, as we did, a woman in a pink jumpsuit offered to let us buy her one, too. We declined. We chomped away on Ace's tender ribs as we returned to the car. The meat was subtly sweet and coated with a sauce that was hotter than the lady in the pink jumpsuit.

As we buckled up, Dr. LaFong pointed to a kid playing out on the sidewalk. "See that eight-year-old kid? You and him are the only two sober people on this block."

Rating: Real good.

Augusta

SCONYERS' BAR-B-QUE

o 2511 Windsor Spring Road o (404) 790-5411
o Open Tues.–Thurs., 10 A.M.–9 P.M., Fri. and Sat., 10 A.M.–10 P.M.
o Closed Sunday and Monday

Something there is about barbecue and politics. They've been intertwined since old Tom Lincoln threw a sheep in the pit and cooked it while his son Abe worked the crowd. The tradition continues. In the Tidewater area of Virginia state legislators have been known to rip their pants jumping the fence to get to Pierce's Pitt Bar-B-Que, which is located in sight of the interstate but a fair clip from an exit. Kenneth Melear, owner of Melear's Barbecue in Fayetteville and chief magistrate of Fayette County, plays host to most of the county officials every morning for breakfast. And in Augusta, the politicians get together every Saturday at Sconyers', a cavernous barbecue joint just off Tobacco Road in the southern part of town. Sconyers' was the pick of the late Roy Harris, a Georgia kingmaker who was instrumental in putting Jimmy Carter in the statehouse and later in the White House. He and his buddies called themselves the Southside Rednecks, and every Saturday they would meet at a local real estate office, knock down some bourbon, and then head for Shorty's Bar-B-Q, a hole-in-the-wall famous for its food and its flies. "Shorty had one of them old-time places, and you go down there and you fight the flies and everything and eat barbecue," Harris told a Detroit newspaper in 1977, shortly after his boy Jimmy had taken up residence in Washington. "So we cussed Shorty out one Saturday and said, 'Shorty, you've got to get rid of these flies.' Shorty went out and got him a contractor and built him a nice room, air-conditioned it, got rid of the flies. Then his barbecue wasn't any good. So we left Shorty."

And moved to Sconyers'. Harris and the Rednecks held court

there every weekend until not long before his death in 1985. The Rednecks still eat there every Saturday.

Sconyers' isn't just huge, it is damned near ridiculous. "Joint" is definitely not the word for it. There are six dining rooms, one with a glass roof, of all things. The place seats 425 customers, just ten shy of being able to hold the House of Representatives. And if they were all to show up one Saturday, Larry Sconyers would figure out a way to squeeze the other ten in. Sconyers recognizes the incongruity of barbecue in a Taj Mahal. "Most places like this, the barbecue's not worth two cents," he says. "We've managed to convert a hole in the wall into a first-class restaurant and not let the barbecue lose its flavor."

The reason Sconyers has been able to maintain quality is simple: he is a barbecue fanatic. His car license plate reads "No. 1 Pig." He wears a huge gold pig ring and a gold chain with a pig on it. But it is more than just being crazy about pork barbecue. Sconyers is also mighty particular. He mixes up all his sauce himself—won't let anyone else touch it. And he supervises the cooking, which he believes is the most important part. "It's the meat, not the sauce, that gives barbecue its flavor." He buys only hams, which are high on the hog, and cooks each one for at least twelve hours over wood coals. He has patented his cooking process: standing the hams on end so they can cook in their own juices. He stumbled upon the method. One weekend he had such a large catering order that he couldn't fit all the hams on the pit. So he turned a few upright, fully expecting them to take longer to cook. To his amazement they cooked in the same length of time and were even more tender. Now Sconyers cooks all his meats, chickens, ribs—everything—standing up. "It burns every single bit of the fat out of the meat."

Sconyers serves up a chopped pork sandwich that will melt in your mouth, if you try to savor the flavor too long. The meat is chopped into fine chunks and then smothered in Sconyers' tangy sauce.

The Rednecks aren't the only politicians who swear by Sconyers'. In 1980 they catered a congressional luncheon on the White House lawn. Every February they cook for the Georgia General Assembly. Huge crowds of barbecue eaters don't bother Larry Sconyers. In 1986 alone he cooked 15,000 pigs. He says his record for one sitting is 2,168 people. That was a Georgia Power Company luncheon, and he says he got all 2,168 hungry workers through the serving line and fed in fifty-five minutes. "They only had an hour for lunch."

Rating: Real good.

Directions: From I-520 take exit 6 (Peach Orchard-Windsor

Springs Road). Take a left at the light. You will see Sconyers' down the road on the left.

Brunswick

THE GA. PIG

o U.S. 84 o (912) 264-6664
o Open daily, 9 A.M.–9 P.M.

The GA. Pig is proof that you can manufacture atmosphere. This dilapidated joint has the look, the feel, even the smell, of a place that's been in business since Johnson was president. We're talking Andrew, not Lyndon. But "Franchisor" Ed Powers didn't open it until 1977.

Powers has "barbecue joint" down pat: dusty gravel parking lot, ramshackle building, dim lighting inside, uncomfortable picnic tables, noisy ceiling fans, pesky flies, even a pair of surly, septuagenarian waitresses who gave us a hard time on our check. Our total came to three dollars and sixty cents, and we paid with a ten-dollar bill. "You have any ones?" snapped our hostess. "Three, but we don't have the sixty cents," we apologized. "Well, that don't do me any good, does it?" she sneered. We added a T-shirt to the tab to get within range of her cash register change.

It was worth the degradation. The meat was as good as we've ever had. If it hadn't been for several chewy outside pieces that we had to pull out, the GA. Pig would get our top rating. As it is, make it a "real good plus," and we'll give it another chance for the second edition.

The two ancient marinaters brush the meat with a baste while it cooks on an indoor brick pit oven right behind the order counter. They use only hickory and oak for the fire. If you're a mind to, you can stand

PORKLORE o Barbecue Don't Go High Class

Jonathan Weld, an Englishman, visited the young United States in 1799 and wrote to his friends back home, "The people are extremely fond of an entertainment which they call a berbecue. It consists of a large party of people meeting together to partake of a sturgeon or pig roasted while in the open air, on a sort of low hurdle, over a slow fire; this, however, is an entertainment confined chiefly to the lower ranks."

and watch while they fish the meat off the pit, pull the pork, chop it, and then shower it with liquid sweetness. The meat is then grilled in the bun so it all comes out toasty hot, fresh from the pit. Pavlov's dogs won't have anything on you if you stand and watch. And the sandwich lives up to its promise. In fact, there was only one thing missing in our visit to the GA. Pig: Bette Davis. She should have walked in, dropped her purse and her shoulders, and said it all: "What a dump." And what a great dump.

Rating: Real good plus.

Directions: Take Exit 6 (U.S. 84) from I-95 and head east. The GA. Pig is on the north side, half hidden in the piney woods.

Jackson

FRESH AIR BARBECUE

o Highway 23 o (404) 775-3182
o Mon.–Thurs., 7 A.M.–7:30 P.M.; Fri.–Sat., 8 A.M.–9:30 P.M.;
    Sun., 8 A.M.–8:30 P.M.

If you got directions to the Fresh Air back in 1929 and it has taken you this long to getting around to going, the directions would still hold. It has been in the same location, in the same building, that long. "People bring their kids in and say, 'Your grandparents brought me in here when I was your age and it looked just the same then,'" says George Barber, one of the managers. "Other people come in and say, 'I was here twenty or thirty years ago and it's nice to see nothing's changed.'"

Nothing has changed.

George's grandfather, eighty-year-old G. W. "Toots" Caston, bought the place in the forties and still comes in at 4:30 every morning. The pit is still in plain view right behind the order counter. The cooking methods are the same: George Barber cooks fresh hams over a hickory-and-oak fire for twenty to twenty-four hours, then pulls the meat, chops it, piles it on a bun, and ladles it with a tangy ketchup-and-vinegar sauce that is traditional to central Georgia. He says even the tables in the old dining room are the same. "They're at least forty years old. They made 'em from old two-inch beat-up pine board, cut from trees around the area."

The Fresh Air was remodeled once, in 1955. "But about all they did was pour concrete floors and add a little pine paneling on the inside, just those two changes." And then a year ago Barber added on a room to the side. But he made sure he left everything else, all the old stuff, intact. "Basically it's just a shack with an old rustic feel that people associate with barbecue."

The barbecue they associate it with is so good. . . . How good is it, George? "It's not unusual for someone to get a plate of barbecue and Brunswick stew for breakfast."

Rating: As good as we've ever had.

Directions: Go south from the town square on Hwy. 23. It's three miles deep into the heart of the Georgia woods, sort of in the middle of nowhere. When you see the American Woodmark Corporation sign, you are almost there. It usually stays open a half hour later in the summer.

Milledgeville

HOOK'S BAR-B-Q

o 713 Sandersville Rd. (Hwy. 24) o (912) 453-2452
o Open daily 7 A.M.–11 P.M., but there's fresh barbecue on
   Fri. and Sat. only

Milledgeville is Flannery O'Connor's hometown. It's not where she was born, but it's where she lived from the time she was thirteen and where she wrote most of her stories and novels. It's also where she wrote this paragraph: "The anguish that most of us have observed for some time now has been caused not by the fact that the South is alienated from the rest of the country, but by the fact that it is not alienated enough, that every day we are getting more and more like the rest of the country, that we are being forced not only out of our many sins, but of our few virtues. This may be unholy anguish but it is anguish nevertheless."

If she were alive today, living in Milledgeville and looking out the window of her writing room toward town, the phrase "unholy anguish" wouldn't begin to cover her feelings. Her Milledgeville is now virtually indistinguishable from a small town in Anywhere, U.S.A. She could look east out her window and see a Holiday Inn parked on Hwy. 441 N just across the street. She could look north and see Showplace Mobile Homes. And she could look south and see a Miracle Mile, crowned by a giant mall, where the franchised bookstore has her stories on the regional interest shelf below Lewis Grizzard's collections of humorous columns.

The South she lamented has been shoved out of town. To find it you need to drive out past the look-alike Pizza Factories and franchised Super Burgers. You need to head to Hook's Bar-B-Q.

Flannery O'Connor never frequented Hook's Bar-B-Q—that we know of—but the hero of her novel *Wise Blood,* Hazel Motes, certainly would have. Once you see Hook's, it isn't hard to believe that Hook's and O'Connor inhabited the same terrain. Going to Hook's Bar-B-Q is like taking a step way back in time, before paved roads and franchises, to when there was a distinguishable South. Hook's is a general store—very general—with juke joint trimmings: a juke box, dinette tables, beer signs. If you aren't too picky about choice of brands, you can buy a bar of soap or a box of cereal or a can of motor oil. Stop by during the week and you would think the store was just an old man's hobby about to peter out. But stop by on the weekend and Hook's is jumping. "Some people come as early as seven in the morning on Friday to get box lunches for work," says Mildred, who stays with George Hooks and helps around the store and house next door.

The end of the week is when George Hooks does what he does best: cook. He starts at five in the morning on Thursdays in the dawn's early light. With a small paring knife he cuts the excess fat off two or more whole hogs. Then he and Mildred split the hogs and lug them up on the pit, skin-side up. Hooks's pit will hold up to a dozen whole hogs, but it is usually filled only on the Fourth of July weekend. They don't take the meat off the fire until Friday morning at seven. That's when the line forms outside the smokehouse door. You see, George Hooks doesn't pull the pork for you, although he will if you want him to. He prefers to let his customers pull their own pork. He gives each one a pair of tongs and a plate and lets them have at it. That's the way he's been doing it for forty years.

Hook's is the only barbecue place we've found where you pull your own. Pulling, or pig picking, is a tradition at church barbecues throughout the South, but this is the only commercial establishment we could find still doing it that way. If the thrill of pulling your own is enough excitement for you, then we recommend Hook's mild sauce. It's quite enough, a dangerous yellow color with black specks suspended ominously in a nitroglycerin-thin liquid. But if you're ready for the whole adventure, ask for the fiery-red hot sauce. We won't venture a guess as to what's in it besides peppers, vinegar, and salt. We think maybe we're better off not knowing.

George Hooks is not the best of interviews: he's a tad deaf and a tad blind. At seventy-five, his body is beginning to betray him. He doesn't talk much, but he doesn't have to. His barbecue and his barbecue customers talk for him. And they all agree, George Hooks can cook that barbecue. Mildred says he learned to cook half a century ago as a young man, shortly after he moved to Baldwin County from neighboring Washington County. He and his new bride bought the place in 1929, and he still lives there today. He had sold a milk cow to get a down payment for the land. At the time it was just woods, but over the years he has cleared it by hand. For two decades he farmed in the daytime, hunted at night, and barbecued on the side. He worked long and hard because he had to support a wife, a son, and his brother's children. He built the store in 1949, and ever since then he's been barbecuing out back in a rusty tin shed.

His wife is dead now and the children are grown. But he still has his barbecue pit. And his loyal customers. "Beer and barbecue, that's the thing," he says. It has not been an easy life, as his stooped shoulders attest, but Hooks has no complaints. He says he lives by God's pattern: "He ain't put nothing out there that's not for some good."

Rating: As good as we've ever had.

Directions: Being the headstrong journalists that we are, we decided to find our own way to Hook's. We followed our usual method: we went to the town square, looked for a sign to Sandersville, and took off after it. It was Ga. 24, the right road, no question about that; we just didn't understand the way they number the houses in this part of Georgia. We figured 713 Sandersville Road would just be a little hop, skip, and a jump out of town, seven blocks. But what long blocks. Hook's is ten miles out of Milledgeville. If you're going east, it's on the right-hand side of the road. It's a nondescript little country store with a single Fina gas pump out front. Hook's is open daily, but there's fresh barbecue only on Fridays and Saturdays. Before heading to Hook's, make sure the cassette player in your car is in good working order. In this part of the South you find radio preachers even on FM.

Why Ty Ty, Georgia, Isn't in This Book: Talk about your barbecue-crazy little town. That's Ty Ty: 618 barbecue-loving people and

PORKLORE ○ You Want That Hot, Don't Ya?

Most barbecue joints serve mild sauce with their sandwiches. If you want it hot, you have to ask. We once heard a customer complain about the mildness and comment, "What's the point?" Does it have to be hot to be good? No. Jack Dempsey, the south Georgia barbecue king, puts it this way, "It used to be hot, hot, hot—all anybody wanted was hot sauce. Now about the only ones who want it hot are the boozeheads."

three barbecue stands, A. W. Cox Store, Bob's Barbecue, and Jack Dempsey's (no relation to the boxer). That low a ratio—one barbecue place for every 206 people—is rare, even in a barbecue-crazy area like south Georgia.

Jack Dempsey's is the best-known of the three. "People always say your trip won't be complete if you don't stop at Jack Dempsey's place," says Dempsey, who's been cooking barbecue since 1929, when he was nine years old. "We're like 'The Wabash Cannonball,' known quite well by all."

Dempsey's deserves its reputation. Writer Jim Dodson, who used to work in Atlanta, recalls the time he stopped in for a couple of Dempsey's renowned she-goat sandwiches. "I ate one and left the other under the seat of my pickup truck for three days. When I got it out and ate it, it tasted even better."

After an extraordinary she-goat sandwich at Dempsey's, we ventured across the street to the grocery store for a local opinion on Ty Ty barbecue. The clerk told us the people in Ty Ty prefer Bob's or Cox's. "Anytime the churches have a barbecue they get Bob to cater it. Dempsey's is too strong."

We backtracked toward the interstate and turned up the narrow road to Omega. We had to try these other two. After driving about two-and-a-half miles we found **A. W. Cox Store,** a low-slung building exactly what a country store is supposed to look like, tucked on the side of the road at a four-way stop. Once inside we had to clear our throats and bang around a bit before Cox appeared from the living quarters in the rear.

Cox douses his pulled-pork in that orangish sauce that south Georgians so love: a combination of tomatoes, mustard, vinegar, and spices. The mustard keeps it from getting too sweet, the tomatoes from getting too bitter. Tasty is the word.

We said our good-byes and turned left on William Gibbs Road heading toward **Bob's**. If you close your eyes for just a half second to savor Cox's sandwich, you're liable to miss Bob's. He has a little stand in back of his house on the right side of the road. You have to drive all the way up the driveway.

Bob's orange sauce was a dead ringer for Cox's sauce. And Bob's pulled pork was just as exquisite as Cox's.

With all due respect to the natives of Ty Ty, all 618 of you, we rank Ty Ty barbecue like this:

1. Jack Dempsey
2. A. W. Cox
3. Bob

We were planning to include Dempsey's as one of the hundred top barbecue places. Then Jack was in a serious car accident and he has been closed down, at this writing, for eight months. He tells us he still has plans to reopen, but the date isn't firmed up.

So what we're going to do is tell you that Jack Dempsey's barbecue sandwich ranks right up there with George Hooks' and Harold Hembree's as the best Georgia has to offer. Cox and Bob are right behind, and if we were listing the top 150 in the country, both would probably be on the list.

When Jack reopens, it will be well worth a trip on Interstate 75 to U.S. 82 (exit 18), and west from there into Ty Ty (about eight miles). Dempsey's is the easiest to find: he's right in the heart of downtown Ty Ty, such as it is, at the stoplight. To get to the other two places you'll have to backtrack on Hwy. 82, heading east. (Sorry, this is the only way to direct you. There's almost no chance you will spot the road first time past.) As soon as you get outside the town limits—you'll know, believe us—turn right on the first paved road. It is the Omega–Ty Ty Road. Cox Store is about two and a half miles down on the left at the four-way stop. The intersecting road is William Gibbs Road. To get to Bob's, turn left on William Gibbs and go a mile or so up the road. Watch closely: Bob's has just a little sign on the right side of the road.

KENTUCKY

Fountain Run

TOOLEY'S

o U.S. Hwy. 100 o no phone
o Fri.–Sun., usually from lunchtime until dark

There's a feud raging in the hills. But this time it isn't the Hatfields versus the McCoys. It's Tooley versus Tooley, and it's a barbecue feud. In Fountain Run, Ky., population 342, there are two competing barbecue joints. Two barbecue joints in a town where the major industry is yard sales, where the Country Inn Restaurant, whose sign says OPEN 7 DAYS, is closed on Sunday, and where there is a College Street but no college.

Tooley's, on West Highway 100, is run by Mrs. Sarah Tooley. George and Ova's, just around the bend on Highway 98, within shouting distance, is run by Mrs. Tooley's daughter Ova Kirk. And at the intersection of Highway 100 and Highway 98, there are dueling signs urging barbecue lovers in opposite directions.

Monroe County, wherein Fountain Run sits, is barbecue country. The competition is already intense. There are nine barbecue joints in this small (population 12,353), isolated county. Monroe Countians love barbecue, and they have created their own unique style. "We've got barbecue you can travel far and wide and not find any like it," says Monroe County Sheriff Bev McClendon. Monroe County barbecue chefs slice pork shoulders about the thickness of a Bonanza steak, slow-cook the slices over hickory coals, and then "dip" or "sprinkle" them with a hot vinegar-based sauce. "Dipped" means dunked in the sauce, and that generally means pretty hot. "Sprinkled" is more like an uptown Presbyterian baptism: just a little sauce dribbled on. They serve the meat on white bread, and it looks for all the world like a pork chop sandwich. But the smoky, fiery taste is definitely barbecue.

No one knows how the ketchup-based sauces managed to surround but not penetrate Monroe County. There is no ketchup in Monroe County sauce. "It's just vinegar, lard, butter, salt, a little sugar, cayenne pepper, and red pepper, all cooked up," says McClendon. For years barbecue was found only at church picnics and at meetings of the Sportsman's Club. Then in the fifties it started going commercial. Mrs. Tooley's was one of the first barbecue stands.

"I started in '55," she says. At first, she and her son and daughter ran the place. "Then they had got tired of it and quit and I kept it up. I cooked outside 'til they made me put a building up. Kelly Carter—Do you know him?—he was the little health man, and he closed me down for a while." To get back on the right side of the law, she put up a galvanized tin shed with a pit inside. Her original outdoor pit stands beside her present building.

PORKLORE ○ Sauce and Slabs

One day it was the teenage hangout in Louisville, Ky. The next day it was closed and the owner was going to jail. In the early thirties, local police closed Ed Land's Bar-B-Que and hauled Land off. He ended up serving time in prison for putting embalming fluid in his meat. "There was no refrigeration then," recalls Thelma Tabler, who was one of the teenagers who enjoyed going to Land's. "Everyone used an icebox. He was just trying to help the meat last longer."

In 1979 daughter Ova decided she wanted to rejoin the family barbecue business. "I wanted to go in with her, but she didn't want to," says Ova. "She's sort of old." So when mama rebuffed her, Ova moved up the road and opened up a place with her husband. And thus began the barbecue feud. It's not a shooting feud. Or even a sniping feud. When asked how they get along, both mother and daughter give the same answer: "We get along just fine."

But it is a competition nonetheless. So far, the mama is ahead. "I still only charge three dollars," says Mrs. Tooley. Then she looks across the bottom land that separates her place from her daughter's. "Everybody else is three-fifty."

Rating: Real good.

Directions: From I-65 take U.S. Hwy. 100 all the way through Chapel Hill and Scottsville to Fountain Run. Be aware that the road jogs left when it joins up with U.S. Hwy. 31 E, two miles south of Scottsville. And watch the signs carefully in Scottsville. It's easy to miss the turn to Fountain Run. Tooley's is on U.S. Hwy. 100 just before you get to town. It's open only Friday, Saturday, and Sunday. "I don't have no hours," says Mrs. Tooley. A good bet is she'll be there from around lunchtime until dark.

P.S.: Fountain Run is pretty far off the beaten track. Odds are you won't get back this way again. While you're here, drive around the bend and try George and Ova's. Decide for yourself who's winning, mama or daughter. Then, if you have time, drive on over to Gamaliel (and pronounce it guh-MAIL-yuh) to **Uncle Bow's**. He cooks the same style as Mrs. Tooley, but his sauce is a tad hotter. Uncle Bow's is named after the bow and arrow, the favored hunting equipment of the men who gather at Uncle Bow's on fall mornings. Uncle Bow's is on U.S. Hwy. 100. Don't worry. You can't get lost in Gamaliel.

Kutawa

KNOTH'S BAR-B-Q

○ U.S. Hwy. 62 ○ (502) 388-9282
○ Open March–Nov., Mon.–Sat., 11 A.M.–8 P.M. ○ Closed Sunday

Is it kuh-NO-th's or Kuh-nawth's or what? How do you pronounce it?

"They pronounce it every which way," says owner Hugh Knoth. "It's NOth's. But we don't care how they pronounce it as long as they keep coming."

They've been coming since 1966, when Hugh's parents opened

Knoth's. "It was just about the time Barkley Dam was finished. Dad had a guy come down from the Old Kuttawa Springs Barbecue—it's closed now—and show him how to cook. The guy worked with Dad just one day. You can't really learn barbecue in one day. It's really something that takes time. You've got to do it a lot to learn how. And the more patience a person has, the better job he does. So Dad kept at it and taught himself how to cook it right."

And like father like son. Knoth's cooks up the sweetest meat we found anywhere. Then they lather it up with a sauce that is as sweet as the meat. Knoth's cooks pork shoulders and beef over wood coals in a low-heat open pit for about fourteen hours.

The one time it did matter whether or not they got the pronunciation right, they did. It was 1969. Knoth's had only been open three years when Ed McMahon mentioned to Johnny Carson on the *Tonight Show* that he had eaten some real good barbecue at a place called Knoth's in Kentucky. "Supposedly he had been here," says Hugh, "although we didn't know about it at the time. The next day after he said that on TV there were ten carloads of people down here from Princeton [Ky.] to tell Dad about the show. Dad always said that was what broke it open for the business."

From then on everybody in western Kentucky knew about Knoth's. It became so famous that Hugh acquired the nickname Hot Pig. "I was in fourth grade and my little league basketball coach said, 'Knoth, why didn't you bring me some of that hot pig?' And from then on everybody called me 'Hot Pig.' I was kind of heavy anyway, and people would yell, 'Sooeey, sooeey, Hot Pig.' I didn't like it then. And it kind of wore out when I got to be a senior in high school. But I wouldn't mind if people called me that now."

Rating: Real good.

Directions: Take U.S. Hwy. 62-641 south from I-24. It is on U.S. Hwy. 62 about half a mile east of Barkley Dam. Hugh says that before Memorial Day and after Labor Day, when school is in session, they usually close at 7 P.M.

P.S.: When they talk about barbecue in Kentucky, the first town they mention is Owensboro, its mutton made famous by Calvin Trillin in a *New Yorker* article. Experienced barbecue pilgrims will add Paducah. The best-kept secret is Hopkinsville, a tobacco town of 27,-000 that is home to a dozen good barbecue joints, the best of which is **Pete's Bar-B-Q**. Pete is Milton Bussell, Sr. "Everybody's always called me Pete. I don't know why. So I named the restaurant Pete's." Pete's is in a faded brown block building no bigger than a one-car garage. It's part roadhouse, part soul-food diner, and part-social club.

Pete learned barbecue when he was a teenager. "I just picked it up from friends and added a few tricks of my own." He cooks over wood coals in an open pit, slowly smoking the meat for twelve to fourteen hours. "Or until it falls off the bone." Then he adds his own sauce. "It's tomato-based, and has eleven herbs and spices which, of course, I can't name for you." Pete has mild, hot, and extra-hot versions. But unless you have asbestos gums, we recommend starting on the low end of the heat scale. When he pours this molten sauce over his shredded mutton, it combusts, producing a smoky-good sandwich guaranteed to please even those who can't stand the thought of eating a cute little sheep.

It is real good. To get to Pete's Bar-B-Q from I-24 take Exit 88 (U.S. Hwy. 41 Alternate) into town. Watch the numbered streets, which intersect with 41A. It's a little tricky getting to Pete's. When you see Sunflower Mills looming ahead, it's time to start looking to your right. Pete's is just a block off U.S. Hwy. 41 behind the Social Security Administration Building and the Horseshoe Bar on the south side of town. The address is 822 East 21st Street. It's open Monday through Thursday, 10 A.M. to 8 P.M.; Friday and Saturday, 10 A.M. to 1 A.M. Closed Sunday. (502) 886-4764.

Owensboro

Mutton Mania: There is nothing like your first taste of barbecued mutton.

To truly understand this, you must visit Owensboro, Ky., early on the second weekend in May. You will see, looming out of a whirling haze of hickory smoke, tinged pink by a hint of dawn, cement-block firepits the size of small garages, filled with hot coals and built smack down the center of a street overlooking the Ohio River. They will be covered with hundreds of pounds of succulent, sizzling slabs of mutton that have been cooking all night long.

Mutton is the meat God meant to be barbecued. It's not at all like the milky, delicate taste of lamb; it tastes rich, grown-up. And its earthy flavor marries with the smoke of the hickory and the fire of the dip. It's not just good; it's perfect. This is not an idly held opinion in Daviess County, where Owensboro is situated; it is a devout belief of the greatest solemnity. In these rolling hills of western Kentucky, it is a belief that has fostered a dedicated rebel band of backwoods barbecuers, men for whom the heresy of pork and beef is only barely tolerated, for whom the word "barbecue" means mutton—and nothing else. Once these pit men labored in relative obscurity; Owensboro isn't "on the way to" much of anywhere. But national attention, and

○○○

PORKLORE ○ Intellectual Barbecue

For his master's thesis at Western Kentucky University, John Marshall wrote "Barbecue in Western Kentucky: An Ethnographic Study."

○○○

hungry tourists, descended on the town after a 1977 Calvin Trillin story about mutton in the *New Yorker*. The secret was out, and Owensboro was ready. If you can't make it in May to the International Bar-B-Q Festival, the men (and women) will be glad to sell it to you in scores of restaurants crowded into this little city. It's barbecue's quirkiest tradition: Western Kentucky mutton.

THE MOONLITE BAR-B-QUE INN

○ 2708 Parrish Ave. ○ (502) 684-8143
○ Mon.–Sat., 9 A.M.–9 P.M.; Sun., 10 A.M.–3 P.M.

"In the wintertime, Owensboro restaurants probably serve thirty to forty thousand pounds of mutton a week," says Ken Bosley, who (along with his parents, two brothers, and sister) owns the largest of those restaurants. "In the summer it probably goes up to a hundred thousand pounds a week." For those not mathematically inclined, that's fifty tons a week—or about two pounds a week for every man, woman, and child in town. But Owensboro isn't just any town. "We claim Owensboro as the barbecue capital of the world, and the Chamber of Commerce promotes it that way," Bosley says. "I think our claim is in the mutton."

Bosley's restaurant is "Kentucky's Very Famous" Moonlite, and it is not just big, it's *big* big—as in forklifts, delivery trucks, and Building No. 2. The restaurant got that way by combining the love of mutton with another Daviess County passion—a good deal. Much of the meat served here is in the $4.59 all-you-can-eat buffet. A price like that means the Moonlite's rambling, paneled dining rooms tend to fill up with businessmen, visitors, families, barbecue pilgrims, and the occasional uniformed softball team halfway through a Saturday double-header. There's a lot of food set out besides barbecue: potatoes, beans, chicken livers, salads, and desserts. But the typical diner's meal seems to consist of three courses—barbecue, barbecue, and barbecue. "I've eaten here often enough to know that you don't take any salad," one softball player said, although he had saved room for the homemade cherry pie served in a huge cast-iron skillet and the soft ice cream served from a self-serve machine with a warning sign: MACHINE HAS A TENDENCY TO THROW FITS. USE AT YOUR OWN RISK.

The Moonlite's mutton is served chopped and simmered in a mild tomato sauce, and it runs a bit on the strong side. You'd never suspect you're eating chopped pork with this wild-eyed funky flavor. But there are three sauces you can mix into the meat to adjust its flavor, temperature, and horizontal hold. There's black dip, a watery Worcestershire number; a sweet tomato sauce; and a Vesuvian version that's appropriately named Very Hot Sauce. Use it sparingly, or you'll singe the little silk flowers at your table.

Rating: Real good.

Directions: To get to the Moonlite from the nearest interstate (I-64), take U.S. 231 south across the bridge over the Ohio and turn right. Go to Frederica St. and turn left. Then go to Parrish Ave. and turn right. It's about three miles up the road. There are lunch and dinner buffets most days.

OLD HICKORY PIT BARBECUE

o 338 Washington Ave. o (502) 926-9000
o Sun.–Thurs., 9 A.M.–9 P.M.; Fri.–Sat., 9 A.M.–10 P.M.

In every great barbecue town, there's the place you *have* to visit and the place you *ought* to visit. In Owensboro, you ought to visit the Old Hickory; it serves the best mutton in town, which most likely means the best mutton on the planet Earth. Here mutton is sold the way it should be, sliced "off the pit." This is mutton the way mutton lovers eat it—no sauce for a disguise, no tricks. It is tender, touched with the ruby hues of hickory smoking, and not the least bit dry. In fact, fresh, hot mutton is as rich and delicious as an aged beef steak and, cooked right, a lot more tender. It has a very faint musky aura that mixes with the hickory aroma in subtle, satisfying ways. The slices are lean and absolutely luscious. Sometimes outsiders will think of the meat of the mature sheep as "gamey" or "icky." These are people who simply have never eaten mutton this good. Toss your Four Seasons filet in the trash; this makes steak superfluous.

Actually, getting masterful mutton at the Old Hickory is something akin to destiny. Owner Harl Foreman, Jr., is a fourth-generation barbecuer; his family started in the business in 1918 when great-grandfather Charles cooked for one of the churches and ran a blacksmith shop. The wisdom of pit-tending is a family heirloom: "It's passed down," Foreman says. The Old Hickory recently moved to a new place that looks a bit modern and rootless, but the cooking hasn't changed a bit. "We cook all night," Foreman says. "I designed my own pit, and I built this building for barbecue."

Rating: As good as we've ever had.

Directions: To get to the Old Hickory from the nearest interstate (I-64), take U.S. 231 south across the bridge over the Ohio and turn right. Go to Frederica St. and turn left. Stay on Frederica south until you hit 25th St. Turn right onto Washington Ave., and you're there.

P.S.: There is a belt of mutton barbecue across western Kentucky. Owensboro is the undisputed capital, but good versions are to be found elsewhere—like the **Ky. Pit Bar-B-Q** on U.S. 41 in Henderson, Ky. A ramshackle, red-and-white wooden barbecue stand, this place features mismatched tables and chairs scattered under a huge shade tree for dining out. Starling McClure has been cooking here continuously, more or less, since 1946, and that's the way the place feels—like a 1940s roadside shack. Except this one sells hot, spicy mutton sandwiches that put some of the big boys' stuff to shame. Lean and not the least bit gamey, these generous sandwiches are made from mutton trimmed so much that they actually lose a little money on each one they sell. "We sell them because people demand them," a counter worker said. Demand one yourself. The shack is set back incongruously from a busy commercial strip at 2850 N. U.S. 41. It's just across the bridge over the Ohio and is open Monday through Saturday, 10 A.M.–2 A.M. (502) 826-7491.

Paducah

STARNES BAR-B-Q

o Joe Clifton Dr. o (502) 444-9555
o Mon.–Sat., 8 A.M.–9 P.M. o Closed Sunday

It was midafternoon of a mild February day: not lunchtime, not barbecue season. But Starnes Bar-B-Q was packed. Both the booths were full. And there was only one seat left at the counter. Starnes Bar-B-Q is simplicity defined. A U-shaped counter surrounds a drink case and candy counter. There is a booth wedged in on each side where the counter meets the wall. On a cold day you might be able to squeeze thirty people in.

"Me and Daddy started this when I was twelve," said Larry Starnes. "I'm forty-five now." When Starnes Bar-B-Q opened its doors for business in 1954, a filling station was the only other business on Joe Clifton Drive. Now the street has been widened and turned into a Miracle Mile. There are ten fast-food restaurants within a city block of Starnes', everything from Pizza Inn to Arby's to the ubiquitous McDonald's. But on this day, the only one with a full parking lot is Starnes. "Every time they opened a new one, I figured it would cut into our business," said Starnes. "But it hasn't yet."

Starnes is the best example going of Paducah-style barbecue. Starnes cooks his meat over red-hot coals in a pit out back. He prefers hickory wood for its distinctive flavor and believes that slow-cooking is the only way. But he doesn't believe all the stories he hears about barbecue fellows cooking meat for hours on end. "Anybody says they get up at four in the morning to start the fire, I just shake my head. I read this one story where the fellow said he cooked his meat twenty-four hours. I drive by his place every day and I know better. We cook ours ten or twelve hours. But I don't get up at four A.M. to start it. We Starneses are lazy."

Starnes' meat is pulled from the bone and chopped fine, then piled on a piece of Bunny-brand white bread. Another piece of bread is stacked on top, and then the sandwich is grilled. At first blush the grilled sandwich looks like something you would order at an airport coffee shop. It takes a couple of bites to get used to barbecue on toast, but once your taste buds accept the difference, you're hooked. There's only one sauce available, a hot, tomato-based one developed years ago by Larry and his father. It's not ninth-ring-of-hell hot, but it does make a statement. Bonnie the waitress will ask if you want any of it on your sandwich. The best answer is "yes." It's just a sprinkle, but it's plenty enough to heat up the meat. "Other areas they use the sauce like gravy," said Starnes. "Ours, you use it like a seasoning."

Starnes offers pork, beef, and mutton sandwiches. Paducah, after all, isn't far from the mutton country of Owensboro. "I just sell mutton as an accommodation for a few folks who ask for it. I don't really believe in it." Drinks come in the bottle straight out of the drink case. People in Paducah will tell you Starnes barbecue is the best anywhere in the world. None of the people who say that have been all over the world. In fact, from the directions Donna, who works at Starnes, gave us to get to the restaurant, you may wonder if they have even been to town. Okay, so they don't know roads. They know barbecue.

Rating: Real good.

Directions: These directions courtesy of Donna at Starnes. "Take the Lone Oak-Mayfield Exit off I-24. Turn right, toward Lourdes Hospital. Go through four traffic lights (about two miles) to the stop sign at the railroad viaduct. Turn right under the viaduct onto Jefferson. At the first traffic light take a left onto Joe Clifton Drive. Go six blocks until you see the bowling alley. The next thing on the right is Starnes."

Waverly

PEAK BROTHERS DRIVE-IN RESTAURANT

o U.S. 60 o (502) 389-0267
o Mon.–Thurs., 8 A.M.–10 P.M.; Fri.–Sat., 8 A.M.–midnight;
  Sun., 8 A.M.–8 P.M.

It takes some mighty fine barbecue to get a rise out of a Texan, but Buddy Peak's mutton sandwich not only brought thanks from a Texan, it pleased a president. And Buddy has the letter to prove it.

"Earle C. Clements, who was a politician from around here, used to bring Lyndon B. Johnson and Ladybird to eat our barbecue. She wrote me a letter one time that she thought Texans knew everything about barbecue but she found out they didn't when she come to my place." It was a prized letter and Buddy kept it framed on the wall for years. "I almost lost it when this place burnt down four or five years ago. One of the fellows run back in the fire and got it."

Peak Brothers has been satisfying barbecue lovers of all stripes and all places of origin since 1948, when Buddy and his late brother, Barker, bought a closed-up restaurant and opened it as a barbecue stand. "I told my dad what I was going to do, and he laughed and said, 'Why, you never even fried a hamburger.'" The two brothers hired the janitor at the local school to teach them how to cook barbecue. "He cooked around at church picnics and all. He was going to stay with us a week or two and he ended up staying twenty-some years. His wife told me he'd go home at night worried we were going to burn the meat up while he was gone. He done the worrying for us in our younger days. Now I'm doing it." Buddy has pretty much turned the place over to his son, Eddie, and his daughters Debbie and Irene. But he still comes in for an hour or so every morning. "I think it's just a habit," says Eddie, "because he sure doesn't stay long enough to do anything. When the work starts and customers start coming in, he leaves."

Buddy taught his children how to cook over a wood-fired open pit. Eddie says mutton is their big item. "But we've cooked everything but a seal on these pits. We've cooked a lot of venison, bear, coon, even possum; believe it or not, they tried one of those on us one time." Peak's specialty is chopped mutton moderated with a sharp, vinegary sauce. "It's highly seasoned," says Buddy. "Some times more than others. Sometimes you get somebody new making it up and they stump their toe and get it real hot."

Rating: Real good.

Directions: Waverly is almost one of those places that you can't get to from here. From Evansville, Ind., take U.S. 41S to U.S. 60 South. Waverly is 7 miles past Corydon. Peak Brothers is right on U.S. 60 on the north side of town.

LOUISIANA

Baton Rouge

JAY'S BARBECUE

o 4215 Government St. o (504) 343-5082
o Mon.–Sat., 10 A.M.–9:55 P.M. o Closed Sunday

There was a sandy-haired guy on one of the five metal stools at the counter in Jay's. Sitting next to his sweet, shy bride-to-be, he had brought her to the little barbecue joint where his mother had always taken him—not as a test, perhaps, but just the same, he had ordered her some ribs and was watching her eat with more than casual interest. Marriages can survive many things, it became obvious, but a serious disagreement about good barbecue may not be one of them.

It would be hard to break up at Jay's, however. Jay's has real good barbecue. And Jay's also has Floyd J. LeBlanc, Sr., a thoroughly entertaining pit master who has been cooking for more than thirty years, ever since he started at age fourteen. In a profession full of slow-talking characters, Floyd is permanently stuck on fast-forward. He will chat with customers, customers' little children, salesgirls from down the street, and someone just looking for change. He will joke and josh, sometimes carrying on a phone conversation at the same time. "Hey! Don't you go talkin' to me that way!" he said, laughing into the phone. "I'm bad! I drink barbecue sauce every day for a living, so you *know* I'm bad!"

Floyd LeBlanc is a big deal in Baton Rouge. Awards have been presented; film crews have filmed. But all that is almost incidental to a man who genuinely and completely loves barbecue, who says, "Barbecuing is like getting up and going to school every day; you are always learning something new." For Floyd that includes smoked alligator tail, which is not featured on the menu, as well as beef, ham, pork, turkey, ribs, and chicken, which are.

There are barbecue cooks who understand barbecuing, but who don't eat it much; they'll tell you it's like working in a candy store.

But Floyd LeBlanc is not one of those people: "How could you ever get tired of barbecue?" he wondered aloud. "I eat it every day. I eat it for *breakfast* every day. There are so many ways to fix it, so many kinds of meat. I eat it dry, I eat it on toast—this morning, I mixed it with potato salad and ate it that way."

One recommended way to eat it is in one of his Barbecue Po-Boys. This is one hefty sandwich, built on a French-style loaf with handfuls of delicately pecan-smoked beef or pork (or both), sliced thin and tender, and dressed with anything from lettuce and tomato and cheese to a simple slosh of Floyd's tonsil-tweaking, tangy sauce. It's an excellent sandwich, and just one of the things at Jay's that has attracted attention.

"A fellow tried to talk me into opening up a place in California," Floyd said. "He said just to tell him how I cook the meat and do that sauce, and he'd set things up out there." It wasn't that Floyd had anything against California, but he turned the man down. "Some of this stuff is written down," he explained, "but a lot of it's just up in my head. And telling a man all your secrets on cooking is like letting him borrow your wife. It just doesn't work that way."

Rating: Real good.

Directions: The original Jay's on Government St. is where you'll find Floyd LeBlanc. There's an exit onto Government from I-110 as it passes through Baton Rouge. There are other locations at 5734 Sherwood Forest and 9817 Greenwell Springs.

Lafayette

THE A & B HENDERSON BAR-B-Q LODGE (AND GATOR COVE)

o U.S. 90 o (318) 264-1373
o Mon.–Thurs., 4 P.M.–10 P.M.; Fri.–Sat., 4 P.M.–10:30 P.M.
o Closed Sunday

Barbecue has a seafood soul brother—a dish with origins almost as humble and a following almost as fanatic, a dish so delightfully spicy and so satisfyingly sloppy that any stuffed shirt in the vicinity is sure to catch a drip. The nice thing is, at A & B Henderson you can eat them both: smoky barbecue and steaming crawfish.

The barbecue came first, a pit with a tiny dining room built about seven years ago. And then the offshore drilling boom hit the Gulf, bringing hordes of hungry oil workers into the area. When the dust settled, the original pit had acquired a big new dining room, plus a second pit with its own dining room, a landscaped courtyard, offices, party rooms, and the Gator Cove, a cavernous hall where crawfish is king. Now, the Gator Cove often outdraws the Bar-B-Q Lodge: During prime crawfish season (roughly November through May), the waiting crowds sometimes line up for two hours in the parking lot.

On the sunny summer afternoon we visited, the huge complex was almost deserted. Inside the lodge (which looks the way a lodge should, with A-frame timber ceilings and a big stone fireplace), the hats outnumbered the heads. This was due to the A & B's "gimme cap" collection, scores of baseball caps, with commercial messages, nailed to the walls and rafters. There are caps from Hawaii, from the Melmar Tools Co., the NRA, and, of course, the A & B Henderson Bar-B-Q Lodge. We headed for the cafeteria line for a cold beer and an A & B Special, a tasty sandwich on a toasted bun that was loaded with bits of barbecue, many nicely burnt, and a splash of molasses-dark, tart tomato sauce. They won't say what's in the sandwich, but it tasted like a mixture of beef and pork, and it tasted real good, especially with the "dirty rice" that had more barbecue bits mixed in. Beef, ham, smoky-pink pork ribs, and rather pedestrian sausage also are on the menu.

But instead of ordering more barbecue, we headed through the courtyard and over the hill to Gator Cove, where an order of crawfish was boiled on the spot in a massive, open iron kettle. Crawfish and barbecue make an enjoyable, earthy surf-and-turf combination, the crawfish painfully hot and powerfully spicy. This may be the only place on earth to try it, and try it you should.

Rating: Good.

Directions: The Lodge and the Cove are on U.S. 90 just east of Lafayette and just past the small airport.

Ville Platte

THE PIG STAND

o 318 E. Main St. o (318) 363-2883
o Tues.–Sun., 6 A.M.–11 P.M. o Closed Monday

The salty, smoky spare ribs were coated with a bright orange, homemade baste. They were served at an aging table with three brands of hot sauce, plus a bottle of peppers and onions—in a spare brick building with only a Coca-Cola sign announcing its presence. A classic barbecue joint, right? Well . . . no.

The Pig Stand Restaurant is a classic *Cajun* barbecue joint, and there's a difference. It's not just that the cooks and friendly waitresses chatter in French, either. A Cajun rib dinner is a wonderful experience full of surprises, and the ribs themselves are just part of the fun. Take the first course: It's true that most barbecue dinners don't include (or even allow) a first course, but the Pig Stand's oyster gumbo is reason enough to reconsider that tradition. Available à la carte, the gumbo arrives in an immense flat bowl, savory with the flavors of a buttery, mellow roux, and studded with plump oysters. It manages to seem sinful and satisfying and vaguely healthful all at the same time. It's the perfect setup for a Bar-B-Q Spare Rib lunch—as long as it's Tuesday, Thursday, Saturday, or Sunday, the only days the Pig Stand serves ribs. The strip of pork spare ribs is cooked just short of chewy, smoked pink and very salty, with a cumulative spicy heat. But the ribs aren't the hottest thing on the plate; that honor goes to the smothered potatoes, a luscious casserole of potatoes and cheese with stingingly hot greens cooked all through it. For three bucks, ribs and a superlative side dish may seem sufficient, but the Pig Stand also tosses in some rich "rice stuffing" dense with crumbs of liver. And some meltingly soft and sweet butter beans (baby limas). And a heap of white rice with a dark roux gravy. It's generous and genuinely delicious.

While patting one's protruding tummy, a short after-dinner promenade may be in order, and just a few hundred feet down the street, at 434 E. Main St., is Floyd's "Nationally Advertised" Record Shop, jammed with Cajun music, blues, oldies, and scenic postcards of Martian Klansmen wearing what appears to be aluminum foil on their heads. You could do worse than to walk out of there with Rockin' Sidney's "My Zydeco Shoes Got the Zydeco Blues." And if you walk briskly in the hot Louisiana sun, you may make room for more oyster gumbo. For dessert.

Rating: Pretty good.

Directions: The Pig Stand is on East Main St., which is the part of U.S. 167 that's one way south through town. It's right next to Reed's Superette and Slaughter House.

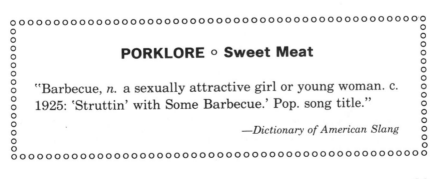

PORKLORE ○ Sweet Meat

"Barbecue, *n.* a sexually attractive girl or young woman. c. 1925: 'Struttin' with Some Barbecue.' Pop. song title."

—*Dictionary of American Slang*

MISSISSIPPI

Clarksdale

ABE'S BAR-B-Q DRIVE-IN

o 616 State St. (U.S. Hwy. 61) o (601) 624-9211
o Open daily, 9 A.M.–9 P.M.

Raymond Gibson, Jr., remembers growing up in Clarksdale, Miss., and padding down to Abe's Bar-B-Q just to watch Abe slice the meat. "He sliced the barbecue so thin you could read the paper through it." Pat Davis, Abe's son, says that wasn't unusual. "Daddy kept the knives sharp, and he could slice the meat so fast people came to watch him. A man came in one time and asked him if he wanted to buy a slaw machine. Daddy said, 'What's that?' The man said, 'It'll cut up your slaw for you in five minutes.' Daddy said, 'I don't need it.' 'Why's that?' the man wanted to know, and Daddy showed him. He could cut that cabbage right to the tip of his fingernails and he could do it quickly. The man watched for a minute and then turned around and said, 'No, you don't need it.' "

Abe was Abe Davis, an immigrant from Lebanon, who opened his first barbecue stand in 1924. He quickly developed a reputation around north Mississippi for top-notch barbecue, and over the years the reputation has only grown. In fact, when the rock group ZZ Top stopped off at Abe's recently, it was Billy Gibbons, a member of the band, who asked for an autograph, instead of the other way around.

When Abe died, sons Pat and Abe, Jr., took over the operation, and they've been running the place since 1960. About the only difference that we could see is that there's no one in the kitchen now who can handle a knife with quite the artistry that Abe could. Pat recalls, "It used to be the bus had a one-minute stop out here. The bus driver would run in and order a sandwich. Daddy would cut it and have it ready in twenty seconds."

We could go on at length about Abe's magic knife. Instead, let's talk about Abe's barbecue. The meat is flaky-tender. Abe's prepares it a little differently from many barbecue stands. "We cook Boston butts over hickory from ten in the morning to four in the afternoon," says Pat. "That gets most of the grease out. Then we refrigerate it, slice it cold, heat it on the grill, and chop it." They squirt the meat with a tangy sauce made from ketchup, Worcestershire sauce, and vinegar, top it with a rough slaw, and serve it on a grilled bun. How does it taste? The best recommendation we can offer for Abe's is an unsolicited one that we happened to observe. One of Abe's car hops was scraping the grill and came up with a tear of meat. He scooped it onto the chopping board, squirted it with sauce, and devoured it.

Rating: Real good.

Directions: From I-55, take State Rt. 6 west to U.S. Hwy. 61, then head south to Clarksdale. Abe's is on the left (east) side at 616 State St., which is U.S. Hwy. 61. (In 1987 Abe's opened a second location in Oxford, Miss., run by Pat's son and son-in-law.)

Gulfport

AN-JAC'S FAMOUS BAR-B-QUE

o 1700 22nd Street o (601) 863-5762
o Mon.–Sat., 8 A.M.–7 P.M.; Sunday, noon–5 P.M.

It has been two decades since Hurricane Camille tore through the Gulf Coast, but her destruction is still a topic of conversation in those parts. "People that haven't seen a hurricane can't imagine," says Jack Meeks, the "Jac" of An-Jac's. The "An" is wife Anne. "It's like a tornado times a hundred, plus it's five or ten miles wide instead of sixty yards, and it lasts four or five hours." Anne and Jack Meeks and their son Michael had been living in Gulfport, on Mississippi's Gulf Coast, only six years when Camille crash-landed in 1969. Jack recalls, "I drove in toward town the next morning, and there were three ocean-going vessels two hundred and fifty yards inland. There was not a bird, not a sound. For two days after that, all you heard was the buzzing of chain saws. The birds didn't come back for a year and a half." Camille's 172-mph winds killed 256 people, caused $1.4 billion in damages, and left scars that still haven't healed, but her black cloud had a silver lining. It made An-Jac's Bar-B-Que famous. "We fed all the clean-up workers," says Michael. "I went all up and down the beach that week giving free barbecue poor-boys to the highway patrolmen who were here to prevent looting."

An-Jac's was one of the few businesses to remain open during those tumultuous days. And people remembered. An-Jac's went from a hometown place to a barbecue stand that lived up to its middle name. "Little did we know when I had the sign painted," says Jack. "I had the guy paint 'An-Jac's Famous Bar-B-Que,' and he said, 'What do you mean, famous? You haven't even got outside Gulfport.' And I said, 'But we will.' "

Jack knew it because he knew how hard his family was willing to work. When they lived in north Mississippi in the early sixties, the Meeks gave new meaning to the term "moonlighting." During the day

Jack worked a snack-food route and Anne ran a nursery. When Michael got home from school in the afternoon, he and his mother would begin making sandwiches. Meanwhile his father was out driving a paper route. When Jack got home, they would pile in the car and begin delivering their ready-made sandwiches to little stores all over the area. "My supper would be a Chocolate Soldier and a day-old sandwich at midnight," remembers Michael.

So when they took over the Gulfport grocery store, Jack began working on a new item to add to the menu, a barbecue sandwich. He knew how to cook the meat. So he set to work on the sauce. "I kept adding and taking away 'til I got it like I wanted it." The way he wanted it was sweet and hot, a lot of both. He got it right. It's especially potent on an An-Jac stack, a pile of thick juicy chunks of hickory-smoked barbecue, swimming in a sea of An-Jac's sauce.

The sauce is so popular that Jack bottles it and sells it in grocery stores in the Gulf area. Still, there are some deprived areas. When we were there, a woman from Shreveport, six hours away in Louisiana, was buying a case of sauce. "I'm down to one bottle in my old case."

Rating: Real good.

Directions: From U.S. Hwy. 49, the main road into Gulfport, it's eight blocks east on 22nd Street. There are billboards directing you from either direction on U.S. Hwy. 49. If you're lucky, you'll visit on a day when Pearly is working the sandwich counter. She is the sweetest waitress this side of heaven.

Vicksburg

GOLDIE'S TRAIL BAR-B-QUE

o 4127 S. Washington St. o (601) 636-9839
o Mon.–Thurs., 11 A.M.–9 P.M.; Fri.–Sat., 11 A.M.–10 P.M.
o Closed Sunday

How's this for the name of a barbecue place: Goldie's Trail Bar-B-Que? You can almost see Gene Autry galloping up on Champion, the palomino rearing up, Gene waving his ten-gallon hat, the grizzled trail cook clanging the triangle, ranch hands lining up with their dinner plates.

But Goldie's Trail Bar-B-Que is on the greenhorn side of the Mississippi, near a bluff overlooking the mighty river. There is no hitching post, no bunkhouse, not even a souvenir saddle next to the cash register. It's a simple cafe decorated with framed pen-and-ink drawings from Vicksburg's Civil War past. And Goldie wasn't a grizzled cook straight out of a scene from *Wagon Train*. He was Gola Marshall, a Missouri native who learned to cook barbecue in Arkansas. "The sauce recipe was passed down in his family," says his nephew, Randy Wright, who has run Goldie's since Marshall's death in 1982. "Goldie's father gave it to him in 1949. Goldie refined it and went into the barbecue business in 1953 in Waverland, Ark." Goldie opened the Mountain View Inn, a little liquor store and restaurant. "Then the county went dry on him," laughs Wright. So in 1960 he moved to Vicksburg, the hometown of his wife, Wright's aunt.

And Goldie's has been there ever since. "In the sixties and seventies this was the teen hangout, like Arnold's on *Happy Days*. Now those kids are grown up, and they bring their kids in here." They want their kids to learn to love the barbecue they grew up on, and Wright tries to comply. "We do things the same way Goldie did. We peel our own potatoes for the potato salad. We still use Goldie's pits." They slow-cook pork shoulders, Boston butts, ribs, chicken, beef brisket, and sausage over hickory. The brisket and sausage are a nod to Goldie's barbecue training west of the Mississippi, as is the sauce—a thick, rich Texas-style accent that tastes as good as it looks, and it looks good. A serving of Goldie's thin-sliced pork barbecue is as beautiful as a Mississippi spring. When it is spread out on a plate, it looks like country ham covered with a thick brown gravy, waiting for a serving spoon full of grits and a *Better Homes and Gardens* photographer.

Rating: As good as we've ever had.

Directions: From I-20 take exit 1A, Washington St., north. It's about 500 yards down on the right.

NORTH CAROLINA: East

In North Carolina barbecue is right up there with basketball as a thing people argue about. That's because North Carolina has developed two distinct barbecue styles, and practitioners of each are divided along geographical lines. *Down East* barbecue, the oldest style of barbecue in this country, appears in the coastal regions of the state. It originated in those days when people thought tomatoes were poisonous and refused to eat them. When the early settlers wanted a seasoning for their barbecued pig, they chose English ketchup, a vinegar seasoned with oysters and peppers and other spices, but containing no tomato. That's still the sauce they use Down East. The Piedmont area has produced *Lexington style,* named after its town of origin, Lexington, N.C.

Let's begin with the most elementary question: Where is Down East? Dennis Rogers, columnist for *The News & Observer* in Raleigh, says, "A lot of people will tell you that U.S. Highway 1, which cuts through Raleigh, is pretty much the dividing line between eastern and western North Carolina barbecue. From Raleigh east, including Raleigh, is Down East. From Raleigh west is Lexington style."

Down East they cook the whole hog, with no baste, over hickory coals, then "pick" the meat off the bone, chop it into fine hunks, and coat it with a thin, hot vinegar-based sauce. The traditional side dishes are Brunswick stew, cole slaw, cornbread, and boiled potatoes cooked with paprika. "Our folks around here eat an enormous amount of barbecue," says Rogers. "It is a standard at social gatherings. What the politicians call the rubber chicken circuit, around here is pig pickin'. You can even rent cookers from U Haul. Rufus Edmisten lost the recent governor's race, and I'm sure it was because he made the statement right before the election that he was sick of barbecue. There ain't no way in hell you're going to be governor of North Carolina if you don't love barbecue."

You wouldn't think that an area with a barbecue tradition that dates to pre–Revolutionary War days would break so easily with that tradition. But Rogers says, "We're having a real problem here in eastern North Carolina because so many of the places have gone to gas. They'll lie to you and tell you it's because of the health department, but it's because it's easier."

Melton's in Rocky Mount, the first place to sell barbecue on the street, now cooks with gas instead of wood; so does Bill's in Wilson and Doug Saul's in Nashville. A number of places still cling to the old ways, and we have singled out a few of the best.

Goldsboro

WILBER'S BARBECUE

o Highway 70 o (919) 778-5218
o Daily 6 A.M.–9 P.M., except Sunday, when it's open
   6 A.M.–2:30 P.M. and 5 P.M.–9 P.M.

When the fish are running off Emerald Isle, N.C., Eddie Williams starts getting antsy. Williams, the industrial recruiter for the Johnson City, Tenn., Chamber of Commerce, keeps a trailer at Emerald Isle for those fishing urges. But it isn't only the fishing that attracts him to that part of the world. There's a barbecue place—Wilber's.

Williams, a Tarheel by birth, has been a Tennessean for twenty-eight years now, but he says his barbecue heart is still in eastern North Carolina. "They've got some good barbecue around here in Tennessee, but they use that sweet sauce. I like Wilber's 'cause it's hotter."

Williams isn't afraid to step into the North Carolina barbecue feud that has been simmering for decades. He says the Down East style is best and thinks the people of the western part of the state would agree, if they wouldn't let their pride get in the way. But he says he has seen them with their guards down. "My sister's son had a wedding in High Point recently and Wilber catered it from Golds-boro." The distance between High Point and Goldsboro is only 140 miles, but it's a lot farther than that in the barbecue world. You see, High Point is on the buckle of the western North Carolina Barbecue Belt, eighteen miles from Lexington. And Goldsboro is almost the center point of the Down East barbecue area. And never the two shall agree, especially when it comes to barbecue. Williams cackles when he recalls, "Most of the people at the wedding were from around High Point but that didn't slow them up when it came to eating Wilber's."

Wilber's reputation extends far outside of North Carolina. Rick Patterson, assistant director of college relations at Marietta College, which is in Ohio, still has the book of matches he picked up at Wilber's in 1979. "I have kept it to this day in case I came near Goldsboro again. Wilber's is the best I've ever had and I was raised on the Ridgewood barbecue." (See Bluff City, Tennessee, for the Ridgewood restaurant.)

Wilber Shirley, owner and founder of Wilber's, works hard at holding onto that reputation. "My wife says I married the restaurant and left her." He is in every morning by nine and seldom leaves before eleven at night. And that's six days a week. On Sunday he may be there as early as six in the morning. Wilber stresses that Wilber's is a family place. "We don't allow no alcoholic beverages on the prem-ises. Never have had them. We don't believe in that stuff. We've found that people who say they like to party still want some place they can take their preacher."

Wilber cooks twenty-eight whole hogs at a time over live-oak coals. He built a special cookhouse out back, some fifty or sixty feet from the restaurant. It means a little more running back and forth from cookhouse to restaurant, but Wilber says, "It keeps fire insur-ance premiums down." Insurance premiums are one of the few places Wilber cuts corners. He sure doesn't on his sandwich. Wilber's sun-burned sauce is thin as rainwater, with a vinegar base, red pepper for tone, and black pepper for fire. Wilber's isn't a flavoring sauce, it's a flavor-enhancing sauce that soaks into Wilber's creamy chopped pork and seems to disappear. Don't miss Wilber's long, worm-shaped hush puppies. They may not look appetizing, but once you start eating them, you can't stop. And top it all off with Wilber's banana pudding.

The only complaint we have about Wilber's is the parking lot. Not just that it's always full, which it is, but that it is gravel and unmarked and, well, a mess. Eddie Williams says, "I've never gone by when the lot isn't about full. He does the business. But he still can't afford to pave his parking lot." Wilber has fixed up the inside over the years. It's not high class; with its knotty pine paneling, high-pitched ceilings, and exposed wooden beams it looks more like a Rod and Gun club. He's had to keep on adding dining area. There are now three dining rooms, and Wilber says he can seat "three hundred twenty-eight or three hundred twenty-nine, depending on how fat the three hundred twenty-eighth person is."

Rating: As good as we've ever had.

Directions: It's four miles east of Goldsboro on Highway 70. Look for a dust cloud and a parking lot full of cars parked this way and that way. For Wilber's banana pudding recipe, see the chapter Side Dishes toward the end of this book. For his sauce, see the mail order section.

New Bern

MOORE'S BARBECUE

o Highway 17 South o (919) 638-3937
o Mon.–Thurs., 10 A.M.–8 P.M.; Fri.–Sat., 10 A.M.–8:30 P.M.
o Closed Sunday

Why are so many barbecue places Down East converting from wood to gas? Tom Moore, the manager of Moore's and son of the founder, offers some insight and some hard figures. It's a dollar decision. "We cook lots of meat two or three times a week rather than a little bit every day," says Tom. "That's because the wood's so expensive. It costs us almost two hundred dollars for each cooking session: sixty-five dollars for wood, sixty-five dollars in labor and fifty dollars in processing and cutting meat." The reason Moore's holds out for wood is because Tom thinks it's worth it. "The secret to cooking barbecue is using live-oak coals."

It was a lot simpler when Tom's dad, Big John Moore, first got into the barbecue business in 1945. "Dad borrowed thirty-five dollars to buy a pig and got someone to cook it," says Tom. "When he sold the barbecue, he paid off the cook and bought another pig." Big John kept plowing his profits back into his business until he was able to open a small restaurant in a converted filling station. Over the next three decades Moore's moved from place to place, finally settling into its current location in 1972. It's nothing fancy—a brick building with an order counter in the center and dining rooms on each side.

It's all self-serve: You order at the counter, grab your drink out of a case by the door, and carry your food to one of the long family-style tables. "There's no table service and no tips," says Tom. "That's so you can have a good meal for under three dollars."

The specialty of the house is the chopped pork sandwich, lightly seasoned with a Down East–style sauce. "We don't use ketchup because it has a distinct flavor of its own," says Tom. "These are all flavor enhancers. And we use red pepper instead of black because it's not as hot and it's digestible. Black pepper isn't digestible."

It is a memorable meal, and that's the way founder Big John Moore wants it to be. Big John, who got his nickname because he is five feet ten inches and weighs two hundred and twenty pounds, says, "I like to tell my customers, 'When you think of a pig, think of me.' That way they remember me and my barbecue."

Rating: Real good.

Directions: Moore's is two miles south of Highway 70 on Highway 17 South. Go past the mall, past Tom's Factory Outlet Mobile Homes, past Jim Walter Homes, past Oakwood Mobile Homes, and it's on the left just before you get to the Mercedes dealer. The hard part is getting to New Bern. Highway 70 from Kinston to New Bern has to be the most boring road in America. It is flatter than a slow cat on an interstate. And it must have been built during Lady Bird Johnson's reign of terror against billboards. There are none, only an endless row of trees ten yards off the road bed. When there is an occasional break in the tree row, you can see twenty yards inland. Where there is another row of trees.

Pittsboro

ALLEN & SON'S PIT-COOKED BAR-B-QUE

o No. 1: Highway 15-1501 o (919) 542-2294
o Mon.–Thurs., 9 A.M.–8 P.M.; Fri., 9 A.M.–9 P.M.; Sat., 8 A.M.–9 P.M.
o Closed Sunday

o No. 2: Highway 86 o (919) 942-7576
o Mon.–Sat., 7 A.M.–8 P.M. o Closed Sunday

o No. 3: 3 mi. south of Graham o (919) 578-5270
o Mon.–Sat., 8 A.M.–8 P.M. o Closed Sunday

"We still do barbecue the old-fashioned way," says Brenda Allen, who is not the Son of Allen & Son's, but the daughter. "We cook over red-hot coals that we fire up every thirty minutes. We use hickory wood only. We have it delivered in logs and my brother saws it, splits it, and chops it." Her brother is the Son. Her late father, James Allen, started Allen & Son's in 1968. To incorporate he needed at least three people, so he used himself, his wife, and his son, hence, Allen & Son's. Brenda says she wasn't offended. "My brother was at home and I was going to college. I'd always intended to do something else anyway." Her father died in 1977. But at Allen & Son's they still cook the meat his way, slowly for eight hours. There are three Allen & Son's stands,

PORKLORE ○ Barbecue Bowl

In 1981 North Carolina's 6th District Representative, Gene Johnston, and South Carolina's 6th district Representative, John Napier, got into a barbecue feud. Johnston charged, "What little barbecue South Carolinians produce, they ruin with that awful mustardy sauce they drown it in down there." And Napier countered, "Hogwash." Johnston and Napier decided to settle the matter with a duel. But not with pistols. With barbecue. And thus was born the Congressional Barbecue Bowl. The first one was held on April Fools Day 1981 with a dozen entrants from each state. A panel of impartial congressmen from Georgia and Virginia were asked to serve as judges. And they offered a typical political solution, declaring it a draw. So everyone kissed his sister and went home. And the politicians, as usual, got a free lunch.

But this barbecue feud wouldn't die. So the next year Johnston and Napier conducted a second Barbecue Bowl. This time a dozen stands from North Carolina and eleven from South Carolina shipped in entries. And this time there were eight congressmen serving as judges. Doug Clark, Johnston's press secretary, said at the time, "It's probably the toughest decision these congressmen will make all year." By a unanimous vote, the judges picked Short Sugar's of Reidsville, N.C., the winner, with Big D's in Hemingway, S.C., second. "North Carolina barbecue is the real thing, clearly superior to the mustardy concoction prepared in the lower Carolina," crowed Johnston. But the Barbecue Bowl didn't really settle the matter. Napier claimed foul, pointing out that two of the judges, Representatives Charles Whitley and Bill Hendon, were from North Carolina.

but there is no master pit for all three places. The barbecue is fresh at each of the three restaurants because each has its own open pit. And you can taste the freshness. The finely chopped pork, as white as preacher's hair, is piled on a bun the size of an offering plate and then baptized with that trademark Down East pepper-vinegar sauce. The meat will melt in your mouth if you try to savor the flavor too long.

Because all three Allen & Son's restaurants are within a twenty-mile radius of Chapel Hill, they are favorites of University of North Carolina students and faculty. But since UNC attracts people from all over the world, Allen & Son's is sometimes patronized by people who aren't that familiar with barbecue. Brenda laughs at some of the things they are asked. "One man wanted to know, 'Can I get some barbecue that isn't frozen?' Another one ordered a 'hushpuppy sandwich.'" Once someone even asked her to put some barbecue on top of a cheeseburger. But her favorite was the woman who asked about the banana pudding: "Do you use *real* bananas?"

Brenda spends most of her time at No.1, which she swears has a ghost. "We've decided it's dad looking over everything, making sure we're doing it right." They are. And Down East they are one of the few left doing it that way.

Rating: Real good.

Directions: To get to Allen & Son's No. 1, take Highway 15-501 south from Chapel Hill. It's about nine miles. If you are coming north from Pittsboro, it's about six miles. To restaurant No. 2, take exit 165 south off I-40-65. It's about six miles down Highway 86. From Chapel Hill take Highway 86 north about five miles. To get to No. 3 take exit 148 (Highway 54) off I-40-65. It's about three miles south of Graham.

NORTH CAROLINA: West

Where is the barbecue capital of America?

People who live in Memphis say their city is and point with pride to their Annual Memphis in May World Championship Barbecue Cooking Contest, which annually draws 300,000 spectators. The Chamber of Commerce of Owensboro, Ky., begs to differ. It promotes its city as the Barbecue Capital of the World and points to its annual International Bar-B-Q Festival, which is held the week before Memphis's. Texas adopts that label for the entire state. There are almost as many places calling themselves the barbecue capital of the world as there are barbecue joints proclaiming they have the best barbecue in the world.

Where is the barbecue capital, if there is such a thing? Is it Memphis or Dallas? Birmingham or Owensboro?

Let's examine the empirical evidence. Per capita consumption of barbecue would be the best indicator, but we don't have such a statistic. So we will have to look at the number of commercial barbecue restaurants. We searched phone books from around the country. Memphis? The Memphis Yellow Pages lists eighty-three barbecue restaurants. That's a lot of barbecue restaurants, but sheer numbers aren't enough. If they were, then whoever has the most, wins. But we think the barbecue capital must be the place with the most restaurants for its population. Owensboro? The Yellow Pages lists eleven barbecue joints for a population of 54,450. Fountain Run, Ky., can make a strong case for being the capital: It has two barbecue joints for a town of 342 people. That's one for every 171 people. (For comparison's sake, the average subdivision would have to open four barbecue joints.)

No other town can come close to that ratio. But Fountain Run's two stands are not open every day, just weekends. So we looked for a town with a large number of barbecue joints, at least double figures, for a small population.

And we kept coming back to one name: Lexington.

Lexington, North Carolina. And Lexington, Tennessee.

Lexington, N.C., a town of 15,711, has 16 barbecue places, one for every 982 people. Lexington, Tenn., a town of 5,934, has 10 barbecue places, one for every 593.

We're not picking a barbecue capital in this book, but you could make a strong case for either Lexington. Lexington, Tenn., would be ahead on the per capita scale. But Lexington, N.C., has something of its own to counter with: a style so distinctive that it derives its name from the town and so pervasive that when people talk about western North Carolina barbecue they are talking about the Lexington style—pork shoulder, pulled and chopped, smeared with a red sauce made from vinegar, pepper, salt, sugar, and tomatoes, crowned with a red slaw made with the sauce, and served on a hot bun.

LEXINGTON BARBECUE NO. 1

o 10 Highway 29-70 South o (704) 249-9814
o Mon.–Sat., 10 A.M.–9 P.M. o Closed Sunday, holidays, and for a
   week around the Fourth of July

Why is barbecue so popular in Lexington, a small town twenty miles south of Winston-Salem? "Tradition," says Wayne Monk, owner of

Lexington Barbecue No. 1. "It just got rooted so long ago. People here know what good barbecue is." Lexington barbecue started in the late 1910s with Sid Weaver and Jesse Swicegood, who began cooking under pitched tents in a vacant lot across from the courthouse. All of Lexington barbecue is descended from these two men and their disciples. "At first they only cooked when court was in session and there was a crowd in town," says Monk. Davidson County was farm country, and the farmers would come to town during "court week" to watch the goings-on and trade horse stories. By the mid-twenties the farmers were coming to town every Saturday, and Weaver and Swicegood and their tents were there to meet them. Soon factory workers and school kids were eating barbecue, and it became a week-long proposition. In the thirties, health regulations forced Weaver and Swicegood to add tin sides to their tents. Swicegood trained Warner Stamey and Conrad Everart (the original owner of Lexington No. 1); Weaver trained Alton Beck and J. B. Tarleton. Every current barbecue restaurant owner in Lexington was trained by one of these four or by someone who was.

We ate at all the Lexington barbecue places, all sixteen of them, and we can tell you, you won't go wrong no matter where you pull in. Monk is right: Lexingtonians know their barbecue. If we had to pick one from the pack, it's not a hard decision. We would choose Lexington Barbecue No. 1, or Lexington No. 1 as it is known. (If you really want to sound like a native, call it Honey Monk's. That was its original name. Honey was owner Wayne Monk's nickname.) Monk is a barbecue purist. "We do everything basically the same way I was taught thirty-five years ago." Monk is a descendant of the Swicegood school. He learned from Warner Stamey, who bought Swicegood's business in 1938. "When you start cutting corners, finding a faster way to do it, you're hurting yourself." That's why Lexington No. 1 hasn't switched to gas or electric cookers. That's why it doesn't make sauce in an eighty-gallon kettle. That's why it doesn't leave cabbage unrefrigerated. "We make the sauce in small pots because we can control the quality better. And if you let cabbage sit out, you get an acid taste in your slaw." Lexington No. 1's sauce, which Monk sells in the restaurant under the Smokehouse label, is Lexington-style sauce in its purest form: vinegar thin with peppers for sizzle and ketchup and sugar to temper the spices and hold down the lawsuits. The Hot & Tangy version puts out more heat than a trailer fire.

Like Stamey and Swicegood before him, Monk is training his descendants and competitors. "I don't know how many have left here and gone into business, six or eight anyway." No matter how many leave and open up competing restaurants, Monk says it doesn't make any difference. His business just keeps on growing. "I'm serving about all I can cook. They moved my interstate on me three years ago. I lost the tourists but picked up local business. The only thing that affects my business is ice on the road." Neither rain nor snow nor dark of night keeps the locals from turning into Lexington No. 1. Just ice. That's quite a compliment from the barbecue connoisseurs of Lexington, N.C. Frankly, if we lived in Lexington, we'd try to make it through the ice, too.

Rating: As good as we've ever had. Good enough that Monk was invited to cook for the 1983 Economic Summit held in Williamsburg, Va.

Directions: Head south on old Interstate 85 (now called Highway 29-70 S). Go past Sky City. On the right you'll see a big sign: HOME OF LEXINGTON BARBECUE AND NATIONAL OUTLET.

Oak Ridge

LEO PHELPS

o At the Oak Ridge Horse Show; held Easter weekend at the Horse Show grounds, just off N.C. 68

There are two things Leo Phelps doesn't like to wear: his shoes and his teeth. But there is one thing he is proud to wear: the label of Barbecue King of Guilford County, N.C. Leo says Guilford, which adjoins Lexington's Davidson County, is the forgotten county of N.C. barbecue. "And everybody I talk to prefers our barbecue here in Guilford County. It's better than that Lexington stuff."

Leo has been cooking for more than half a century. He started out by helping his uncle Arch Pegram. "I got up about eighteen or twenty years old and my uncle he says, 'What you doing Saturday?' He'd wanted me to go with him, help him cook. It got to where he'd take me every weekend to fire up his coals for him. He taught me all about barbecue cooking."

He also taught Leo about barbecue sauce, including passing on the family recipe. Leo believes that sauce is the key. "It's 80 percent of it. Anybody can cook the meat—just don't burn it and get it done. Sauce is the secret. I've had many a person drink my sauce right out of a cup; really, just turn it right up. I give a lot of it away at Christmastime, and the people say I couldn't have given them anything any better. This one fellow told me he cooked a steak the other day and he said he got to wondering how some of Leo's barbecue sauce would go on that. He tried it and he said, 'Lord God, that was good.'"

It takes Leo about five hours to cook up a batch of his secret sauce. "A fellow who owns a barbecue place asked me how long I cooked it. I told him, and he said he can't afford to go to the trouble to cook it that long. I told him it's worth the trouble." Leo may not be telling his sauce recipe, but it's not hard to figure out the main ingredient. His carport is overrun with empty vinegar jugs. Leo cuts the vinegar's tartness with tomatoes and something sweet, maybe brown sugar, giving the sauce a sweet-and-sour taste that will make you pucker and smile at the same time.

During his fifty years of cooking barbecue, Leo has seen a lot of changes. "Used to we'd dig a hole in the ground, put the hickory and oak in it, lay a grate down, put the meat on the grate. Then they went to charcoal. Now most of them cooks with gas. It cuts the time way down. Used to it took us twelve hours. Now they can do it in about seven and a half." Leo has even made a few changes himself—in his sauce. "You've heard it said you can make things better or worse. We made our sauce better."

Ask anyone in Oak Ridge or nearby Summerfield about good barbecue and they will point the way to Leo's house. "He has a real reputation around here," says Wilson Browning, treasurer of the local volunteer fire department. Leo has built his reputation on free-lance cooking, never opening his own place. "All we did was cook for local people, the horse show, the fire department. It helps the fire department out." In fact one of the great mysteries in Guilford County is why Leo never opened his own barbecue place. Leo pulls at his bib overalls, spits out a dip of chewing tobacco, and shrugs. "Aw, I didn't want to get into that health business. And it'd be too much trouble."

Leo was once a weekend institution during the summers in Guilford County. But at seventy-two, age is slowing him down. He suffers from diabetes and arteriosclerosis and has had to cut back on his cooking. "I'm gradually letting it go because I can't stand up as long as I used to. But I've cooked enough if I never cook no more. Now, me and my assistant cook about five or six times a year, plus the horse show." Leo says he is passing his secrets down through his assistant, Chuck Jones. "Chuck, he's been helping me for fifteen years, and he can make the sauce just about as good as I can."

We asked to buy some sauce from Leo. He hobbled outside in his sock feet—"Got a blister on my toe that keeps coming open"—to where he keeps his stock in unlabeled gallon jugs. We didn't want a whole gallon, so he dug around in a pasteboard box until he found what he was looking for—an empty fifth of Ancient Age whiskey. As he transferred the sauce from the gallon jug into the bottle, we noticed there was still a dribble of Ancient Age at the bottom. We understood what he meant by "all that health stuff." Hey, maybe that's the secret ingredient.

Rating: As good as we've ever had.

Directions: The Oak Ridge Horse Show is now Leo's only regularly scheduled cooking, although he occasionally cooks for the fire department benefits.

Reidsville

SHORT SUGAR'S PIT BAR-B-Q

o 1328 South Scales St. o (919) 349-9184
o Mon.–Thurs., 6 A.M.–9 P.M.; Fri.–Sat., 6 A.M.–10 P.M.
o Closed Sunday

"If they were to film a remake of *American Graffiti,* this would be the place to film it," says Reidsville native Roger Carter. "It hasn't changed since I was a teenager in the fifties." Short Sugar's, which opened the summer of 1949, is still in the same location, still has a drive-in, and still has curb service. There is even a curb boy who looks old enough to have started working there when the place opened.

When Short Sugar's opened its doors and parking lot in 1949, Reidsville's teenagers quickly descended. It was soon the teen hangout. It was also a teen hangout that parents could approve of. "Johnny wouldn't sell alcohol and wouldn't open on Sunday," says Mrs. Biddie Overby, widow of Johnny Overby, one of the cofounders. "He said, 'If you can't make a living in six days, you'd better quit.' He also said, 'If I don't want to go to church myself, I don't want to keep anyone else from going.' "

Short Sugar's got its odd name from Johnny's late brother Eldridge. They were originally going to call the place the Overby Brothers Drive-in, named for Johnny, Eldridge, and Clyde Overby, who had all decided they wanted to open a pit barbecue restaurant. But in June 1949, two days before the grand opening, thirty-four-year-old Eldridge was killed in a car wreck. So the two surviving brothers decided to honor Eldridge and name the restaurant after him. Eldridge's nickname had been Short Sugar. There are varying tales about how he acquired such a moniker. One thing all the stories agree on is that he was short. They diverge on the Sugar part. It was either because of his infectious laugh or because of his reputation as a ladies' man or because he wasn't a ladies' man and the ladies liked to tease him: "Come on, Short, come on, Sugar."

Short Sugar's has expanded a bit over the years. But the place still has the look of the fifties. And Carter says the sandwiches still taste just the way he remembers they tasted in the fifties. Mrs. Overby credits that consistency to "the sauce and the care we take cooking the meat." The sauce is the same one created by Johnny Overby in 1949. It's a thin concoction, about the color and consistency of prune juice, but with considerably more firepower (and without the aftereffect). The recipe is still known only to Biddie and one of her daughters, but we can tell you it has that undeniable Lexington-style taste—an immediate blast of vinegar with a lingering sweetness, kind of like dipping a dill pickle in ketchup.

There's no hiding the care they take in cooking the meat. The pit is in plain view behind the counter. They serve their barbecue chopped, sliced, or minced, heaped on a Merita bun, seasoned with the thin vinegar-and-ketchup sauce, and topped with slaw. And for an after-sandwich treat there's an out-of-this-world lemon pie with vanilla wafer crust.

Reidsville is off the beaten interstate path, but that hasn't prevented Short Sugar's from getting the recognition it deserves. In 1982 it was the winner in a congressional barbecue contest (See page 72.) And people from all over make the detour to get some of Short Sugar's barbecue. David Wilson, a son-in-law of Johnny Overby and one of the current owners, says the most famous customer is probably Lash LaRue, the old cowboy, who whips by on occasion.

But the most unusual customer came by a few years ago. A hearse lead a funeral procession in for curb service. Everyone inside bolted to the windows to see what was going on. "Did someone die from the barbecue?" a prankster asked. "Maybe it was his last request: He wanted to take some with him," another quipped. That wasn't it. Nor was it a barbecue-famished hearse driver stopping in for a quick sandwich before the trip to the cemetery. It was the twenty-year reunion from the local high school. The teenagers of Reidsville can't get Short Sugar's out of their system, no matter how old they get.

Rating: Real good.

Directions: Take U.S. 29 to 87 S. Turn south on Scales St. Go past the Harris-Teeter market. It's on the right and is the only thing for miles around that looks like a fifties drive-in.

SOUTH CAROLINA

Greenville

BEACON DRIVE-IN

o 225 Reidsville Rd. o (805) 585-9387
o Mon.–Sat., 7 A.M.–11:30 P.M. o Closed Sunday

There used to be a billboard in Palm Springs, Calif., that read YOU ARE ONLY 2,300 MILES FROM THE FAMOUS BEACON DRIVE-IN, SPARTANBURG, S.C. And when we would see it, we would speed up. We could hear the Beacon's ringmaster, J. C. Strobel, urging us to "Move, move, move."

It's a fine line between being obnoxious and being humorous, and J. C. Strobel straddles that line every day as he runs the cafeteria at the Beacon. When the column of customers gets slow, J. C. gets quick. "Next, next, next," he barks at the bewildered tourist. "Let's move on. Come on, come on, come on, down the line." You are standing there feeling insulted and wondering if J. C. even heard your order, when suddenly he cocks his head sideways, turns and spits, "Hey Fred! Three outsides, two slices, five cheese, two with slaw, two chili cheese with, two without, three burgers with, one without, hash aplenty." And before you know it, he is handing you a plate that holds your order, right down to a tee.

J. C. may be the Eighth Wonder of the World—the human collator. He'll store up twenty orders in his head, sort by categories, then output them in one breath and turn back to the line, ready for more. "Let's move on, next, next, next." J. C. doesn't own the Beacon, but for regulars, he is the Beacon. John White is the owner. White opened his first Beacon in 1947, three buildings ago. "We wore those other places out," he says. J. C. is the Beacon's Confucius. There are little hand-lettered J. C. SAYS signs tacked on every bare spot. J. C. SAYS: IT'S FINE TO PASS IN LINE. J. C. SAYS: LET'S MOVE ON. J. C. SAYS: LET'S DON'T BOOGIE JIVE, LET'S MERCHANDISE. J. C. seems to have a one-track philosophy.

The Beacon is a drive-in of the old school: the longer the menu the better. There are sixty-six different sandwiches, twenty-four side dishes, thirty-one plates, fifteen desserts. When J. C. says, "Chilicheese," he wants a cheeseburger with chili on top. "With or without" is with or without bacon. "Pork-a-plenty" is a sliced pork sandwich with french fries and onion rings (which are cooked with the skin on).

But the item that gets top billing on the menu, and deservedly, is the barbecue. You can order regular ("Slice"), the crunchy crust ("Outside"), or "Beef Slice." It all comes the same way: mountains of meat overflowing a softball-size bun and smothered in a tart tomato-vinegar sauce.

Yes, J. C. can be obnoxious. But when you are trying to stampede 12,000 people through a cafeteria, which is how many the Beacon serves on an average Saturday night, you have to keep them moving, moving, moving, next, next, next.

Rating: Real good.

Directions: From I-26 take Exit 22, Reidsville Rd., east. The Beacon is two miles down on the right. It's open daily, but "never on Sunday." Except on Easter, when the Beacon's sunrise service annually draws 5,000 to the parking lot. (There's free watermelon afterward.)

Holly Hill

SWEATMAN'S BAR-B-QUE

o S.C. Route 453 o no phone
o Only Fri.–Sat., 11:30 A.M.–10:30 P.M.

We've never met anyone who wasn't repulsed at the first sight of a mustard-based barbecue sauce. "Yellow barbecue!" they exclaim. "Ugh!" Mustard-based sauce is a South Carolina phenomenon. In fact it's a central South Carolina phenomenon, confined almost exclusively to a sixty-five-mile radius of Columbia.

If you're ready to give yellow barbecue a toss, we suggest you start with the best. H. O. "Bub" Sweatman serves a bright yellow meat that

PORKLORE o Truth in Barbecue

South Carolina's state legislature passed a Truth in Barbecue law in 1986, requiring barbecue restaurants to purchase a sticker that tells customers if they cook with wood or with something else and if they cook whole hogs or part of, but not the whole, hog.

is like nothing you've ever tasted. This is not ballpark mustard spread on pork. Bub's sauce is made from a seventy-five-year-old family recipe. The sugar, or honey, or whatever it is Bub puts in it, cuts the mustard's natural pungency and meshes nicely with the pork's natural sweetness.

Bub is a third-generation barbecue man. "It's in his blood," says his wife Margie. "And once it's in your blood, you can't get it out." He tried to get it out in the early seventies. He quit barbecuing and devoted his full time to farming his 2,500-acre spread. But by 1977 he was itching to get back to it. So he bought a dumpy old house and converted it into a weekend barbecue place and country restaurant. It looks the part. The planks are weathered, the porch is swayed, the steps are worn. Out back you find the open pit, surrounded by a screen shed. Douglas, the cook, says they burn oak limbs down into coals, shovel them into the pit, and then cook whole hogs all night Thursday and all night Friday.

Bub, being of farmer stock, is a practical man. He wants to offer value. But he also wants to clear a little profit. So he's had to change his all-you-can-eat buffet policy. It is now all-you-can-eat-from-one-plate. There is even a hand-lettered sign to remind: TAKE WHAT YOU WANT, BUT EAT WHAT YOU TAKE. LET'S KEEP FOOD PRICES DOWN.

Rating: As good as we've ever had.

Directions: Take U.S. Hwy. 176 to S.C. Route 453. It's about 3½ miles down on the right, surrounded by ancient oak trees and an expansive field. If you're coming from the other direction . . . aw, don't come from the other direction. It's too much trouble to direct you that way.

Lake City

OWEN'S BAR-B-Q

o The old 378 business route o (803) 394-8771
o Mon.–Sat., 8 A.M.–3 P.M. o Closed Sunday

The sign on the door said OPEN 8 A.M. But though it was already 9:30, the door was still locked. It was our second trip to Owen's, and we were afraid we had missed connections again. Then we heard a voice from inside say, "Just a minute." We could see Chessie Owens scurrying between the tables, wiping her hands on her apron as she came to open up. "I keep it locked whenever I'm in the back. You never know who might come in on you." We plopped down in a dinette chair and were admiring the picture of Jesus propped on the air conditioner, when Sherman Gibbs, her longtime pitmaster, came puffing in. "Oh, whew, I thought you were the Health Man," he said. Mr. Gibbs had been outside mowing the lawn when we drove up, and apparently there is some regulation about mowing and cooking.

It took two trips and several passes to make sure it was the right place, but it was worth the trouble. Even though Owen's is right out on the road, it is still difficult to spot. The white block building is nondescript. It looks like an old country grocery. If it weren't for the pig painted on the side, you could whiz by and never remember passing it. "There used to be a sign out front, but after the old man died, we did away with it because it reminded her of him," said Mr. Gibbs. The old man was Mellon Owens, who opened the place in 1946 as a grocery store and filling station. "We didn't start cooking barbecue until '52," said Mrs. Owens. Owen's looks like it is still 1952. The tired dinette tables, the worn counter stools, the faded green walls, look the same as they must have been back then.

"Mellon always loved barbecue," said Mrs. Owens. "When he passed away [in 1975], I didn't know what to do. People said I ought to keep the business up to have something to do. I didn't care too much about it, but it was all I knew how to do." She has had help keeping the business up from Mr. Gibbs, who has worked for the Owenses for almost fifty years. "We just about raised him. He started here when he was twelve." Mr. Gibbs worked his way up from errand boy to pitman. Now he cooks barbecue as well as anybody in the state. He cooks the way he learned from Mellon Owens, slowly, allowing the meat to bask all night in an open pit. Mr. Gibbs learned his lessons well. His meat is as tender as Mrs. Owens's heart. And her sauce is as good a match for the meat as Mellon must have been for her. She tops the marriage off by grilling a bun with the meat inside. It comes out crisp and steamy.

Many of the local people have asked Chessie to open up again for dinner like she used to, but she wants no part of that. "I could do more if I stayed open later, but I just can't do it anymore. It's all I can do to get lunch."

Rating: Real good.

Directions: If you're coming from the east, when the bypass forks off Hwy. 378, stay left on the old road. Owen's is about a mile up the road on the left. If you're coming from any other direction, go through town and out on the old 378 business route. It's one mile east of town.

West Columbia

MAURICE'S PIGGIE PARK

o 1600 Charleston Highway o (803) 796-0220
o Mon.–Thurs., 10 A.M.–11 P.M.; Fri.–Sat., 10 A.M.–midnight
o Closed Sunday

One look at Maurice's Piggie Park might convince you that the BB in BBQ stands for Big Business. Maurice's Piggie Park is Big Business, and Maurice is the Colonel Sanders of barbecue. He offers curb service, a drive-through window, and a sit-down dining room. Or, if you don't live in the area, he'll ship it to you via Federal Express.

Piggie Park is success porcine-ified. The parking lot is full. The line is long. The service is fast. If it weren't for that smoky smell, you would swear you were in a McDonald's. Everything says: fast food chain. But, though it is fast, it isn't a chain. It is just successful, and we don't believe in penalizing success. We know that barbecue snobs sniff at nice places, wondering if perhaps the owner isn't spending more time on the books than on the barbecue. But facts are facts: If you beget a better barbecue sandwich, people are going to beat a path to your door. Why not pave the path?

That's what Maurice has done. He has branched out and expanded and remodeled. But he still takes care of business—barbecue—by letting whole hogs smolder for eighteen to twenty-four hours over hickory coals. When the meat is done, his workers pull it, chop it, and then coat it with Maurice's "million dollar secret sauce." It's a thick, ocher-colored sauce, definitely made from the bitter center of a mustard seed, but cut with sugar, which makes it as sweet as iced tea.

If you want to try some, you can. Maurice packages what he calls "gourmet microwave barbecue," which sounds like somebody's idea of a bad joke, but tastes absolutely delicious. All you need is a charge card and a phone. Federal Express will deliver it to your door tomorrow morning. (See the section on mail order in the back of this book.) Call before midnight, so you won't forget.

Rating: Real good.

Directions: From I-26 take exit 113. Go east on Airport Rd. Piggie Park is about a mile down the road at the junction with U.S. Hwy. 321. Don't worry, you can't miss the giant Flying Pig sign.

TENNESSEE

Bluff City

THE RIDGEWOOD

o U.S. 19E o (615) 538-7543
o Tues.–Thurs., 11:30 A.M.–7:30 P.M.;
  Fri.–Sun., 11:30 A.M.–2:45 P.M.; Fri., 4:30 P.M.–8:30 P.M.;
  Sat., 4:30 P.M.–8:25 P.M.; Sun., 4:30 P.M.–7:30 P.M.
o Closed Monday

People magazine called it the best barbecue in the country.

Proving that even barbecue has trouble getting respect from its own, the local newspaper said it wasn't even the best barbecue in the area. Who's right? Who has the best barbecue? Is it the Ridgewood restaurant in Bluff City, Tenn., as *People* proclaimed? Or is it Bare's Barbecue, in nearby Bristol, which was the choice of the reporter on the scene from *The Kingsport Times-News?*

The two barbecue joints are twenty minutes apart, assuming it isn't shift-change time, making a barbecue battle an easy task. So here we go with round one: the Ridgewood vs. Bare's. Both serve up east Tennessee-style barbecue, which favors sliced pork meat on buns as big as baby moon hubcaps with gobs and gobs of tangy, ketchup-based sauce.

First stop: the Ridgewood.

To find the Ridgewood, you need a tour guide. We picked Bruce Haney, a chemical engineer in nearby Kingsport and longtime observer of the east Tennessee barbecue scene. "The Ridgewood is not the well-kept secret it used to be," said Haney. "Yuppies discovered it after the *People* magazine write-up. It was the first time people in Bluff City had ever seen a Volvo."

It was almost closing time, which for some odd reason is 8:25 on a Saturday night, when we pulled into the Ridgewood's parking lot. "Turn off your headlights," Haney warned. "If Mrs. Proffitt sees those lights she's liable to run and lock the door." Mrs. Grace Proffitt, the legendary owner of the Ridgewood, runs her place with an iron hand. Haney said his wife would no longer patronize the Ridgewood after a closing-time incident. "My wife refuses to ever go back. One night we stood in line for an hour, waiting to get in. It was hot. She was fussing with our year-old baby the whole time. And when we finally got up to the door, Mrs. Proffitt shut it in our faces, said she'd served all she was going to that night."

Tales of Ridgewood rudeness are legendary. There is the story about the eight executives from Tennessee Eastman Corporation, who stopped in before heading to the airport eight miles away. Donnie Boggs, another east Tennessee barbecue aficionado, picks up the story. "Four of them got there first, and the waitress seated them. When the other bunch arrived, she put them at a table on the other side of the room even though it was early and there wasn't anybody else in the place. She left and they got up and moved a couple of tables so they could all sit together. Well, they waited. And they waited. And the waitress never came. Finally they looked over by the door and there she was, tapping her foot. She gave 'em that evil eye and said, 'When you'uns get in the seats I set you in, I'll serve you.' "

On this night the door is open; Mrs. Proffitt is behind the counter wearing a Jesus-loves-you smile. And the waitresses are hustling to help us. "The staff is much more polite and accommodating than they used to be back when the Ridgewood was the only barbecue place around," said Haney. "Mrs. Proffitt has trained a lot of competition, and now she has to be nice. But if you're a longtime customer I'm sure she'll still insult you and slam the door in your face, for old times' sake. When they were the only game in town, it was kind of interesting. It was like going to the Don Rickles Restaurant. I kind of miss those days."

The Ridgewood has the look of something built in the days before planning commissions. It is a diner that has sprouted wings. To get to the restrooms you have to go outside. "And in the wintertime they are colder than damnit," said Haney. The best seat in the house is the booth across from the front door. From there you can watch the 300-pound cooks sweat over the grill. "They've got these extra-wide aisles so that two of them extra-wide waitresses with trays can pass each other," said Haney. "The waitresses aren't as heavy as they used to be, but they're still a little heavier than average, even for a barbecue joint."

The menu advises that the Ridgewood has been serving up barbecue "since 1948." We ordered pork sandwiches with Mrs. Proffitt's barbecue beans on the side. And we weren't disappointed. The sandwiches arrived hot and juicy, a skyscraper of meat four layers thick, piled on a plump Kern's bun and ladled with enough sauce to drown a small dog. "They fairly much float that meat in sauce," said Haney. "They have some very definite ideas about how much sauce to put on it. You will notice there are no sauce dispensers on the tables."

The sauce was thick and tangy, and you could tell that several bottles of ketchup had given their lives so that we might enjoy barbecue. It was spicy, but not dangerously so, about a five on a one-to-ten hotness scale. The beans were out of this world. There seemed to be a pound of lean meat cooked in with them.

We paid up and, on the way to the car, Haney observed that the Ford we had landed next to had a CHUB license plate on the front. "If you frequent the Ridgewood very often, you could be the next candidate for a 'Chub' license plate," he said.

Next stop: Bare's.

Bare's Barbecue is housed in a former Fass Brothers Fish House, on Volunteer Parkway in Bristol, Tenn., just down the road from the Valleydale meat packing plant and Kern's bakery. "If they run out of pig or buns, they don't have far to go," said Boggs. The pit is out back, and on a clear night you can singe your eyes before you get inside.

Boggs had warned us that Bare's was "an uptown place. Chairs with carpet [upholstery] on them. A fountain. Baskets and art prints on the wall. They use Royal Doulton china. They even take charge cards." For a barbecue joint veteran, Bare's was intimidating, even off-putting. There were ferns hanging above the fountain. To Bare's credit, all the ferns were dead.

The Bare's barbecue sandwich looked exactly like the Ridgewood's. But favorable comparisons end there. The sauce was ketchupy, but not as tasty as the Ridgewood's. It was also blander, about a three on our hot scale. Bare's used leaner meat, which is not always what you want in a barbecue joint. (Ask your doctor.) Its beans were bigger, but less flavorful than Mrs. Proffitt's.

Ah, but the final course. The Strawberry Bare was a strawberry shortcake served in a fruit jar and it was gooooood, as Andy Griffith used to say. And may still. But dessert still didn't swing the verdict. *People* magazine is right. Bare's is good. The Ridgewood is better.

Rating: Real good.

Directions: To get to the Ridgewood, "You'll have to get to Bluff City on your own," said Haney. "I don't presume to tell people how to get there because, frankly, I don't know which direction they're coming from. Once they find Bluff City, it's a snap. You just run the stop sign on SR 37 and turn left toward Elizabethton on 19E. And there it is."

Greenbrier

OLD FASHION BAR-B-Q

o 395 U.S. Hwy. 431 o (615) 384-5077
o Fri.–Sat., 9 A.M.–dark

There's just a small sign in the front yard, one of those portable jobs that barbers use to let people know they're in. OLD FASHION BAR-B-Q OPEN it reads. It's easy to miss it when you are barreling down U.S. Hwy. 431. The little sign gives no indication of what a treat the barbecue pilgrim has in store. Old Fashion Bar-B-Q is Richard Jones's place. He sells his velvety chopped pork from an old metallic gray bread truck parked on blocks in the driveway of his ranch home. He cooks it in the hollow down behind the house. He learned the art of cooking barbecue sixteen years ago from Sam Chatman, an old church friend. "I thought I had it. My friend would never tell me I had it, but he would leave me alone, so I figured I must have it." Jones *knew* he had it when his friend divulged his secret sauce recipe. "He was getting on in years, and he didn't want to die without someone having that recipe."

Jones has it. His chopped pork sandwich is almost a half-pound of tenderness, with a crisp vinegar flavor. A little fat woman, who was sitting in the driver's seat of the van while she waited for Jones to prepare her order, said it best. "I used to go that place in Springfield, but once I found this place I quit them. His meat here is nice and moist but it's not greasy."

Old Fashion is a weekend-only, take-out place. Jones farms during the week. He says he loves people and loves to talk to them. "But if I have to have people come in and sit down, I'd have to have two restrooms and follow a lot more rules. I just rather do it this way." The old fashion way.

Rating: As good as we've ever had.

Directions: From I-24 take exit 35 (U.S. Hwy. 431) north. It's about four miles up on the left. The number, but no name, appears on the mailbox. If you're coming from Springfield, it's about eight miles south on U.S. Hwy. 431.

P.S.: Dolly Loyd made us a list of all the country music stars who have frequented her **Center Point Pit Barbecue** cafe in Hendersonville, just north of Nashville. It reads like a first draft of the Country Music Hall of Fame: Faron Young, Conway Twitty, George Jones, Alabama, Johnny Cash and June Carter, Slim Whitman, Billy Walker, Roy Orbison, String Bean, Tanya Tucker, Glen Campbell,

Ray Stevens, Ricky Skaggs, Little Jimmie Dickens, Bill Monroe, Red Foley, Tammy Wynette, Minnie Pearl, Jerry Reed, Bobby Bare, Roy Acuff, Waylon Jennings, Barbara Mandrell, the Louvin Brothers, Roger Miller, Willie Nelson, the Willis Brothers, Grandpa Jones, Jimmie Newman, Tom T. Hall, Lefty Frizzell, the Kendalls, the Oak Ridge Boys, Mel Tillis, Dolly Parton, Archie Campbell, Boots Randolph, Chet Atkins, and George Morgan. Loyd has been a pork purveyor since 1965, when she and her late husband, Bill, opened Center Point. "Johnny Cash was one of my first customers," she says. "He still comes in." Her place is down the road from the Johnny Cash Museum and Conway Twitty's amusement park, Twitty City.

Over the years all these Hall of Famers and future Hall of Famers have come in for one reason: Dolly's barbecue. Her chopped pork, oozing with a rich-tasting tomato-and-vinegar sauce, will stand on its own. But when she serves it on her cornbread pancakes, it's time to make reservations for the Barbecue Hall of Fame induction ceremonies. It is real good. To get there, take Exit 96, Two Mile Pike, east from I-65. Turn north at the Rivergate Mall onto U.S. 31E. It's on the left, just inside the Hendersonville city limits sign, at 1212 West Main St., between Bobby's Bare Trap souvenir shop and Rose's Guitar Center and across from the Colonial Drive-In Theater. It's open daily, 8:30 A.M.–9 P.M. (615) 824-9330.

Knoxville

BROTHER JACK'S

o 1710 University Ave. o (615) 522-4684
o Thurs.–Sat., 2 P.M.–1:30 A.M.

Not every freshman at the University of Tennessee joins a fraternity or sorority. But every one of them goes through an initiation. It's not hell week; it's hog heaven. Long before they learn the school song or the names of all the football starters, UT freshmen learn directions to Brother Jack's.

Brother Jack's has been a UT institution since 1947. Everybody has to go at least once, usually that first year. Chris Wohlwend remembers how it was when he was at UT in the mid-sixties. "Sometimes we'd take dates with us. Not only would the girls not go inside, they wouldn't even wait in the car for us. They insisted we give them the keys so they could drive around." The days of the sawdust floor are past. It's concrete now. But it's still Brother Jack's. There are still Brother Jack's hand-lettered signs: NO SPITTING ON FLOOR. NO COMBING HAIR IN KITCHEN. NO PLAYING CARDS AND CUSSING. SING, BROTHER

JACK. ("Sing" is really "Signed," but Brother Jack made a typo when he was painting.)

And it's still Brother Jack doing the cooking.

When we visited, Knoxville was celebrating Riverfeast, an annual barbecue cook-off. "Why aren't you down there?" one customer ribbed. Brother Jack just shook his head. All those ribs smoking down at the Riverfeast hadn't hurt Brother Jack's business. If anything, Riverfeast had whetted appetites for some real ribs. Brother Jack pointed to a couple of packages of meat. "That's all I got left for the weekend," he said. And it was only midafternoon Saturday.

We ordered what we had ordered twenty years earlier on our first visit: a rib sandwich. "You want that hot, don't ya?" Brother Jack grinned. He has been asking that question for forty years and the answer is always the same, "Yeah." He chopped four ribs off a slab, plopped them on a piece of light bread, and then squeezed on a dabble of sauce. Brother Jack's hot sauce is a sweet heat that perfectly complements his lean, pink ribs. The sandwich reminded us of what UT student Tom Jester had said twenty years earlier about Brother Jack's rib sandwich: "Good ribs are like a skinny girl: the closer to the bone, the sweeter the meat."

Rating: Real good.

Directions: From I-40 west, go north on the 17th Ave.-Western Ave. exit. Go left (west) on Western Avenue, then right at the light on University Ave. Brother Jack's is the first building on the right. The most noticeable lettering on the building says FRESH MEAT.

Lexington

B. E. SCOTT'S BAR-B-Q

o Highway 20 o no phone
o Wed. 11 A.M.–usually Sat. afternoon

The sun is just starting to smear its yellow stain across the eastern sky over Lexington, Tenn., when Early Scott's alarm clock jangles. Scott lifts himself to the edge of his cot and mashes the button down. It is not his first spell of interrupted sleep. And it won't be his last. All night long he will rouse himself to tend his barbecue pit. It is a grueling method of cooking: burning hickory strips down to red-hot coals, spreading those coals evenly in the fire bed under searing meat that's been mopped with a spicy vinegar varnish. After a quick nap, he's up and doing it all over again. There are easier ways to cook barbecue. He could buy a new-fashioned gas pit, which cooks the meat with clean heat. He could convert to electric heat and smoke the meat with hickory chips. But Early Scott doesn't want to take the easy way out. Early Scott isn't just an old-fashioned barbecue cook, he is an artist. And his is a dying art. There aren't many cooks like Early Scott left. Twenty years ago every barbecue joint cooked pretty much the same way, the way Early Scott still cooks, with patience and with pride. But ingenious manufacturers have devised shortcuts: pressure cookers to cut the time, electric cookers to eliminate the constant stoking, gas cookers to keep the heat even. Scott rejects shortcuts. He grows all the vegetables he uses in his sauce. He mixes the sauce up in small batches, so each will taste the same as the one before it. And when he is cooking, he even sleeps by the pit, so he can keep the fire constant all night long. "Early once told me, 'A man that won't sleep with his barbecue isn't serious about his cooking,'" says his friend Robin Beard.

Maybe it is the competition that has kept Scott serious. Lexington, a town of barely 6,000, has ten barbecue joints. And none of the places are slouches when it comes to cooking. But Scott is the acknowledged master. A string of cars will swing through his parking lot on days he is closed, just on the chance he may have some leftover meat. "Don't have any of that bobba-que?" each asks. He waves and shakes his head no.

Scott cooks over an open pit, covering the meat with the pasteboard from appliance cartons. He cooks whole hogs mopped in his sour pepper baste. When the hogs are done, he hand-pulls the meat. He serves it just like that, on a plate or on a bun. "I've got hot sauce if people want it. But the sauce has already been cooked into the meat, so it's seasoned."

After we told Early Scott's story to a friend, she asked, "So how's his barbecue?" Then she immediately withdrew the question. "What am I asking? Anybody who cooks like that has to make great barbecue." Early does. His pulled-pork sandwich, hot off the grill, is so good it will make your eyes roll up in your head.

"It's a lot of trouble to cook this way," Scott says. "A lot. Gas and electric are cheaper and not as big a mess, but it don't taste the same. It's not the same."

Rating: As good as we've ever had.

Directions: From Interstate 40 take Exit 101 (Highway 104) south to Lexington. Go west on Highway 20 toward Jackson. B. E. Scott's Barbecue is on the left about a half mile west down the road. It's the third barbecue place you'll pass, after Brooksie's and Beech Island. Scott's is open from Wednesday 11 A.M. until he sells out of meat, which is usually early Saturday afternoon. There is no phone: "He don't want to be bothered when he's cooking that barbecue," says his sister-in-law Tina.

Memphis

The Wets and the Drys: There are 1.3 million Elvis stories in the King's home city, and all but thirty-seven of them are dull. "He passed us one time in his Cadillac and waved," said the squat woman squatting at the gates of Graceland. "I lived over behind Graceland," said the waitress at Harry's Barbecue. "And I'd get off the bus right there. So one time I stopped at the guardhouse and talked to the guard and asked him if my teenagers could meet Elvis sometime. He said he thought they could. So I'd stop by there at least once a week and talk to him. But we never did set a time. Then I was riding home on the bus one night and I heard that Elvis had died."

Zzzzzzz.

But barbecue stories are something else. We've never heard a dull barbecue story in Memphis. There's the story of the skydiving barbecue team at the 1983 Memphis International Barbecue Festival. To pick up as many showmanship points as possible, they arrived on judgment day via plane; all four cooks and the (dressed) pig jumped toward Tom Lee Park. Unfortunately, a puff of wind took the pig's parachute into the Mississippi River. But these were no rank amateurs. They had a backup pig waiting on the ground.

We could go on. But we'd rather get right down to business, and in Memphis that means barbecue. Memphis has two divergent barbecue traditions: the wet style and the dry style. Proponents of the wet style—let's adopt the style newspapers use when reporting on a mixed-drink referendum and call them The Wets—believe the secret is in the sauce. They prefer a rich-looking paste made by mixing equal

---

PORKLORE ○ Is Barbecue Kosher?

"We are always allowed to eat porkfish," said Paul Skolnick, the only Jewish competitor at the 1987 Annual Memphis in May World Championship Cooking Contest where contestants are not allowed to cook any meat except pork.

---

parts tomato sauce and vinegar and then seasoning with onions, peppers, and anything else in the cabinet that looks spicy.

The Drys scoff at sauce on the finished product. "If it's cooked right, you don't need no sauce," says Lucious "The King" Newsom, who cut his teeth on Memphis rib bones. The Drys use a paprika rub on their meat before cooking, giving the finished rib a gritty crust.

They'll barbecue anything in Memphis. Coletta's serves a barbecue pizza. Brady and Lil's has barbecue spaghetti. Both taste pretty much as you would expect them to. Memphis may have gotten more of our attention than any other barbecue hotbed. Vince is a native Tennessean and he has been eating Memphis barbecue since his high school basketball team played in the state tournament there in 1965. In addition, we made four separate pilgrimages to Memphis because no sooner would we get back home and start writing up the Memphis section than some Memphis barbecue fool would call and tell us about another barbecue discovery. Memphis barbecue fanatics, which seems to be anybody in Memphis who still has his teeth, never quit searching for that Perfect Rib.

CHARLIE VERGOS' RENDEZVOUS

o General Washburn Alley o (901) 523-2746
o Tues.–Thurs., 4:30 P.M.–midnight; Fri.–Sat., noon–1 A.M.
o Closed Sunday

We think we have found that perfect rib. And it's been in plain sight all along. It's at Charlie Vergos' Rendezvous. Vergos has been serving ribs in his downtown rathskeller since 1948. He is the dean of the Dry School. The 'Vous's ribs are rubbed with a paprika-and-spice mixture that bakes on crispy and holds the juices in until your bicuspids set them free. There is nothing like them anywhere. For a dry rib these are the best and have been for four decades. (You can try them yourself. See the mail order barbecue section.) Vergos's noisy, claustrophobic cavern is a study in tacky. Every inch of the walls is gilded with old signs, old newspapers, old business cards, the kind of collection you might find at a museum without a curator. Go early, or be prepared to wait outside in line, where you can smell the hickory smoke and listen to your stomach rumble.

Rating: As good as we've ever had.

Directions: If you look for the 'Vous at 52 South Second St., its official address, you could die hungry. It is actually on the General Washburn Alley, which runs parallel to South Second Street between Second and Third. The simplest directions: Go to the Peabody Hotel on Union Ave. Look straight across the street. See that alley where everyone is heading. It's half a block down on the left.

GRIDLEY'S BAR-B-Q

○ 4101 Summer Ave. ○ (901) 775-2351
○ Sun.–Thurs., 6 A.M.–11 P.M.; Fri.–Sat., 6 A.M.–midnight

If you want your ribs wet, the choice is Gridley's, a chain-esque pit founded in 1975 by the late Clyde Gridley, former controller for Loeb's Barbecue. He and his family spent weeks in the kitchen working on their sauce and they didn't come out until they had it right. Gridley's paints its ribs with a sweetish sauce that is baked into the meat.

And for a wet sandwich, you don't even have to move the car. Gridley's is it, with a giant bunful of chopped pork, slopped up with a mild Memphis sauce. Okay, it isn't as giant as it used to be. Recently Gridley's dropped some prices, at the same time decreasing portions. But regardless of the size, they are just as messy and just as good as they've always been. Gridley's has expanded to four locations and ships ribs anywhere there is an airport (see the section on mail order barbecue in the back of the book).

Rating: Real good.

Directions: Summer Ave. is Exit 12A off I-40. Head west until you smell the hickory.

LEONARD'S

○ 1140 S. Bellevue Blvd. ○ (901) 948-1581
○ Mon.–Sat., 10 A.M.–5 P.M. ○ Closed Sunday

The waiters at Gridley's, all decked out in gold jackets and bow ties, will remind you of another era. But if you really want to be reminded of another era, head to the original Leonard's on South Bellevue Blvd. Leonard Heuberger, the man who put the Leonard in Leonard's, is acknowledged as the creator of the Memphis-style barbecue sandwich: chunks of pulled pork, mounded on a bun, covered with vinegar-and-tomato sauce, and crowned with cole slaw. Leonard's neon pig— MR. BROWN GOES TO TOWN, it says—has been a beacon on Bellevue since 1922. The original place, and two others, are now owned by a local corporation, but many of the cooks are the same ones Leonard hired back in the days when his chief competitors were the Pig 'n' Whistle, Miss Culpepper's, and Willie King's.

Rating: Real good.

Directions: Take the Union Ave. exit east from I-240. Turn right

PORKLORE ○ Pig Latin

Our language is rich in porklore. There may be more folk
expressions using pigs than any other animal.

He's as independent as a hog on ice.

What's time to a pig?

It's like buying a pig in a poke.

I'm in hog heaven.

He bled like a stuck pig.

She was frisking about like a pig in clover.

She's as happy as a pig in paradise.

I could do that in less time than a pig's whistle.

You been eating high on the hog.

You can't make a silk purse out of a sow's ear.

I feel hog-tied.

He's as fat as a pig.

For us it's whole hog or none.

---

on South Bellevue. Leonard's is on the corner of McLemore and Bellevue.

PAYNE'S

○ 1762 Lamar Ave. ○ (901) 274-9823
○ Mon., Tues., Thurs., 11 A.M.–9 P.M.; Wed., 11 A.M.–6:30 P.M.;
    Fri., 11 A.M.–11 P.M.; Sat., 11 A.M.–9:30 P.M. ○ Closed Sunday

Any Memphian, even a recent refugee from Arkansas, can direct you
to the 'Vous, Gridley's, or Leonard's. But only the true barbecue
connoisseurs in town know about Payne's, a plain-as-vanilla place
making do in a converted filling station in Mid City. Memphis native
Tommy O'Brien introduced us to Payne's in 1980, and we have been
careful not to spread the word, until now. We didn't want the sweetness of success to spoil the sass of the sauce. But word has leaked out.
"You can't get in there at lunchtime," says Memphian Dennis Sigman. "Now, I don't go by that. I rate places not by how many people
are there, but who is there. When you see guys leave construction
sites, when you see trucks from the power company, plumbers'
trucks—and they are all at Payne's every day—you know it's got to
be good."

Payne's is better than good, better than real good. It's as good as we've ever had. The secret? You can't get any fresher meat than Emily Payne serves. She keeps it toasting on the rack until you order. "It's the best wet barbecue sandwich I have ever put in my mouth," says Sigman. "Just talking about them, I can almost taste that hot mustard cole slaw that runs down your arm. For a rib sandwich, wet ribs on a piece of a bread with mustard relish, we're talking good eating."

Rating: As good as we've ever had.

Directions: There's a Lamar Avenue exit off I-240. Head west and watch the building numbers. It's the one in the converted filling station.

VIRGINIA

Clinchport

FRIENDLY'S MARKET & RESTAURANT

o U.S. Hwy. 23 o (703) 940-4000
o Mon.–Thurs., 5:30 A.M.–11 P.M.; Fri.–Sun., 5:30 A.M.–midnight

Sometimes there's a bend in the road on the way to barbecue fame. Raymond Gibson, Jr., owner of Gib's Ribs in Louisville, trained as a French chef before realizing he preferred the pit to the pâté. The Brandons, Dave and Dottye, owners of Brandon's Bar-B-Que in Plantation, Ky., had Wall Street in their sights. But they took their fancy degrees—his in international finance, hers in mathematics—and traded them in, an even swap: pork futures for pork sandwiches.

Charles Fugate was on the fast track with a *Fortune* 500 company. He had all the baggage: an M.B.A., a middle-manager's post, a company car. But shortly after turning forty, he decided to quit the corporate rat race. He moved back home to Clinchport, Va., to farm with his father and run Friendly's, a barbecue place-general store. And we thank him for it.

There's nobody named Friendly at Friendly's; it's just the way everybody in the place acts. The cashier asks you how you've been; the hostess makes sure the seat suits you; the waitress calls you honey. The restaurant and the store are jointed at the potato chip rack, so that the place is as much a social center as an eating establishment. There are construction workers beginning the day with red eyes and black coffee, farmers stopping by to pick up a bale of barbed wire, district judges taking a break from the bench to down a little barbecue. And Friendly's has it all, from barbed wire to barbecue, from antacid to gas. All served up with a friendly glow. It used to have a friendly shine. "When we started, we'd wax the floors once a week," says Fugate, "but we found out people didn't want to come in and scuff them up. So we stopped that. We're still a clean place, the health inspector and his boss eat here all the time, we just don't wax the floors so often."

Friendly's has only been in business since 1985, but already it has established a reputation for its generous barbecue sandwich. Fugate slices juicy hunks off a pork shoulder, masses them on a Sunbeam bun, and blankets it in an amiably sweet, ketchupy sauce. Cole slaw is available if you want it, on the side or on the top. Fugate swears by it. "It's so good I could eat it with my cornflakes."

Fugate fires up his cooker at nine in the morning. "We romance our meat all day long." He finally takes it off the hickory fire as the eleven o'clock late news is coming on. When he's cooking, everybody in the Clinch Valley knows it. He puts out more smoke than the last-place car at the dragway. "Once this woman was in here and she had been watching that smoke the whole time with a nervous eye. Finally she got up the nerve to ask the waitress what had been on her mind. 'Is everything all right?' she asked. 'Or am I in a burning building?' "

Rating: Real good.

Directions: Friendly's is on U.S. Hwy. 23 one mile south of Clinchport. The nearest interstate is I-81, but that's about thirty miles away. If you don't know the area, your best bet would be to exit I-81 at U.S. 23 and follow it all the way to Clinchport. If you do know the area, then we don't have to give you directions, do we?

Lightfoot

PIERCE'S PITT BAR-B-QUE

o 137 Rochambeau Dr. o (804) 565-2955
o Open daily: 10 A.M.–9 P.M. in the summer,
    10 A.M.–8 P.M. in the winter

Let's say you take our advice and decide to give Pierce's barbecue a try. And let's say you are heading down I-64 when you realize you've lost the directions. Never fear. You won't have any trouble spotting Pierce's. It's the only barbecue joint we've seen that's painted like a beach umbrella. "We call it U Haul orange and Ryder yellow," says J. C. Pierce, son of the founder and current manager. "They're our trademark colors." Those traffic-stopping colors and the enticing aroma from Pierce's hickory-fired open pit have cost many a trucker seventy-five dollars. You see, for years there wasn't a nearby exit. So truckers and state legislators alike would park on the interstate shoulder and jump the fence. J. C. remembers one little old lady who got her dress caught on the barbed wire, got a ticket, and still tried to get over the fence. "The policeman told her to move her car but she refused. 'If I have to pay a seventy-five dollar fine,' she said, 'I'm at least going to eat. Go ahead and tow the car!'"

Pierce's opened in October 1971 as a take-out joint. It was just a little ten-by-fourteen-foot shack that Doc Pierce, J. C.'s father, had constructed in the middle of a vacant field. "We had a guy painting our sign for us and we noticed he was misspelling the word 'pit.' When we went to correct him, he said, 'If you don't like the way I spell you can do it yourself.'" The Pierces decided they liked the unusual spelling—Pitt—and had their restaurant name trademarked that way. Pierce's has expanded four times since it opened and now seats eighty-five inside and forty-three outside. Doc Pierce turned the business over to J. C. back in '81 after quadruple bypass heart surgery. But that doesn't keep him from traipsing in and out a lot.

Pierce's hasn't changed its cooking method the entire time it has been in business. They still cook slowly on an open pit in a building twenty yards behind the restaurant. They use mostly hickory, with a little oak mixed in. The meat is cooked for eight hours, then pulled from the bone by hand, cut in small chunks, and variegated in Pierce's spicy tomato-based sauce. J. C. says Pierce's will always cook with wood, even if it takes longer and costs more. "Dad used to say, 'The difference between cooking over a pit and cooking on a gas cooker is like the difference between homemade biscuits and canned biscuits.'"

Rating: Real good.

Directions: If you're traveling I-64 eastbound, take Exit 55 (right), then take a quick left onto the service road (which is Rochambeau Dr.); Pierce's is one mile on the right. If you're traveling from Virginia Beach (I-64 westbound), take Exit 56 (left), then take a quick right onto the service road (Rochambeau Dr.); Pierce's is three miles on the left. Pierce's is closed for the holidays, from Dec. 23 to Jan. 2.

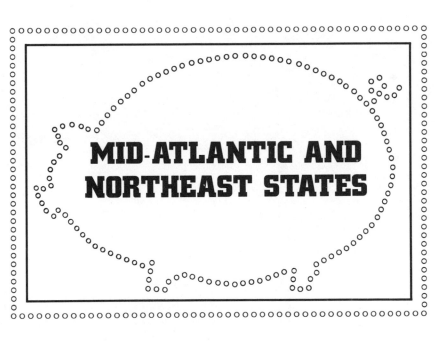

MID-ATLANTIC AND
NORTHEAST STATES

CONNECTICUT

Stratford

STICK TO YOUR RIBS

o 1785 Stratford Ave. o (203) 377-1752
o Tues.–Sat., 10:30 A.M.–7 P.M. o Closed Sunday and Monday

If you had told us a year ago that we would be recommending barbecue by an English hairdresser, we would have told you . . . well, we
can't print what we would have told you.

Then we made the short hop off America's busiest interstate, I-95,
to Stick to Your Ribs. Maybe these English know something about
food after all.

The decor at Stick To Your Ribs is Hard Luck Drive-In. If you
remember what McDonald's was like before it added eat-in areas,
you've got it. But the food is Good Fortune Good. It'll stick in your
memory as well as to your ribs.

Owner Robert Pearson, an Englishman and a former hairdresser
who once had a salon in Bloomingdale's, got the idea to open a barbecue joint when he was traveling the south for Sassoon. "I used to do
a lot of teaching in my travels. And a lot of it was done on Sunday or
Monday. I'd get into town on Saturday night and I'd want to go out
and party." Often as not the locals would take him to a nearby barbecue joint. Soon he was a convert.

But he wasn't content to be just a convert; he wanted to spread
the gospel into the northeast. "I wanted to open an authentic barbecue place. There are lots of barbecue places around but very few,
especially in this neck of the woods, that are authentic and cook solely
with wood."

He started looking for a location in New York City, where he lives.
"It was going to cost $110, $120 a square foot. I'd never been in the
food business before. I'd never been in an industrial kitchen for more
than an hour. But I knew that at those prices if I made one mistake
I'd be out of business."

He landed in Connecticut by chance. At a party he met a man who
offered him an attractive deal on a closed-up hamburger stand in
Stratford. "He said, 'Listen, it sounds as if you should come and get
some experience.' So I came up and looked at the place. It looked
awful. There were masses of old equipment, old refrigerators inside.

I ran back to New York with my tail between my legs and said it was not right for me."

Then Pearson began to recall all the great barbecue places he had eaten at in the south. "I realized the best barbecue places were all on the wrong side of the tracks and all were funky and all had white-collar professionals eating in them. I go to Texas to Red Bryan's or Angelo's, and there are guys sitting at tables making big deals."

He decided the run-down drive-in was right. His next problem was developing a product. He used his friends as guinea pigs. "I would have dinner parties over the weekend and get people who were interested in food to test my sauces." He estimates he concocted at least a thousand different experimental sauces before he narrowed it down to the three basic varieties he uses in the restaurant: mild, medium, and mad (hot). The names tell it all.

Stick to Your Ribs is the barbecue eclectic's delight. Pearson serves everything from west Texas barbecued rattlesnake to North Carolina pork sandwiches. His specialty is a Texas-style sliced beef sandwich that will parch your throat and make you long for a Lone Star beer.

PORKLORE ○ Barbecue in USA

For *USA Today* readers, who are accustomed to a lot of cold, hard facts, here are the numbers on barbecue. Sorry, no pie charts or bar graphs.

We Love Barbecue

In 1986 there were 6,412 barbecue joints in the USA. (Source: Restaurant Consulting Group of Evanston, Illinois)

Barbecue is on the Upswing

The number of people who ate at a barbecue restaurant in 1986 was up 38 percent from 1985. (Source: National Restaurant Association)

Who Eats Barbecue?

The people most likely to patronize a barbecue restaurant are men between the ages of eighteen and twenty-four, women employed fulltime, and residents of the South. (Source: National Restaurant Association)

Pearson says he continues to refine his barbecue. He has even added a fourth sauce, at his customers' insistence.

"My hot was designed so you would still be able to taste the food through it. But I had a whole bunch of guys standing here beating their chests, saying, 'That's not hot, come on.' So I added my 'mean' sauce, which I think is much too hot for human consumption."

We can vouch for that. It is hot enough to make you forget Connecticut winters.

Rating: Good.

Directions: Take Exit 31 east off I-95. That's Stratford Avenue. You'll see Stick to Your Ribs up the road at the corner of Stratford and Honeyspot.

MARYLAND

Baltimore

CAFE TATTOO

o 4807 Belair Rd. o (301) 325-7427
o Wed.–Sun., 4 P.M.–11 P.M. o Closed Monday and Tuesday

This is the kind of barbecue town Baltimore is: The same month that *Baltimore* magazine picked the Wharf Rat as the best barbecued rib restaurant in the city, the new owners dropped the item from the menu. Actually, that's being a little harsh on Baltimore. It has something of a barbecue tradition: Woody's, out on Pulaski Highway, has been around for thirty years. It's the rib joint of preference for professional wrestler Haystack Calhoun when he's in town. The Dixie Pig, down south at Fort Meade, was Oprah Winfrey's favorite joint when she worked in Baltimore. Leon's Pig Pit has had many owners and many names—Leon's, Kenny's, and now Lake Trout—but its reputation for good ribs has remained steady among inner-city barbecue lovers. And ask a longtime resident and you'll probably hear about the Corner Stable's ribs, up north in Cockeysville.

We're here to tell you that while all four of these places serve Good Barbecue, there is only one place in town where you can find Real Good Barbecue: the Cafe Tattoo—or the Tattoo Cafe, take your pick.

Why the flip-flop name? Because it is really two places in one. "If you go in the front door, it's the Cafe Tattoo, and if you go in the back door, it's the Tattoo Cafe," says Bob Moody, a transplanted Arkansan who began an in-depth search for good barbecue after he moved to Baltimore in 1987. "If you go in the front, you are in the barbecue joint; if you go in the back, you are in the tattoo parlor, which is run by the barbecue guy's wife." The barbecue guy is Rick Catalano, and his wife is Elayne, the Dark Lady. "I call her the Dark Lady because in the tattoo field you have to have a nickname, and basically she doesn't come out until the sun goes down," says Rick.

Elayne, who is a dead ringer, no pun intended, for Morticia Addams of TV's *The Addams Family,* is the brains behind the barbecue business. Rick readily admits it. "If it weren't for her, I'd be sleeping in a cardboard box over some steam grate." He is chief cook and bottle-washer, but it is Elayne who concocts the sauces. She has the gustatory equivalent of perfect pitch. "A friend went to Arthur Bryant's and brought back his sauce," says Rick. "She went in the kitchen and came back later and said, 'Here it is.' She had duplicated it exactly."

Rick doesn't use the Bryant sauce in the cafe, but he does offer a choice of four other sauces: a tangy tomato-based sauce; the same style sauce with some heat to it; a spicy version; and Rick's award-winning Black Jack sauce, blended with Jack Daniel's sour mash whiskey. Combine the four sauces with the four kinds of ribs that Rick cooks—baby back, St. Louis style, sparerib tips, and what he calls Black Jack beef ribs (mesquite smoked with a dash of Jack Daniel's whiskey)—and you have sixteen different possibilities. The ribs are just part of the appeal at the Cafe Tattoo. There's Rick's shredded beef sandwich with the meat cooked into a pocket of the bread. There's his award-winning chili, which comes in three styles: regular, hi-test, and unleaded. And there is Elayne's side venture, tattoo artistry.

The Cafe's homey sixties feel is another part of the appeal. With his ponytail and his amphetamine-pace storytelling, Rick reminded us of comedian George Carlin. It only added to the overall effect when he told us about his wedding day back in 1969. "Elayne and I were going to go to Woodstock for our honeymoon. But by the time we got out of the reception, they were saying on the radio that all the roads were blocked, so we didn't go. It was just as well. Everybody we knew who went came back with walking pneumonia."

Since our first visit, Rick has moved the Cafe down the street. Elayne's tattoo parlor is no longer in back. She has moved upstairs. But you can still fill up on hot barbecue and cold beer and, if you get the notion, go upstairs and get Elayne to stitch MOTHER in your bicep.

Rating: Real good.

Directions: From the north take Belair Rd. (Exit 32) off I-695 and follow it all the way in. Belair Road is also U.S. 1. From downtown take I-83 to Exit 6, North Ave. North will veer left and become Belair Rd.

MASSACHUSETTS

Sunderland

BUB'S BAR-B-QUE

o Route 116 o (413) 259-1254
o Sun.–Thurs., 4 P.M.–9 P.M.; Fri.–Sat., 5 P.M.–10 P.M.

Bub's is the best barbecue joint in New England. Granted that isn't much more praise than calling someone the world's tallest midget. We found only eight legitimate barbecue places in New England, although we did hear rumors of two others. But Bub's belongs. He isn't in this book just for geographical symmetry.

Howard "Bub" Tiley opened his roadhouse in 1977, shortly after he returned from a vacation in Florida—a twelve-year vacation. It had started as a two-week tour but he enjoyed it so much he stayed and stayed. Bub's began as your basic barbecue stand, with waitresses and all. But soon Bub converted it into a cafeteria with a self-serve line. "Getting rid of waitresses, you get rid of a lot of trouble." The cafeteria line begins in front of the pit, where Bub himself takes your order, and then winds around to the drink bar (yes, they do have beer), stops at the cashier, and then circles back to the steam table, which Bub keeps overloaded with slaw, beans, fries, and rice.

You carry your own tray to one of the varnished pine picnic tables, plop down, and then dig into Bub's piquant pork sandwich. Bub chunks his meat, then lathers it in an apple-red tomato-based sauce that is flavorful without overwhelming the smoked meat. If you are of the slaw-on-top persuasion, Bub has white slaw at the self-serve steam table. Bub got his sauce recipe when he was managing a golf course in Plant City, Fla. He used convict labor to maintain the greens and fairways, and one of the convicts gave Bub his mother's recipe.

Bub's is a popular hangout for Amherst students. That explains the free jukebox. It doesn't explain the odd mixture of hard country and hard-core rock, from Crystal Gayle to Jody Watley, from Little Richard to Little Jimmy Dickens. Bub's itself has been celebrated in song, although it's not on the jukebox. In 1983 Jeff Holmes, a professor of music at nearby University of Massachusetts, composed "Bubs," a jazz piece, and it was performed in concert locally.

Like many of your new generation barbecue men, Bub cooks on gas. If you are opposed for religious reasons, we suggest you not make the trip. Bub's not one to argue with. Remember, this is a man who got a convict to give him his mother's recipe.

Rating: Real good.

Directions: Take Exit 24 from I-91 North and wind around east on Route 116. Bub's is about three miles down on the left. You can't miss it. It's a brown, squatty roadhouse with yellow trim.

NEW YORK

New York City

Big Apple Que: Barbecue came to New York City in 1977. That was the year Barry Farber, New York radio talk-show host and North Carolina native, got the idea that he could satisfy his hunger for some of his native cuisine and also make some money. Let's let Farber tell the story. "I have a theory—never believe a fact unless it's supported by a theory—that foods have blister power to reach beyond their boundaries and make friends. The food with the greatest blister power is pizza. Pizza broke out of Italy and conquered the world. The lowest blister power is Philadelphia scrapple. It's not sold one yard outside the city limits. It's just bad. Estonian codfish heads have low blister power. Second to pizza, North Carolina barbecue has the greatest blister power on Earth. If properly presented, it will conquer the world."

So Farber took his theory to his friend Alex Parker, who owned a building on Times Square. "I told him, 'I've got a product that is the next pizza.' " Farber explained his blister theory, and the next day the two were flying down to North Carolina to let Parker taste the theory. "Alex didn't want to eat the barbecue. It was so good, he just wanted to put his head down in it." With Parker convinced, Farber arranged to have Fuzzy's Bar-B-Que in Madison, N.C., package chopped pork in Dixie Cups and send it to New York every night by air express.

Parker had already rented his Times Square space to a Greek restaurant, but as luck would have it the man was behind in his rent. "So Alex goes to the guy and says, 'Tony, I want you to put this (barbecue) in your restaurant for me. We want to see how it goes.'" Farber went on the radio and advertised this great place in Times Square that had authentic North Carolina barbecue. And sat back and waited for the fame and adulation, and also money, that should naturally accrue to someone who had brought the Real Thing to the Big Apple. But it didn't happen. "I began getting hate mail from North Carolinians. They would hear me say it's authentic North Carolina barbecue on the radio and they would drive down from Yonkers and White Plains and then the guy would serve it to them on a cold bun with no slaw. The Greek seemed to be going along like a Viet Cong who knew his rights by the Geneva Convention. Every day it was no rolls or old rolls or cold rolls or 'We forgot to make slaw.'"

The Great North Carolina Barbecue in New York City Experiment ended when Farber took a prominent North Carolinian to try out the place. "And the Greek served him authentic North Carolina barbecue on a bagel. Authentic *pork* barbecue on a bagel! If Moses had seen that, there would have been another commandment."

A decade later, barbecue is still an alien dish in New York City. There are a lot of places that serve ribs, but not very many that serve barbecue. We're not even sure they know what barbecue is. You look up "barbecue" in the Westchester suburban phone book, and you find Scarsdale Oriental Food Market and Poultry Time. And in all the guide books, under "barbecue" they seem to talk more about the "ambience" and the "restaurant concept" than the pork. Tell us about the barbecue, damnit.

PORKLORE ○ How Do You Eat a Rib Sandwich?

Everybody knows how to eat ribs, but what do you do when you first encounter a rib sandwich, a menu item favored at many urban barbecue stands? These directions courtesy of the Raineshaven Barbecue in Memphis, Tenn.: "First you take off the top piece of bread. Then you separate the ribs and take 'em one at a time in your hand. You run the rib this way and then back this way, sort of like eating corn on the cob. Then you go for the slaw. And you use the bread to sop up whatever is left over."

Undaunted, we ate our way around Manhattan Island, testing every place that was even rumored to have barbecue. Pig Heaven fooled us into thinking it was a barbecue place. Pig, hell. It's a Chinese restaurant. We had some unusual barbecue experiences in New York. It was the first place anyone with a British accent had ever asked us how we wanted our sauce (Dallas BBQ). And it was the first place we ever had barbecue accompanied by a drink with a little umbrella in it (Carolina).

All told, we ate two hundred and sixty dollars' worth of New York City barbecue in three days. We could have taken that same money and lived for six months on North Carolina or Texas barbecue. There are some valiant efforts going on there. Dallas BBQ, Home on the Range, Texarkana, and Tennessee Mountain are all working on it. Carolina, on West 46th Street, might even be able to make it in a small Carolina town, providing the people didn't mind eating their barbecue off a lettuce leaf. That doesn't mean New York doesn't have barbecue. It just means you may have to spend two hundred and sixty dollars finding it. Not including cab fare. And tips.

THE PINK TEA CUP

o 42 Grove St. o (212) 807-6755
o Sun.–Thurs., 8 A.M.–midnight; Fri.–Sat., 8 A.M.–1 A.M.

When Charles Raye bought The Pink Tea Cup in 1979, he introduced Greenwich Village to the kind of barbecue he grew up eating in his native Georgia. "In Georgia they do barbecue the old-fashioned way. Everyone else tries to do the fast-food thing, tries to find a shortcut. But there is no shortcut to good cooking." Now, the purist in us might claim that Raye takes a shortcut because he barbecues with gas instead of wood. But we're going to look the other way this time because, frankly, there isn't much cheap, available hickory wood in his part of town, or any part for that matter. A good barbecue man could burn up all the hardwood trees in Greenwich Village inside of a week, easy.

Raye's barbecue offerings include ribs, chicken wings, pig's feet, and a notorious chopped pork sandwich, the Big Bad John, named for the cook. The Big Bad John has a strong, smoky flavor and a husky sauce that fires your mouth from the first bite. We fell in love with the king-sized Big Bad John. We also fell in love with Jackie, our waitress, who took good care of us, before going back to a table next to the jukebox to break beans.

The Pink Tea Cup is aptly named. It is pink, its waitresses wear pink, and it used to serve on pink dinnerware. "But nobody makes the pink plates anymore," says Raye, "and all of ours are broken." The Pink Tea Cup also lives up to its last name. It could easily pass for a tearoom. But don't worry. Nobody is going to eat a Big Bad John sandwich with the pinky finger up.

Rating: Good (for gas-cooking).

Directions: Grove St. is in the Village. From Seventh Avenue South take Bleecker Street west one block to Grove. Turn left (sort of southwest). It's up the street on the left, between Bedford and Bleecker streets. Better still, take a taxi.

PENNSYLVANIA

Philadelphia

MAMA ROSA'S

o 3838 North Broad St. o (215) 225-2177
o Mon.–Thurs., 10 A.M.–11 P.M.; Fri.–Sat., 10 A.M.–3 A.M.;
   Sun., noon–8 P.M.

o 5531 Germantown Ave. o (215) 848-3860
o Open daily, 11 A.M.–8 P.M.

You're probably asking yourself what a spaghetti place is doing in a book about barbecue restaurants. Don't let the name fool you. Mama Rosa's may sound like an Italian restaurant, but it is barbecue from the word go. And Philadelphians are starting to get the word and go. Owner Walter Ridder has them believing there is more to lunch than cheese steak. He's got them eating ribs and—what?—pig's feet? "The Pennsylvania Dutch love those pig feet. They eat everything except the squeal!"

Mama Rosa's traces its roots back to 1965 when Ridder was running a pharmacy. "My wife, *the* Mama Rosa, had always been a good cook and had always loved cooking. My pharmacy had been broken into a couple of times, and one day I saw an ad for thirty food trucks. On a whim, I bought ten of them."

The Ridders turned them into what Walter calls "hamburger trucks." "They just went around to factories and all at lunchtime." They sold Mama Rosa's hamburgers and chicken. And the factory workers loved them. In 1972 things were going so well that Walter closed the pharmacy and opened the first Mama Rosa's restaurant on North Broad Street. "We sold ribs from the start, but it wasn't a featured item. Pretty soon we were getting so many calls for them we had to make them a regular menu item."

They've moved down the street and added a second restaurant, but they haven't changed the menu. "Ribs and chicken, that's what we are, a ribs and chicken place. That's what our customers want. We have people that come into the restaurant and say, 'We've followed Mama Rosa's ever since you were just a truck in the parking lot of the post office.'"

The secret to Mama Rosa's best-selling ribs? Walter will tell you how they marinate the meat with a dry rub—"let it sit a while." They cook it for four hours in a mesquite wood smoker and add an easy-going vinegar-based sauce. Then his eyes will light up. "The real secret is having someone like Mama Rosa in the kitchen!"

Rating: Real good.

Directions: To get to the North Broad Street restaurant from the Pennsylvania Turnpike, take the Broad Street exit, turn left, and Mama Rosa's is on the corner, a half block up.

To get to the Germantown Ave. restaurant from the Turnpike, take the Norristown–Plymouth Meeting exit and go south on Germantown Pike toward the center of the city. Mama Rosa's is in the heart of the historic district.

VERMONT

Putney

CURTIS' ALL AMERICAN NINTH WONDER OF THE WORLD BAR-B-Q

o Route 5 o (802) 387-5474
o Open daily during the summer, 8 A.M.–9 P.M.

We originally intended to bypass New England. We were afraid they might do something like put clam chowder in the sauce. Or barbecue beavers. Then we heard about Curtis and his Ninth Wonder of the

World Bar-B-Q. We figured we should make the trip just to find out what the Eighth Wonder was.

What we found was not one but two great barbecue joints in New England. Curtis's place lives up to its name; it is a world wonder. And an hour south, down in Sunderland, Mass., is Bub's, which may be the Tenth Wonder.

Curtis' has great barbecue written all over it. He hand-lettered the sign himself: GREAT BAR-B-Q. Curtis operates his barbecue restaurant out of a refurbished school bus. Actually it hasn't been refurbished, just sort of painted and outfitted with a 275-gallon oil drum cooker. "It's comfortable," Curtis says. "And you can drive along and cook at the same time."

Curtis is Curtis Tuff, a Buffalo native who just fell into barbecuing some twenty years ago. "I was working around here, doing odd jobs, when some of the students at Windham School asked me if I knew anything about barbecuing a pig." Curtis didn't, but that didn't stop him from volunteering. He taught himself, and pretty soon his skills were in demand at parties and school functions all around southern Vermont. It was just a small step from that to opening up his pit on a vacant lot beside a Mobil gas station. Now Curtis lives in a mobile home behind the barbecue bus. He says it wasn't easy at first, teaching Vermonters to eat barbecue. "They didn't have no idea what it was. But they're getting there."

Curtis cooks his ribs over a mixture of hardwoods, primarily oak, rock maple, and ash. He doesn't use any hickory—the traditional barbecue wood—though. "That's out. I can't get it. I used to clean off mountains for big apple growers. I did that for twenty-four years, and in twenty-four years I found one hickory tree." All he sells is take-out. No seats in the bus. But you can hang around and watch Curtis cook and eat on one of the many picnic tables he has strewn all around the lot. His ribs are chewy but not tough. You enjoy chewing them. And he adds a lip-smacking sweet sauce that he invented himself. It's an award-winning sauce. Curtis has the award proudly displayed in one of the bus windows: CURTIS' SAUCE, BEST IN VERMONT.

Before we left, we had one last question for Curtis. We told him we knew about the Seven Wonders of the world and now we knew where to find the Ninth Wonder of the world. But we wondered: What is the Eighth Wonder? Curtis turned his head sideways, squinted his eyes, and got this thoughtful grin on his face. "I can't remember the name of it," he said, "but I know it's somewhere down in New York."

Rating: Real good.

Directions: Get off I-91 at Exit 4, the Putney exit. Curtis' is set up on the south side of the Mobil station on Route 5. You'll see the smoke. Although it's open daily during the summer, during the winter, hours of operation depend on the weather and on Curtis.

WASHINGTON, D.C.

Capital Scandals: Once Washington, D.C., was a respectable barbecue town. There was Mrs. Garbine's and Hickory Plantation and Allman's down in Fredericksburg, a list as long as your arm. But times have changed. The first two have closed, Mr. Allman has retired, and his place has switched to electric cookers.

"What's happened here is it's become a quiche-eating town," laments Bob Edwards, host of National Public Radio's "Morning Edition" and a barbecue lover from way back. "You have the two counties with the highest per capita income in the land, Fairfax in Virginia and Montgomery in Maryland. You have all the lobbyists and the big media people. It is quite the rich people's area."

Our barbecue sampling took us all over the D.C. area, as far north as Rockville and as far south as Fredericksburg, west to Purcellville, Va., and east to Waldorf, Md. We had to go that far to find Real Good Barbecue. We found nothing inside the city limits to satisfy our barbecue hunger. At first, Kenny's Best Pit Bar-B-Q on Mt. Pleasant Street seemed promising. Vince was ordering his sandwich when a large fellow in a suit sidled up and tried to fence some stolen jewelry off on the counter man. It would have made a great Barbecue Rule: If they're fencing stolen jewelry at the counter, you can count on good barbecue. Unfortunately, Kenny's meat was tough. Another promising candidate was Charlie Boy's in Sterling, Va. But we arrived too late. They were just putting the stools up on the counter for the last time. Charlie had made a valiant effort. He had fought the good barbecue fight, but he just couldn't make a go of it, running a barbecue joint inside a health club. (He still has a mobile cooker in operation.)

We tried Hog Wild on Capital Hill and the Florida Avenue Grill (which has great food, but not great barbecue) and Thrifty Carry-Out and a dozen others, but we ended up having to drive outside the city limits to find places that met our standards. We found two.

La Plata

JOHNNY BOY'S RIBS

o U.S. 301 o (301) 736-6300
o In warm weather: Mon.–Thurs., 11 A.M.–1 A.M.;
  Fri.–Sat., 11 A.M.–5 A.M. o Closed Sunday
o In cold weather: Wed.–Sun., 11 A.M.–6 or 7 P.M.

If Johnny Boy's had bad barbecue, it might create a new credibility gap in the nation's capital. People wouldn't trust their eyes anymore. For if ever we saw a place that screamed Bar-B-Q, it was Johnny Boy's. Johnny Katsouros and his mother, Sophie, operate their place in an open-air take-out shack edged up against busy U.S. Highway 301 in the tobacco country south of La Plata, Md. There's a tumbledown stack of wood scattered to the side. Paint is peeling off the plank sign. But Johnny Boy doesn't care. "People don't have to read the sign to know it's a barbecue place. If I built a fancy place out of cinderblocks and make it so people can come and sit down, well, you lose something."

Katsouros cooks on an iron grate balanced on cement blocks, an open pit, the kind of barbecue cooker that is prohibited or regulated some places but not in rural Charles County. The ribs and sandwiches are take-out only. You even have to get your drink from a machine. But if it's a hot summer day and you're cruising the open road with the windows down and the radio up, it would be impossible to speed through those billows of Johnny Boy's hickory smoke without stopping to sample the barbecue.

If you stop, your reward is a multitextured minced pork sandwich with crunchies from the crust and delicate morsels from the middle. Or you could choose a generous slab of auburn-colored ribs, reeking of hickory and oak smoke, so good they don't even need sauce, al-

PORKLORE o Barbecue is Good Bidness

In its August 11, 1986, issue *Business Week* magazine recommended that business travelers who were tired of hotel food give barbecue a try. "Of course, barbecue—and the down-home places that usually serve it—won't always impress important clients. But loosening up for an evening might be a big hit with your colleagues."

though Johnny Boy has a strong peppery-hot one with an upfront pop; no surprises later.

Rating: Real good.

Directions: We don't know where you're coming from, so we can't be too helpful on finding U.S. Hwy. 301. If you're coming from the north, 301 is one of the main roads south out of Baltimore. If you're coming from the south, it's Exit 41 on I-95. Either way Johnny Boy's is on the east side of U.S. Hwy. 301, just before you get to the Twin Kiss. It's about a mile south of La Plata in Bel Alton. The hours are loose.

Rockville

O'BRIEN'S PIT BARBECUE

o 1314 East Gude Rd., Rockville o (301) 340-8591
o Sun.–Thurs., 11 A.M.–9 P.M.; Fri.–Sat., 11 A.M.–10 P.M.

o 7305 Waverly St., Bethesda o (301) 654-9004
o Hours same as above

o 6820 Commerce St., Springfield o (301) 569-7801
o Hours same as above

O'Brien's Pit Barbecue is one of those places that we wish we could kiss off as yet another yuppie fern bar that serves barbecuelike food. Barbecue connoisseur Robin Beard disparagingly calls it "one of those institutional-type places." And it worries us that *Washingtonian* magazine ranks it among the area's fifty Very Best Restaurants, up there next to places like L'Auberge Chez Francois and Vincenzo. It gives us chill bumps just typing names like L'This and Chez That. The Bethesda branch of O'Brien's has, and we swear and apologize at the same time, Old West saloon doors. Yup. But it also has Real Good barbecue.

Ken O'Brien hasn't let success spoil his operation. No cutting corners. No parboiling the ribs. No roasting the meat and then smoking it with a handful of wood chips. He uses hickory wood in a closed pit, cooking his meat longer than a Southern filibuster. It is pulled and chopped, then lumped on a bun. You can eat it that way or you can add O'Brien's sauce, a coffee-thin liquid that is sharper than Tip O'Neill's tongue.

Rating: Real good.

Directions: Call the nearest location and ask directions. They're very helpful.

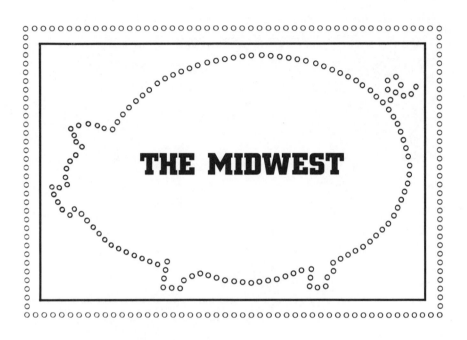

THE MIDWEST

ILLINOIS

Cairo

SHEMWELL'S BARBECUE (DARRELL'S)
SHEMWELL'S BARBECUE (SKIP'S)

- Darrell's: 1102 Washington St. ○ (618) 734-0165
- Open daily, 8 A.M.–9 P.M. (Closes at 7:30 P.M. on winter weekdays)

- Skip's: 2203 Sycamore St. ○ (618) 734-3357
- Tues.–Thurs., 10 A.M.–7 P.M.; Fri.–Sat., 10 A.M.–9 P.M.
- Closed Sunday and Monday

It's not exactly *Dallas,* but there it is in little Cairo, Ill.—Darrell Shemwell's "Shemwell's Barbecue" sitting on Washington Street and, a short six tenths of a mile down the street, Skip Shemwell's "Shemwell's Barbecue," sitting in defiant opposition. Unlike Bobby and J. R. Ewing, the two aren't brothers; Skip is actually Darrell's step-nephew. And they aren't battling to the death. Not quite. "When you teach a child to do something, it doesn't mean he's going to follow it," says Darrell of Skip's sauce. "It's the same recipe," replies Skip. "The difference is in the people that make it. I like the taste of mine better."

Once upon a time, all was happiness in Cairo (pronounced KAY-row). Luther Cashman Shemwell ran a barbecue place in what was then a bustling river town where the Mississippi and Ohio rivers met. Luther had arrived with quite a barbecue reputation: At his first place in Murphysboro, Ill., he had rolled two big fuel tanks together and cut the insides out with a blowtorch for seating. Luther's place in Cairo started doing so well that his son Howard opened up another restaurant. After that, it gets a little confusing. Somewhere in there, Luther retired and then reopened ·in a former Chinese laundry. Luther's other son, Darrell, Howard's half-brother, took over Luther's new place; and Howard's son Skip, Luther's step-nephew, took over Howard's business, building a new place of his own in 1961. That brings us up to the present day and a Cairo that's more of a backwash than a bustling metropolis. In a town of only 6,000, the barbecue competition can get intense. "It's not a family feud," Skip says. "We just don't do business together." But Darrell's pointedly uses as its slogan: THE BEST IN TOWN.

And, appropriately enough, it is. If we can't get the Battling Shemwells back together just for this book, at least we can settle the argument about who's best: Darrell is. The barbecued pork at Darrell's classic lunch counter is smoky and tender, served on bread or bun in a sandwich that's squashed flat on the grill into a dense, delightful, compressed collection of barbecue. And Darrell's sauce is delicious, too—a tantalizing tan with flakes of red pepper and grainy spices suspended in a vinegary mixture. It's pleasantly hot, served in squeeze bottles in a very pleasant restaurant, with metal stools along the counter and tables and booths scattered elsewhere. The palm tree planted in a white Sliced Dill Pickle bucket sort of sets off the decor.

A half mile down at Skip's, things are good, too, but just not quite as good. The lunch counter is newer and less distinctive. The sandwich, also served squashed, arrives between toasted bread almost like a grilled cheese sandwich. But the meat is fattier and slightly overcooked, and the sauce is lighter on the red pepper and heavier on the black. It's good eating, and the potato salad and baked beans are excellent, but it's silver medal stuff.

One more thing: Darrell sells a Shemwell's Frisbee. Skip doesn't.

Rating: Good.

Directions: Once you get to Cairo, the rest is easy. Darrell's place is on Washington St., the main drag through downtown. You can find Skip's just up the road on Sycamore St., which veers slightly to the right. Maybe you'll like Skip's better; if you do, be sure to tell him.

Chicago

South Side Barbecue: When you fly over the city of Chicago into O'Hare International, you may be excused for believing for a moment that you see part of the city enveloped in a soft, romantic fog almost like the gentle fogs of San Francisco. It's probably just your imagination, sparked by the knowledge that Chicago's South Side is a concentrated urban barbecue mecca, smoldering in soulful versions of ribs and hot links, basking in deserved fame, and sending its seductive, distinctive signature upward into the summer air.

Then again, it may actually be Lem's, which puts out more smoke from its tiny spot in the 300 block of East 75th Street than a runaway choo-choo train.

LEM'S

○ 311 E. 75th St. ○ (312) 994-2428
○ Sun.–Thurs., 3 P.M.–2 A.M.; Fri.–Sat., 3 P.M.–4 A.M.
○ Closed Tuesday

○ 5914 S. State St. ○ (312) 684-5007
○ Tues.–Thurs., 5 P.M.–3 A.M.; Fri.–Sat., 5 P.M.–5 A.M.
○ Closed Sunday and Monday

It's possible that Lem's may not singlehandedly be able to fog in the entire city of Chicago, but the place certainly can do a number on a slab of ribs, producing barbecue that is as surprisingly tender as it is distinctively smoky. Lem's ribs are not something a visitor quickly forgets. Wrapped in slick paper and nestled into a cardboard carton on a mattress of greasy fries, these are not just another batch of not-too-bad carry-out ribs. These are the sort of ribs that will lure a man back from Kansas City just to see if his memory is playing tricks on him. These are ribs that make a statement—about daring to be different, about not compromising. But mostly about smoke.

Smoke doesn't just boil from Lem's tall, battered smokestack, which has towered over the shopworn sidewalks of 75th Street for twenty years. It also seems to seep in huge, lazy billows through the building's circular roof itself, giving the whole thing the look of a recently crashed flying saucer. Inside the tiny kitchen, seen from the even tinier carry-out area, the smoke caresses racks of ribs in an aquariumlike cooker with glass on all sides. It's a contraption that would afford a tempting view of the meat inside—if it weren't completely obscured by hickory clouds. That's the way Lem's has been doing it since Miles Lemons started the whole shebang in 1952.

The object of the incendiary attention, the ribs, are an edible masterpiece. They are among the smokiest served anywhere, but they never flirt with the caked-on char that can ruin oversmoked ribs with a chimneysweep flavor. The smokiness of the ribs stops short of stealing the show from the pork, and the pork itself is that agonizingly perfect match of textures that makes good ribs almost impossible to stop eating. The satisfyingly tough exterior is cushioned by a tender, meaty middle that is juicy without being greasy. One food-loving female compared them to the complementary textures of good French bread—slightly crisp and chewy on the outside, pleasantly soft underneath. They really don't require sauce, but Lem's will slap it on or serve it on the side in two varieties—a sledgehammer hot sauce, too much like straight tabasco sauce, and a milder version that leaves at least a couple of taste buds alive for appreciating the meat.

Rating: As good as we've ever had.

Directions: Take 75th St. east off of the Dan Ryan Expressway (I-90 and I-94) as it passes through the middle of Chicago and you'll be lost in Lem's smoke cloud in the space of about three blocks. Lem's also operates a place on South State St., actually the original location.

LEON'S

o 8249 S. Cottage Grove Ave. o (312) 488-4556
o Dining room is open Sun.–Thurs., 11 A.M.–11 P.M.;
     Fri.–Sat., 11 A.M.–2 A.M. o Carry-out is open daily, 11 A.M.–5 A.M.

Although its ribs are one of the best reasons for going there, Lem's is far from alone in Chicago's South Side barbecue scene. In fact, one of the best barbecue *sauces* in the country comes from a place not far from Lem's—Leon's, over on South Cottage Grove Avenue. Both places are locally famous, and both have their ardent followers; but the ribs at Leon's, while tasty and respectable, aren't the distinctive work of art on display at Lem's.

Leon's sauce, on the other hand, is one of the best tomato-based sauces served on the planet Earth. Tell your wine-loving friends that it comes at you in stages, like a fine chardonnay (if chardonnay were hot enough to make you sweat and sigh at the same time). First the sweetness hits, a discreet shot of tomatoey, molasses-rich flavor on the tip of your tongue. Then the barest hints of smokiness begin to creep up on you, and just as you're starting to think you've got the sauce pegged, it whips a roundhouse right to the back of your throat with a delayed-action time bomb that's somewhere between a pleasant, warm feeling and a free tonsilectomy. Get the hot, not the mild. Get it on Leon's ribs if you like, and then get some more to go. A half gallon costs, and we quote, "Eleven something"; a gallon is "Twenty-two something." A gallon is barely enough. After you've finished the ribs, you will find yourself dipping french fries in it, and after you finish your fries, heaven help your fingers.

Leon's, with its bulletproof liquor store built into the entrance (next to the neon pig and the lottery ticket booth), offers an appropriate occasion to mention that the South Side can be intimidating to tourists and Chicagoans who see it only as they flash by on the Dan Ryan Expressway. This is a shame, and a good example of how skittishness can screw up a good meal.

It's true that the take-out at both Lem's and Leon's takes place behind thick protective glass, with the goodies passed out through tiny windows. But you won't find two friendlier places. At Lem's there's no such thing as sitting down (it's carry-out only), but at Leon's there are seventeen tables, a big-screen TV, a bar, and even some hanging plants to make you feel at home. If venturing the few blocks east of the expressway seems daring at midnight, think of South Side barbecue as a summer afternoon sort of thing, born of parks and cookouts—and sample it then.

Actually, Lem's and Leon's are simply two of the best of a whole barbecue colony that stretches roughly from downtown on through the University of Chicago area, often bounded by industry or railroad tracks but filled with pleasant, tree-lined residential streets. In this part of town, on streets like State and Cottage Grove and Halstead and the many cross streets between them, there is a concentration of storefront barbecue shops that rivals those found in any city anywhere. They pop up every two or three blocks in all directions. It is possible to get mediocre barbecue from some of them, barbecue that has been warming too long until it's more like tree bark than pork. But at the best of these South Side eateries, like Lem's, you'll find ribs made by a maestro for a knowledgeable audience.

One footnote: There have been signs of a reverse revisionism in Chicago in recent years. In 1986, *Chicago* magazine named a place up north in Skokie as serving the best ribs in the city. The annointed ribbery, Carson's, has dark paneling, pristine white cloth napkins, intrusive Muzak, and even—this is for barbecue, now—valet parking. If you judge a barbecue place by how kind it is to your automobile, maybe Carson's is the ticket, sticky-sweet ribs and all. But otherwise, head on down to the South Side on a sunny afternoon and sample some carry-out from Lem's. You may drip a little juice on your car seat, but you'll find out what real city barbecue is all about.

Rating: As good as we've ever had.

Directions: Take 75th St. east off of the Dan Ryan Expressway (I-90 and I-94) as it passes through the middle of Chicago. A few blocks toward the lake and to your right from Lem's on 75th St., you'll find Cotton Grove Ave. and Leon's big two-story restaurant, complete with private parking lot, colorful flags, and canopies. There are other Leon's locations in Chicago—after all, Leon's has been in business for forty-seven years—but you might as well stop at this one.

Mt. Vernon

KING BARBACOA

o 918 Gilbert St. o (618) 242-9853
o Mon.–Sat., 10 A.M.–8 P.M. (Tues. until 7 P.M.) o Closed Sunday

Angelo's is more exciting, and Arthur Bryant's is more famous, but you'd have to go a ways before you'd find a place that is just plain nicer than King Barbacoa, especially on a lazy afternoon. There's a picnic table in the side yard of this former doughnut shop, shaded by a big oak tree that has so far escaped the two big barbecue pits out back. And there's a sandbox near the picnic table, making for a parklike setting in a quiet residential area of this southern Illinois city.

Warm July breezes bring the buzzing of distant lawn mowers, and they blow a lovely counterpoint to the delicious barbecue sauce created by Ernest D. Bowman, the king of King Barbacoa. His sauce is a deep brown, with the rich sweetness of molasses and the steady-state burn of cayenne—great on the crusty beef sandwich that's sliced thin and served crisp on an oblong bun. But if it's good on the sandwich, it's even better on the ribs. They are cooked so long you think they'd taste like one of Charlie Chaplin's shoes, but the dark, ruddy brown crust is meaty and chewy without being at all tough. "They're not tough," agrees Bowman. "You can eat them without any trouble. I'm proud of that."

Bowman takes pride in a lot about King Barbacoa, from the name (suggested by his daughter at college and harking back to barbecue's origins) to the history of the place. "I was working at the foundry," Bowman says. "I wasn't making three dollars an hour. I had six kids and just couldn't make ends meet. Something was telling me, 'Try it. Try it.' I told my wife, and she didn't believe we could do it, but I went on. I worked at the foundry and at the barbecue, and my daughter helped. One day I went to the restaurant and my eyes got big: I had

PORKLORE ○ Perfect Pit-ch

Louis Armstrong recorded "Struttin' With Some Barbecue" in 1927, but it wasn't really about barbecue. According to the *Dictionary of American Slang* the "barbecue" Satchmo was walking with was a sexy lady.

But there are two musical tributes to barbecue, "Barbeque U.S.A." by Mojo Nixon and a soul salute recorded on the Stax label back in the sixties. Carla Thomas recorded "I Love Barbecue" everyone told us. But we could never find a record of the song or of a Thomas version. We finally tracked Ms. Thomas down in Memphis, and she sang the song for us over the phone. "But I didn't record it." So who did? "I keep thinking Wendy Renee."

We haven't found Ms. Renee or the record. But we agree with the sentiment: We love barbecue, too.

such a crowd! But I couldn't cook nothing! I didn't know nothing about barbecue! But I was determined that I was going to make that thing work. I quit my job." He allows himself a little chuckle: "It's taken me a long time to learn how to cook meat." But the lessons stuck: The crown that towers over the parking lot isn't just for looks. Bowman earned it.

Rating: Real good.

Directions: To get to the King, take Exit 80 off of I-64. Follow State Rd. 37 north; it'll become 10th St., and the restaurant will be on your right at Gilbert St. Look for a sign with a big guy wearing a crown and a three-piece suit; that's Ernest.

INDIANA

Evansville

PORKY'S

o 6224 Booneville Hwy. o (812) 476-9587
o Mon.–Thurs., 10:30 A.M.–8 P.M.; Fri.–Sat., 10:30 A.M.–9 P.M.; Sun.,
   11 A.M.–7 P.M.

Smack in the middle of an unassuming gravel parking lot in this southern Indiana city, something wonderful has happened. The Sloppy Joe has been elevated to an art form.

The Sloppy Joe, of course, was as close as many people ever came to a barbecue sandwich during their formative years, as the moms of America slid them down hundreds of thousands of hungry throats. A simpleminded conglomeration of ground beef, goop, and bun, the Joe has nostalgia value for dedicated barbecue buffs, but not much more. At Porky's, however, Ron Dunn and Charles Schlensker refused to leave well enough alone; they elevated a simple sandwich to semi-legendary status.

For a dollar-fifty they will sell you a sandwich of "soaks," lovable little nubbins of smoked pork scraps from the cutting board that have simmered in sauce for hours. A soaks sandwich is a delight. It is served on rye bread with onion, some determinedly dill pickle slices, and a side order of potato chips. A little bowl of sauce sits off to one side, intended to be used liberally. In fact, a soaks sandwich hasn't really earned its name until it is so saturated that it is virtually impossible to eat without a fork. By then, it is also virtually impossible to resist.

The pork bits—some burnt and crisp, some crumbly and compliant—are present in a generous heap. The sauce is not exactly hot and not exactly not; it hangs in the back of your throat like a light, fiery fog. And the taste has the sort of tang that whispers to you to take just one more bite.

In most respects, Porky's is a typical better-than-average Barbecue Belt barbecue joint, with glazed white block walls, plastic tablecloths, and plates so thick they'd crack the floor if they ever dropped. A full menu of ribs, pork, beef, mutton, and chicken is offered. But don't be deterred: Stick with the soaks, the best buck-fifty's worth of food in America. And tip your hat to the moms of the world who made it all possible.

One more thing: The potato chips you will have been maniacally munching throughout the meal are Grippo's brand, thin and crisp and just oily enough to go absolutely perfectly with barbecue. They're available from a rack by the door in half-pound sacks to go. Here's a tip: It's hard to carry more than three sacks at once without looking a little silly.

Rating: Real good.

Directions: Porky's is on Booneville Hwy. at Burkhart Rd., between the One-Stop Recycling Center and a propane gas sales outlet. From I-64, take U.S. 41 south a few miles to Evansville, then turn east on Morgan Avenue, which is also Ind. 62 (and, for that matter, also Booneville Highway).

Indianapolis

PA & MA'S BAR-B-QUE

o 974 West 27th St. o (317) 923-1272
o Mon., 11 A.M.–8 P.M.; Tues.–Thurs., 11 A.M.–1 A.M.;
 Fri.–Sat., 11 A.M.–3 A.M.; Sun., noon–8 P.M.

o 1002 East 38th St. o (317) 547-8853
o Mon., 11 A.M.–8 P.M.; Tues.–Thurs., 11 A.M.–midnight;
 Fri.–Sat., 11 A.M.–3 A.M.; Sun., noon–8 P.M.

When you talk to anyone about Pa & Ma's, the first thing they will mention, always, is the sauce. It may be the hottest kitchen sauce we encountered in our barbecue sojourns. "I've seen people stumble in drunk and walk out sober after having some of the sauce," says Joyce Rogers, Pa & Ma's granddaughter and the current owner of the place.

"I've seen people eating it crying, then crying and laughing at the same time, because they can't believe how hot it is." And new customers—well, Joyce warns them not to be overconfident. "I always ask if they've ever tried the sauce. They'll say no, but that's no problem because they can eat jalapeño peppers straight. Then they'll take one bite and start screaming. New customers always scream. But they always like it, too."

Despite its popularity, Joyce refuses to sell the sauce separately. "We won't even give you extra with your meal unless you beg for it. That offends some people. You wouldn't believe the dollar amounts I've been offered for just a small quantity of the sauce." But she won't give in. "There's just too much other work to do to spend time making more sauce." In fact the only time she'll give you sauce on the side is if you order your meat without it. "Then I'll give you what we normally put on the meat." She says she has seen people drain it off their meat, into their own container, and take it home with them. "Those people come back and tell me how wonderful it tastes on lots of other foods."

Pa & Ma's is the Pa, or Ma, take your pick, of Indianapolis barbecue. It has been around since 1940, almost half a century. In 1986 Joyce opened a second restaurant, on 38th Street. But it's the original, on 27th Street, that you'll want to visit. It is in a building that Joyce jokes is "probably two hundred years old." She says people who started going to 27th Street continue going there, even though they may live closer to the 38th Street outlet. "They like the old-fashioned flavor of 27th Street, the paneling, the ceramics, the old tin Orange Crush sign, the candy case for the neighborhood kids."

And also the same barbecue they've been enjoying all these years. At Pa & Ma's they still cook the pork in the open pit they used fifty years ago. "Except we have to follow a few more fire regulations," adds Joyce. The pit is brick, and they burn charcoal while applying a special basting concoction that is different from the hot sauce. "The secret is knowing when to baste," Joyce says. "Once the meat gets to a certain temperature, it starts to swell. That's the time to baste it because the meat is open, and the flavor can soak in." Joyce is a college graduate with a degree in psychology, but she quit her career as a counselor to come back to the family restaurant business. "I grew up in it. Besides it's more rewarding to work for yourself than to follow other people's progress as a counselor, and it's certainly more money."

Rating: Real good.

Directions: To get to the 27th Street location, take Exit 116 from I-65. Go east on 30th St. to Martin Luther King St. Then go south on

Martin Luther King St. to 27th St. It's one way west, and Pa & Ma's is three blocks up on the right.

Terre Haute

BIG SHOE'S

o 1112 S. 12th St. o no phone
o Noon–7 P.M. daily

The hand-painted sign faces the gravel parking lot of this low-slung cinder-block building, a building almost hidden behind impossibly high piles of wooden pallets.

WE BARBECUE EVERYTHING BUT THE BABY. WE BOIL HIM.

As barbecue slogans go, it's the most slyly vicious in the business, but the dark humor springs from a gentle soul in his seventies, a slow-moving bear of a man with the kind face of a basset hound. After a handshake and a friendly hello, the joke is obvious: The baby would be absolutely safe with Big Shoe, although a stray sparerib might be in serious danger.

Big Shoe, christened Ellis Mills, has been cooking up lean, luscious ribs for nearly forty years, ever since the floor in his place was nothing but stamped earth and sawdust. In those days, when Terre Haute was earning its reputation as a wild town on the Wabash, Big Shoe's was the place to go when other places let out. A young Scatman Crothers would drift over from the pool hall across the street, and the joint would be packed with jumping crowds who had no intention of slowing down the party. Finally, in the wee hours of the morning, Big Shoe would turn up the jukebox and punch a particular selection: "You Don't Have To Go Home, But You Can't Stay Here." The throngs would eventually work their way out, and Shoe would catch some sleep before getting ready for another early morning of stoking his big open pit and starting the day's batch of barbecue.

The health department made him put in a concrete floor a while back, and the crowds moved on to other hot spots. Big Shoe's today is a relaxed, almost wistful place where regulars stop in to talk about the old days, or anything else, and his grandson helps him shove the planks from broken pallets into the hooded pit at one end of the low room. The jukebox is shut down, the turquoise booths are worn, and the chipped red floor is dotted with throw rugs. But one thing hasn't changed: the barbecue. Ribs are served in whole racks on enameled metal trays, with just a sheet of butcher paper beneath them and an enameled bowl of sauce on the side. The ribs are lean and long cooked, simmered in big pans on the pit. The sauce is watery and surprisingly sweet, with a lingering kick that might send you running to the soda pop vending machine at the other end of the room.

"Don't let this man fool you," a fellow at the worn counter volunteered partway through his ribs and ice water. "He's the nicest man who ever lived. When I was young, all the teenagers would hang around here to play the jukebox. We'd put our money together to buy ribs. But sometimes he'd fix it so the jukebox would start giving free selections, and if we ran short of rib money, well, we'd never leave hungry."

Big Shoe will chuckle at a testimonial like that, a relaxed rumbling laugh. He has seen a lot in his forty years of barbecuing. Like the time he tried to take a buffalo on the Interstate down to Lexington, Ky., for a big barbecue. But that's another story, and one that you ought to hear from Shoe himself.

Rating: Real good.

Directions: To get to Big Shoe's, take the U.S. 41 North exit from I-70, go right to College Ave., then right on College Ave. to 12th St. The restaurant will be on your right; there's a big shoe on a pole out by the street.

KANSAS

Hutchinson

ROY'S

o State Road 96 o (313) 663-7421
o Tues.–Sat., 11:30 A.M.– whenever they run out of meat

There are barbecue joints with no tables and barbecue joints with seating for 425, but there is only one barbecue joint with exactly one table, and that's Roy's. Of course, that one table seats fourteen in a big circle that fills up most of Roy's tiny dining room, but it's still one table, with all the elbow-knocking and napkin-passing you'd expect when a bunch of hungry people crowd in close with plates of ribs and sausage.

If you order a lot, which it's almost impossible to avoid doing, considering how good the food is, you have to arrange your stuff out toward the center of the table, or else you start crowding into neighboring territory. As a result, part of the conversation tends to be along the lines of "Is this your cole slaw or is it mine?" Still, for true singleness of purpose and devotion to the barbecue code of camaraderie, you can't beat it.

Dining at one big table eliminates whatever pretentions might be left among barbecue lovers. You can't try to look cool, because the telephone repairmen across the way will see the sauce dribble down your chin before you have a prayer of catching it. You can't pretend to stick to your diet, because all those bones pile up in plain view. You can't even hope to come off as a sophisticated barbecue connoisseur, because your slurping and sighs will inevitably join the general chorus. You might as well loosen up and enjoy yourself; everybody's there for the same reason.

The truth is, two tables would be one too many.

What you eat at this one big table are some of the smokiest, most fetching ribs in Kansas. They are slow-cooked and meaty, with the same sort of balance between tough and tender that you get from, say, Mel Gibson. They have enough hickory flavor to attract beavers, but they aren't overcooked. And the sausage is just as smoky, with chunks of plainly visible hot pepper that do some definite hoo-doo to the unprotected tongue. However, the best bite in the place may belong to the beef sandwich, served on big slices of thick toast hot off the

PORKLORE ○ Barbecue Insults

After being told that Bub, of Bub's Barbecue in Sunderland, Mass., had acquired his sauce recipe from a convict in Florida, Arkansas native Bob Moody opined, "That just goes to prove that any convict in Florida knows how to cook barbecue better than anybody in Massachusetts."

"In California they think putting a steak on the grill and flipping it over is barbecue," says Paul Skolnik, a California native, who learned about barbecue at the Annual Memphis in May World Championship Barbecue Cooking Contest.

"Which barbecue is best, that of Texas, North Carolina, or Georgia? That is like asking who is the best outfielder, Linares, Bonds, or Mays?"—Lewis Grizzard, Georgia humorist.

griddle, piled with tender chunks of brisket and doused with a no-comment secret sauce that's molasses dark and tangy.

The homestyle beans are good, too, and there's the world's smallest salad bar off to one side with some salad bar stuff. But watch yourself: If you get the ribs and the sausage and the beef sandwich and the beans and the salad bar—and a beer—you'd better have the permission of the guy next to you. Or else bring your own table.

Rating: As good as we've ever had.

Directions: Once you get to Hutchinson, Kan., which is northwest of Wichita on State Road 96, the rest is a breeze. You just follow State Road 96 west out of town and look for Roy's gravel lot after you pass Erv's Barber Shop and the Silver Dollar Saloon. Roy's, which is actually run by a guy named Mike Armstrong, is open Tuesday through Saturday from 11:30 A.M. until they run out of their 500 or so pounds of meat. That might be 4 P.M.; might be 7 P.M. Just to be safe, we stopped at 11:45 in the morning. The table was full.

Topeka

THE PIZZA PARLOR

o 1919 Seward Ave. o (913) 232-5190
o Mon.–Sat., 8 A.M.–11:30 P.M. o Closed Sunday

As one travels across America in search of great barbecue, a serious problem soon becomes evident: Sure, it's possible to have barbecue for lunch and dinner, but what about breakfast? With most barbecue joints opening midmorning at the earliest, one can easily find oneself faced with nothing for breakfast except healthful fruit and cereal, a disturbing prospect for anyone who hasn't had ribs since late the night before.

Thank heavens for John Ingenthron and the Pizza Parlor. He just may serve the best barbecue breakfast in the nation.

From the beginning, things haven't always gone smoothly for John. Twenty-three years ago, he says, he just wanted to open a little neighborhood beer joint, but the neighbors "fought me tooth and toenail." After a couple of failed attempts at getting a license to sell beer, he tried a different tack. What if, he inquired discreetly of the licensing board, he just opened up a little pizza place and sold beer on the side? That'd be different, he was told; that'd be fine. But just getting the nod for his license wasn't enough for Ingenthron, who never does things halfway. So he backed a big truck up to his place and pretended to haul out all the equipment. But actually he was moving most of it downstairs into the basement. "You beat me," he told curious neighborhood residents who peeked into his apparently empty building. "You beat me fair and square." The truck drove away, and the neighbors went to sleep. The next morning, with equipment hauled up from downstairs, Ingenthron was in business as the Pizza Parlor. By comparison, the story of why a place named after pizza started selling barbecue seems almost commonplace.

But sell it the Pizza Parlor does, and for breakfast, too, starting at eight in the morning. Here's how to make early morning barbecue part of a nutritious meal. Order a rib dinner with beans and slaw. Lots of food groups. Since it's breakfast, you may feel shy about ordering a beer, which is absolutely the best thirst-quencher to drink with spicy food. Okay. Order a "red draught" instead. It's draft beer mixed with tomato juice, served in a mug like a blue-collar Bloody Mary. Perfect for beginning a wonderful day.

The ribs at the Pizza Parlor are wonderful, too, meaty and smoky and sloppy and abundant. The slaw is a standout as well—crisp, fresh, and long-cut with a peppery vinegar taste. But the barbecue sauce is where Ingenthron lavishes most of his attention. He makes it himself in big twenty-five–gallon batches according to a recipe that "cost me plenty," he says. "It takes a long time to make, and it's expensive. We use nothing but the best. It's based on Heinz, which is the best ketchup." Whatever relationship the thick liquid may have had with a bottle is quickly forgotten when you sample the sauce itself: Tomatoey and tangy at first bite, it has a cumulative kick that heats up gradually like an August afternoon. If the drenched ribs don't feature enough of the stuff, a little bottle comes alongside. Odds are, you'll end up using it. It's excellent sauce, made by a guy who has a few definite opinions about sauces.

"Me and my wife like to eat a lot of barbecue," Ingenthron explains. "We were on vacation down in North Carolina. I ordered some barbecue, and they brought it, and I said, 'Where's the sauce?' They pointed to a bottle on the table with a hole punched in the top. Now, you could tell that was just vinegar with some red peppers in it. I went ahead and ate those ribs, but as we left, I said to my wife, 'I don't think I'm going to order any more barbecue on this trip.'"

Back at home in Kansas, he found people trying to copy his pride-and-joy sauce recipe. "One good old boy took some out to Goodyear to have it analyzed," he once told a reporter. "But they couldn't figure it out." So Ingenthron presses on, sending various of his nine kids through college and selling barbecue in his spare, rectangular beer joint. He talks about getting out of the business when the gang has graduated: "I didn't send 'em to college to run a place like this. Any dummy can run a place like this."

But even though Ingenthron can seem crusty at times, like his ribs, he's a little soft underneath. Take the time in October 1985 when a Topeka charity called Let's Help needed some holiday dinners for the elderly. They asked John how much he'd charge them to cook some turkeys, and he said, "Oh, for you folks I won't charge a thing." He opened up the kitchen on a Sunday to smoke four or five turkeys and set his place on fire. He pretty much burned it down. It took him six months to reopen.

One can only hope that, despite adversity, John Ingenthron continues to sell his delicious barbecue for breakfast, and that you, dear reader, have the chance to sample it. There's just one problem: After you eat it, nothing better is likely to happen to you for the rest of the day. You might as well go back to bed.

Rating: Real good.

Directions: To get to the Pizza Parlor, take I-70 to East Topeka and get off on the Fourth Street exit. Take Fourth east past the railyards to Branner; go left on Branner until you can take a right on Seward. The restaurant will be in a small shopping center on your right.

Wichita

SELMON BROS. BAR-B-Q

o 300 S. Greenwich Rd. o (316) 682-2766
o Tues.–Thurs., 11 A.M.–7 P.M.; Fri. and Sat. 11 A.M.–8 P.M.
o Closed Sunday and Monday

When we say the sauce at Selmon Bros. is All-American, we mean it literally. The particular Selmon brothers in charge of sauce concocting are Lee Roy and Dewey, both former All-American football players at Oklahoma University. Brother Lucius played there too, and all three went on to knock heads in the pros for a while. Now Lee Roy and Dewey are back working with their brother Charles, who owns this fine Midwestern barbecue joint, and he has given them power that no monster NFL linebacker could ever hope to equal: With one slug of their Selmon Bros. Fine Bar-B-Q Sauce (Hot), they can lift you up, lay you out, and leave you on your back breathless. And smiling.

If they had made this many people sweat while they were in uniform, the Selmon brothers might have won the Super Bowl. As it is, though, they stir up a superior sauce in an unassuming little spot that also sells good meat to slip underneath it.

But let's get back to the sauce for a second: There are basically two kinds of barbecue sauce in the world, With-ers and Without-ers. The With-ers are the very best sauces, the most sophisticated, because they are designed to be eaten with a particular type of smoked meat, delicately capitalizing on its characteristic flavors to fill in the gaps of the final taste. Like half a jigsaw puzzle, however, a With-er sauce on its own can seem sort of lonely. A good Without-er, however, doesn't need any assistance. It packs the pert flavors of tomato, lemon, and vinegar in with a rollicking shot of hot, a splash of smoke, and a full-bodied meatiness that makes actual food almost unnecessary. It is the barbecue experience in a bottle, a full-color postcard from the pit. A boisterous Without-er sauce is good to have in your refrigerator, so that you can sneak a lick, close your eyes, and think of hickory. Selmon Bros. is a Without-er no one should be without. It's a "commercial" sauce that shows the supermarket standbys how it ought to be done. Yeah, it has a pinch of sodium benzoate as a preservative, but it also cleverly slips in some anchovies with its garlic and onion, resulting in a chunky, cheeky goo that's hot enough to polka with your palate. It's a past Top 10 winner at the national Diddy-Wa-Diddy sauce contest, and the recipient of a gushy fan letter from Gerald R. Ford.

Getting your hands on the stuff is as simple as sending off a letter. Selmon Bros. sauce is available mail-order for $1.40 a pint, plus UPS shipping (see our chapter on mail order at the end of the book). But visiting the place is more fun. Inside the slightly worn former Country Kitchen, the white cement-block walls are dotted with occasional football memorabilia, but the important action takes place on the faded, cafeteria-style plastic trays stacked in a washed-out rainbow of blue, black, red, yellow, tan, and pink. On such a tray, ask them to place a "combo," which will give you ribs, brisket, and hot links in whatever proportions you request. All are very good. The brisket is a bit of a rainbow in itself, with burnt edges, a rim of smoky pink, and a rich brown middle that's tender and just shy of juicy. The ribs are heavy on the hickory, with a tooth-teasing bite to them, and the hot links are finely ground and beefy. The sauce goes perfectly with all of them, of course.

As you leave, get a bottle of sauce to go. Or two. Or more. And be glad that the Selmon brothers played for Tampa Bay. If they were still in football, you'd still be hungry.

Rating: Good.

Directions: Selmon Brothers Bar-B-Q is on the east side of Wichita proper. To get there, exit any of the Interstates onto Kellog (also known as U.S. 54 and State Rd. 96). Just east of the airfield at the

Beech Aircraft plant, go north on Greenwich Rd. Selmon Brothers will be on your right. If they haven't changed the sign out by the road yet, it'll read: BUY OUR UCE AATADI. If you figure out what it means, tell us.

Williamsburg

GUY AND MAE'S TAVERN

o The main street in Williamsburg o (913) 746-8830
o Tues.–Sat., 11 A.M.–midnight o Closed Sunday and Monday

"Guy always wanted to try barbecue," Mae says. "We started as a beer joint, and Guy said, 'If we're gonna stay up here all this time, we might as well build a barbecue.'" That one "might-as-well" changed history for the G & M Tavern, transforming it from a backroads beer bar to a Certified Barbecue Mecca. It opened in 1975, when Guy got out of the service-station business, but now the little brick hole-in-the-wall serves some of the tastiest, tenderest ribs in the Midwest, ribs laden with blushing pink meat so eager to please that it leaps to the lips from a distance of half a foot.

Such delightful dining has not gone unnoticed: Students road-trip for Guy and Mae's ribs from Kansas University, and big wheels roll in from the state capital. The rest of the booths and stools and picnic tables fill up with blue collars, farmers, and famished tourists. And this all happens in Williamsburg, Kan., an eyeblink of a town that you could call "sleepy" if you thought it might ever wake up. Kansas doesn't have tumbleweeds; otherwise, they'd be blowing down the main street of town. In fact, if it weren't for the G & M Tavern, it seems likely the whole main street would blow away.

But inside the paneled walls of the G & M, things are warm and lively, especially warm by the big pit where they lay out those luscious planks of pork. "We started doing one box of ribs a day," says Mae Kesner. "Now we do twelve to fifteen boxes." And what they do to them is downright inspiring, cooking them for four hours over a hickory fire and then letting them sizzle in foil in a special warming oven. "It's the stuff we put on 'em," Mae explains. "The spices and basting with vinegar and painting with marinade. Then we wrap 'em in foil, and that makes 'em tender." How tender? If you pick them up too fast, all the meat stays on the table. Of course, it tastes just as smoky and succulent down there—on top of the foil and old newspapers that serve as plates. At the table the ribs are joined by some sauce—an idiosyncratic broth that shares a lot with vegetable-beef soup.

Frankly, the ribs don't need it. They are pushing perfection pretty hard in their natural state. The only liquid they require is a bottle of the tavern's supernaturally cold beer.

Guy and Mae's looks like what it is: an appropriately dim little bar where wives wouldn't come unless they planned on staying. It does contain the following objects: a Ping-Pong table, a collection of framed clippings, a gushing letter from a Philadelphia attorney tacked to one wall, and a poster advertising a Mud Volleyball tournament. It also contains a staff that's all family and all friendly—Guy's and Mae's daughters Diana, Judy, and Christina, and son-in-law Steve. They're running the place now; Mae is basically retired and Guy passed on in 1985. But the openness and good cheer of the place—and its unforgettable food—are a fitting testament to a man who once explained barbecue to *KS* magazine like this: "Eggs ain't worth a damn without bacon. Barbecue ain't worth a damn without washing it down with beer. And barbecue ain't worth a damn unless the juice rolls down your elbow."

Rating: Real good.

Directions: Guy and Mae's, on the main street of Williamsburg, is next to the boarded-up fire station. To get there, take Exit 170 off I-35 between the towns of Olathe and Emporia.

MISSOURI

Kansas City

Barbecue Central: This is it: Ground Zero, America's premier melting pot of smoke and sauce, the headquarters of hickory, Cow Town Central, the Capital of Que. Where else but in Kansas City could you have the most famous barbecue joint in the world—and it's not even the best in town? Where else could you find hot sauce in the airport gift shop?

Other cities can claim to be the Barbecue Center of the Universe: Lexington, N.C., has more restaurants per square citizen; Lockhart, Texas, has a turn-of-the-century pedigree; Memphis, Tenn., has better ribs; Owensboro, Ky., has better mutton; Chicago has more sizzling sauce. But no place puts it all together like K.C., a one-city crash course in American barbecue. Choosing one joint in Kansas City as the "best" is as pointless an exercise as looking down a row of Rockettes and worrying about who has the best knee dimples. The thing about Kansas City is that you don't *have* to choose: It's all there for the sampling. Lots of places have their strong points, and it's hard to find a loser. But here are the best of the best.

ARTHUR BRYANT'S

o 1727 Brooklyn o (816) 231-1123
o Mon.–Thurs., 10 A.M.–9:30 P.M.; Fri.–Sat., 10 A.M.–10 P.M.;
  Sun., 11 A.M.–8 P.M.

The Best Legend: The barbecue boom of the eighties can be traced in part to a writer for *The New Yorker* who enlisted several score of his better adjectives in praising a dumpy little place in his old hometown as "the single best restaurant in the world." Calvin Trillin brought a writer's sensibilities to Arthur Bryant's, but the legend was already there waiting for him at 18th and Brooklyn.

Arthur Bryant, born poor in East Texas, moved to Kansas City in 1931 and began tending pit. He eventually took over his brother Charlie's restaurant in 1946, and he remained so dedicated to his ribs and brisket that he cooked them on his smoke-stained white-tile pits almost daily until his death in 1982. He served them to Jimmy Carter and Emperor Haile Selassie and shipped them to a New York gathering of French chefs. He served them with a sauce that went beyond inventive to flat-out strange—a fascinating mixture grainy with paprika and a little cayenne, which would cling to the dark, chewy ribs chopped by cleaver-wielding countermen. He served them with beer that was tooth-cracking cold and with rich handfuls of unskinned french fries cooked in sizzlingly hot lard. And he served them without pretension, in a place that had tile floors, linoleum tables, and huge display jugs of sauce, which had separated into countless layers of oil, spice, and vinegar. Such is the stuff of legends, and Bryant's became *the* place to send hungry tourists for barbecue.

It retains much of its charm under Doretha Bryant, Arthur's niece, the current operator. And it still is a mandatory stop on any Kansas City barbecue pilgrimage. But it has become ever-so-slightly . . . cleaner. And the beef seems a bit less burned and more lightly smoked (in fact, on a recent visit, it was almost flabby). And there are T-shirts, too, somewhat of a self-conscious flourish. And even plans for a suburban location. But the basics of cared-for food and cold beer that made Arthur Bryant's a legend are still in evidence, ready to jog the memories of native sons and capture the hearts of travelers.

Rating: Real good.

Directions: To get to Bryant's, take I-70 west to the Prospect exit. Go left on Prospect to Truman Rd. Go right on Truman Rd. to Brooklyn, and then take a left and follow the scent.

BOYD'S 'N' SON

o 5510 Prospect o (816) 523-0436
o Mon.–Fri., 11 A.M.–12:30 A.M.; Sat., 11 A.M.–1:30 A.M.
o Closed Sunday

The best brisket: Before it burnt down in 1985, Otis Boyd's barbecue joint was in an old frame house that looked the part of the Best Place in Kansas City You Probably Haven't Heard Of. Now it's in a fake-brick building with an air of fast-foodishness about it. "We've got a red roof like a Pizza Hut," Boyd admits. But the place is still laid-back and loosey-goosey, despite its other minicalamity: It no longer serves beer or liquor. But the big, metal pit doors are painted a cheerfully extravagant cherry, and the pit is what counts, according to Boyd. "Nobody can top me," he states just as cheerfully. "I'm one of these do-it-yourself guys. I built my own pit." He has been doing it himself since age eleven, when he learned the art from a Birmingham man who put on barbecues for the Baptist churches in Boyd's home state of Iowa. He graduated from a chef's school in Chicago in 1939, and his first restaurant in Kansas City was a soul-food place. "But they kept hollerin' about barbecue," Boyd said, so in 1949 he went "straight barbecue."

Now in his sixties, Boyd sells barbecue worth hollering about— lush, tender brisket with the true taste of Texas, except even more suffused with smoke. With a splash of one of Boyd's five sauces (which he mixes in 100-gallon batches), this is beef that the cruel could dangle in front of vegetarians. It is bubbling over with an intense flavor and possessed of a tender, teasing bite that's always the signal of perfectly cooked brisket. The sauces (regular, hot, smoky, onion, and horseradish) are uniformly delicious, made with tomato paste, not ketchup, and displaying evidence of onion, garlic and other intense flavors (anise? allspice? cinnamon? chili powder?) in a convoluted concoction that also goes well with what may be the best sausage in the city, a beef-and-pork production that is smoked for hours and sold bursting with juices.

Despite nearly forty years of such masterly barbecue, Otis Boyd still isn't on the tourist maps in Kansas City. This is a shame, but it doesn't seem to bother Boyd much. He operates the same way he always has: "My neighborhood keeps me working."

Rating: As good as we've ever had.

Directions: To get to Boyd's, take I-70 west to the Prospect exit. Take a left, go straight through to 55th Street, and look for the red roof.

GATES & SON'S BAR-B-Q

o 1411 Swope Pkwy. o (816) 921-0409
o 11 A.M.–2 A.M. daily

The best ribs: Gates & Son's is what every barbecue purist is afraid will happen to a good place: It branches out, goes fast-food, moves to the suburbs, and starts hollering a rehearsed "Hi! May I help you?" at people who just have one shoelace inside the door. Well, Gates did it all, and still sells wonderful barbecue. "Barbecue doesn't have to be dirty, greasy, and ugly," Ollie Gates is on record as saying. And since a big part of Gates's business comes from people who are grabbing carry-out, the slick "chain" approach is hardly out of place. Besides, Gates is building on a tradition that can go up against any in the city, stretching back to his father, George, who got started in 1946 and ran a place called Gates Ole Kentuck Bar-B-Q. "Used to be there were two places, Arthur Bryant's and Ollie's," says Fred Martin, manager of one of Ollie Gates's six locations. "It used to be, but not now—since Arthur died." Aside from the usual barbecue bragging, he has a point. Piled on a trademark red-and-yellow paper plate, with a bunch of "Struttin' with Gates" yellow napkins lying around, Gates's ribs are the best way to redecorate a living room—or a motel room. The ribs are chewy and meaty, cooked long enough to have gained character but short of requiring an epitaph. The fries that invariably accompany them are greasy and good, suitable for dunking in the little cups of sauce. The sauce, by the way, is a zingy, chili-esque number with oodles of cumin and a nice, rosy glow to it—another idiosyncratic style in a city with more styles than anywhere else.

Rating: Real good.

Directions: There are six locations; ask around for the one nearest you.

THE GRAND EMPORIUM

o 3832 Main St. o (816) 531-1504
o Mon.–Sat., 9 A.M.–3 A.M. o Closed Sunday

The best music: Jukeboxes attest to it, from Stubb's in Austin, Texas, to Mr. Jim's in Los Angeles: The blues is barbecue put to music. And the best place to savor the slow-cooking, saucy pleasures of the blues is at this onetime hotel for transients, where the ground floor has been turned into a six-night-a-week celebration of song and sauce.

A cavernous room jammed late into the night with crowds of dancers, listeners, and drinkers, the Grand Emporium mixes guitar licks with the edible variety. The rich, sweet, smoky barbecue sauce served by "Amazing" Grace Harris harkens back to her New Orleans roots, where she learned cooking from her Creole mother and grand-father. On rib tips, the sauce's dusky pleasures and slow-building sting are such that, even in the dim light from a spotlit stage, it's impossible not to go searching for another dab to soak up with slices of white bread. Aside from sandwiches and slabs, Grace also serves up Creole and Jamaican specials, from curried goat to jerk chicken. At two in the morning on a weekend, she may be out of something. That's okay; eat something else. It's all pure R&BBQ. In fact, the guitarist for the group A.C. Reed and the Spark Plugs was in the food line just as their late-night set was supposed to begin. Was it a simple case of the preperformance munchies? Or might a little sauce on the finger-tips be the secret to spectacular blues riffs?

Rating: Real good.

Directions: To get to the Grand Emporium, ask someone how to get to the fancy Crown Center area. The not-so-fancy Emporium is nearby.

HAYWARD'S PIT BAR-B-QUE

o 11051 Antioch Overland Park, Kan. o (913) 451-8080
o Mon.–Thurs., 11 A.M.–10 P.M.; Fri.–Sat., 11 A.M.–11 P.M.;
  Sun., noon–9 P.M.

The best burnt ends: The Betty Ford Institute has no cure for addiction to burnt ends. The craving for crusty, burned nubbins chopped off the end of a beef brisket can strike without warning, and as close as you can come to effective treatment is to head out into the night to a place like Hayward's Pit Bar-B-Que. Burnt ends are a particular affliction of Kansas Citians; they're not sold in most parts of the country, and barbecue lovers elsewhere seldom seem to realize what they're missing. But enough are eaten here to make beef cattle an endangered species; they were even offered as free appetizers at a place called Richard's. But Hayward's sleek suburban restaurant serves the best in town, each little chunk charred and chewy on the outside, with a juicy and tender interior. They're so flavorful that sauce is served on the side and best ignored.

In fact, take-out is the best way to get them. They are the perfect barbecue munch food, not sloppy like ribs or bulky like brisket, and a sack on the seat makes driving a pleasure. Besides, if you get them to go, you don't have to reconcile dining at Hayward's, a slick brick palace of a restaurant that sports a Chemlawn lawn and etched-glass between the tables. For company, there's a ten-lane intersection out front and vacuformed office buildings and country clubs. Overland Park is such a chichi suburb that they complained when a White Castle hamburger stand wanted to move in. It wasn't that the city council was opposed to hamburgers; but they wanted the White Castle to be beige. It's quite a place for Hayward Spears, a guy from Hope, Ark., "a little old town about the size of my restaurant." He built three pits in his backyard and ran a place down the street before he built this rib-tip Taj Mahal. And there's no doubt that his custom-made rotating hickory pit turns out luscious meat.

But it's better you should stand in the take-out area and stare at the autographed pictures from people like Walter Cronkite ("With toothsome memories") and sneak out of there with a paper sack. Burnt ends are a phenomenon somewhere between addiction and perfection, and they shouldn't be eaten in front of ferns.

Rating: Real, real good.

Directions: Hayward's is on Antioch in Overland Park, Kan. To get there, take I-70 west to the Metcalf exit. Go left about three stoplights to College, then west on College about two miles. It's near College and Antioch.

ROSEDALE

o 630 Southwest Blvd. o (913) 262-0343
o Mon.–Sat., 9 A.M.–10 P.M.

The best barbecue sandwich: Anthony Rieke opened Rosedale Barbecue in 1934, when he was just a pup of about thirty. He kept improving his barbecue pit and finally, in 1949, he designed and built his masterpiece, a motor-driven rotisserie rib-smoker. It was sitting out in his barn untested, and he needed to try some ribs on it. So he did—his own. "I got in the pan. It's like a Ferris wheel," he said. "I rode around in it to see how it would operate." It did just fine, and it still does. Rieke (pronounced "Ricky") is now eighty-four, and using that same oven—and a couple of newer ones—his place sells some of the best barbecue in town. Close to downtown, the Rosedale sells a lot of wax paper–wrapped lunches over its plain sheet metal counter. The tender, tattered beef and pork sandwiches are moist and meaty and served on bread with a substantial sauce that's sweet enough to inspire seconds and sharp enough to inspire doubt. The place is part linoleum lunchroom and part bar, where they were selling beer by the quart in bottles one customer referred to as "elephant tits." Did we mention that it's not real fancy?

Rating: Real good.

Directions: To get to Rosedale, take I-70 west to I-35 west to the Seventh St. exit. Turn left, go across the bridge, and at Seventh St. and Southwest Blvd. go right. It's two blocks down on the right.

St. Louis

CHARLOTTE'S RIB

o 14908 Manchester Rd. o (314) 394-3332
o Tues.–Thurs., 11 A.M.–10 P.M.; Fri.–Sat., 11 A.M.–11 P.M.;
   Sun., 11 A.M.–9 P.M. o Closed Monday

His *nom de barbecue* is Dr. Rollin River. "Herb Schwarz just doesn't sound right in this line of work sometimes," he says. So it was Dr. Rollin River who ventured into the foreign territory of Kansas City and came away with the American Royal Barbecue Cook-Off prize for the best commercial barbecue—a plum that doesn't often go to out-of-towners. Such an award is only to be expected, however, because the good doctor cooks up barbecue that is better than good; the pork sandwich here is one of the best in the country.

Barbecue sandwiches may be ordered a multitude of ways, but consider this: thinly sliced pork piled on a big, oblong seeded bun—the meat so perfectly smoked that it is luxuriously tender inside and seared crisp on its edges, which twist like smoky threads through the maze of thin slices in the sandwich, offering an unexpected cache of crunch in every bite. The sauce lathered on the meat is a tomato-rich homemade concoction with tiny bits of meat floating in it, just spicy enough to make your hair stand up without straightening out your new perm. The bun is so fresh that the FBI could lift your fingerprints from it.

The restaurant that sells such a superlative sandwich is a modest place, outfitted in saloon drag with Western knickknacks and murals.

The picture on the front wall of Dr. Herb's mother-in-law, the late Charlotte Peters, in complete *Annie Get Your Gun* cowgirl regalia, is right in character with the decor. The restaurant's namesake, she was the First Lady of Television in St. Louis for twenty-three years, beginning in 1947. In fact, it was Charlotte, in a burst of investigative journalism, who wheedled the basic recipe for the restaurant's barbecue seasoning from a Roman chef who was a guest on her talk show. This dry rub, used to flavor the meat during its long cooking period, was further modified by Herb's father, Armand Schwarz, a career chef.

There's a regular restaurant kitchen in back that turns out hamburgers, salads, fries, and genuinely homemade pies and cobblers. But the important work at Charlotte's Rib takes place on the screened-in front porch, where a couple of converted oil tanks send meat-scented hickory smoke into the immediate neighborhood and out onto the street to seduce innocent passersby. Hot coals are segregated on one side of the cookers, and the hot air is passed to the meat through mostly closed vents. Marinading is an important part of the cookery here, and Schwarz says it's best to use the meat's own juices, though he also favors a shot of sauce.

Brisket is the trickiest meat to cook, Schwarz says, and he sells a swell beef sandwich, too, along with the C.B. Joe, a combination sandwich of chopped pork and beef. All sandwiches are available on rye, whole wheat, or bun, chopped or sliced, without sauce or with regular or hot. There's also a full range of chicken, rib, beef, pork, and even shrimp dinners. There is freshly brewed ice tea or cold beer, and anything on the menu is available for carry-out.

The pork shoulder is the meat that won the prize for Schwarz, but he's prouder right now of his "charbroiled huge pork steak," an eighteen-ouncer trimmed to sixteen or so. It sounded good; it really did. But what with ordering two more of those scrumptious sandwiches to go, there was hardly time to try it.

Rating: As good as we've ever had.

Directions: Charlotte's Rib is in the western reaches of St. Louis. To get there, make your way from one of St. Louis's many lovely Interstates to I-270 and turn west onto Manchester in the suburb of Des Peres. Drive west a few miles. Roll your windows down. Your nose will tell you when you've reached Charlotte's Rib.

Side trip: Another nifty barbecue sandwich also calls western St. Louis home. It's served at **Chaney's Restaurant and Lounge**, 8224 Olive Boulevard, just east of I-270. If Chaney's had "barbecue" in its name somewhere, it'd probably be famous. The restaurant has a great-looking open pit with a massive hood and chimney. A huge octagon, it's located in its own brick enclosure near the parking lot and is manned summer and winter by J. C. Price, who calls the never-ending hickory and oak smoke "the best advertisement there is." Chaney's is owned and operated by Michael Chaney; it was begun forty-four years ago by his father, Drexel, in a wooden shack. Now it's your basic restaurant-lounge with a long bar and booths and tables and lots of darts trophies all over. But the place sells a pork sandwich that is dark, funky, and fascinating, with piles of burnt-edged chunks floating in a rich, tart sauce that makes your salivary glands ache and beg for more. It's smoky and idiosyncratic—and almost impossible to put down. (314) 993-1716.

C & K BARBECUE

o 1512 Goodfellow Blvd. o (314) 385-5740
o Mon.–Thurs., 9:30 A.M.–2:30 A.M.; Fri.–Sat., 9:30 A.M.–3 A.M.;
   Sun., 9:30 A.M.–1 A.M.

First we'd better deal with "snoots." Snoots are a part of the soul-food barbecue scene in St. Louis that will stare you in the face at the C & K, as well as at any number of other places in town and across the river in East St. Louis. Snoots are deep-fried pigs' noses. You can request an order of "barbecued snoots," and what you'll get is a heap of crunchy fried nubbins, roughly half a snout per snoot, all of them crisp like cracklin's and suitable for snacking, if you're the sort who snacks on snoots. If you're not that sort, you may skip the snoot part of the menu and go on to the ribs, which are distinctive and delicious at the C & K. And you may also thank your lucky stars that you haven't been offered the other regional specialty associated with St. Louis: brain sandwiches.

Anyway, on to the ribs. These are the reason that Ozzie Carr's homely C & K Barbecue fills to overflowing on weekend evenings, with people lined up in the bare, blue Formica waiting room and out onto the bare asphalt parking lot. It's certainly not for the architecture, which is brown plywood and cement blocks, or the surroundings, which tend toward boarded-up storefronts. But the ribs are reason enough to come back.

A small-end rib sandwich arrives in a package wrapped in butcher paper and bulging with goodies. There's the requisite couple of slices of white bread, with saucy ribs sticking out of either end, but there's also a C & K bonus—potato salad, slapped in a heap all over the ribs. If it sounds messy, it is; if it sounds weird, it's not. It's very, very good. The potato salad is creamy and cool, a sweet respite from the smoky ribs. The ribs themselves are smoked long and hard, stopping just short of chewy, and are served in an unusual dark-orange sauce that is packed with pepper—not red pepper, either, but a blizzard of big flecks of good old black pepper. It's delicious and different. But even with the five napkins provided, it's also hopelessly messy. The C & K sells only carry-out, but restrain yourself from eating an order like this in the car. Go home, or to your motel room, and sit in the shower stall. Then stop worrying and enjoy yourself.

Rating: Real good.

Directions: To get to the C & K, take the Goodfellow exit off I-70 and head south toward Martin Luther King Blvd. The C & K is directly across the street from Mr. Austin's Bar-B-Que, where everything looks a little nicer but doesn't taste as good.

OHIO

Middleburg Heights

BIG CHARLIE'S

o 7581 Pearl Rd. o (216) 234-3790
o Open Mon.–Sat., 8:30 A.M.–2:30 A.M. (kitchen closes at 10:30 P.M.)
o Closed Sunday

Over the years Cleveland acquired something of an oafish reputation. A lot of it was deserved. You have to expect derision when your mayor catches his hair on fire during a ceremonial ribbon-cutting. (It actually happened in 1972 to then-mayor Ralph Perk, who was opening a new plant and using a blowtorch instead of the customary scissors.) Or when your river is so polluted it ignites. But with the introduction in 1983 of the National Rib Cook-Off, Cleveland began to make its name as a town that knows, and loves, good ribs. Now the city is stuffed with rib joints: from Baby Sister's Barbecue on the east side to Mama's Boy Bar-B-Q on Lee Street near downtown to the Tick Tock Tavern on the west side.

We enjoyed the sweet, tangy ribs at Harvey's on the east side, and we appreciated the selection at the suburban Mimi's Barbeque Lounge, where you have a choice of five different sauces: sweet, hickory-flavored, onion-flavored, garlic-flavored, or just plain hot. But our choice for the best in northern Ohio is Big Charlie's.

Not only is Big Charlie Maira big (he says he's been Big Charlie since he was nine years old) but so are his portions. Big Charlie says he started cooking ribs when he was in the service. "They called me Goodtime Charlie then." He got his sauce recipe from a fellow soldier who was an Arkansas native. "Some barbecue people have twenty-six ingredients in their sauce. We just have a few ingredients. We depend on our ribs being as tasty as can be. Then the smoke adds a little flavor; the crust adds to it. I believe you do as much as you can with as little as you can. All those other people are doing with their fancy sauces is hiding things."

When he got out of the service, Big Charlie started doing part-time catering. "People would call and say, 'I've got fifteen people out my house. Could you cook?' Pretty soon fifteen became fifty and fifty became a hundred, and it just evolved into the restaurant." Big Charlie's, which Maira describes as "just a little local tavern-lounge-restaurant," opened in 1967. Big Charlie is a treat to watch as he cooks. He is one big fellow and with his Van Dyke beard he could pass for wrestler Captain Lou Albano's tag-team partner. When he's standing by his grill, smoke spewing everywhere, sweat sluicing down his face and plopping onto his already grungy T-shirt, he is a man with

PORKLORE ○ Rib Rah

How's this for confusion: Cleveland girls dressed as Hawaiian hula dancers to promote a Michigan company? That makes mixed metaphors seem okay.

But that was the Rotisserie Girls from Rotisserie Grills of Auburn Hills, Mich., one of the competitors at the 1987 National Rib Cook-Off in Cleveland. The Girls, four Cleveland high school students hired for the festival, were decked out in Hawaiian hula girl outfits. They invited passersby to try their ribs with this synchronized cheer:

"Ours are better,
"You better believe,
"Because ours
"Are guaranteed . . .
"Juicy, juicy juicy."

a mission. "If you're going to be serious about ribs, you need to be serious about being serious," he says. The secret to his savory ribs? The personal touch. "I watch everything that comes off that grill."

Rating: Real good.

Directions: Take Exit 234 (U.S. 42) east from I-71. U.S. 42 becomes Pearl Rd. at Middleburg Heights.

Why Cincinnati Isn't in This Book: Every afternoon for five years, radio preacher the Reverend Deutcronomy Skaggs would go on the airwaves of Cincinnati's WLW-AM preaching against the local barbecue restaurants, claiming they didn't serve barbecue but some ersatz barbecuelike food, shouting that Cincinnati didn't have barbecue, and warning that "If God had meant for Cincinnati to have barbecue, He'd a give it to us a long time ago."

Actually the Rev. Skaggs was just a character in the repertoire of Gary Burbank, a popular Cincinnati radio personality and Memphis native who tired of trying to find good barbecue in his northern habitat.

Burbank tried the Montgomery Inn and he tried Walt's Hitching Post, the two places local folks recommended to him when he asked about barbecue. "Some people at the station took me out to the Montgomery Inn, which they said had the best barbecue in the country. I went in there and ordered a sandwich. When it came, it looked like it had grape jelly or something splashed on it. I called the waitress over and told her, 'Take this back and give it to the poor.' " He tried Walt's and found it no more to his liking.

Burbank had all but given up on ever eating real good barbecue in his adopted town.

Then arrived the Barbecue Missionary.

"I was on the air one afternoon, letting the Rev. Skaggs rail away about Cincinnati barbecue, or the lack thereof. About a half hour later they call me and say there is some guy in the lobby with a platter of ribs."

It was the Barbecue Missionary, Lucious "The King" Newsom, a 64-year-old Memphis native who had spent his entire life spreading the word about barbecue. He had only recently arrived in Cincinnati and was out to prove the Reverend Skaggs wrong by demonstrating that Cincinnati did have real good barbecue—namely, his. Burbank took one bite of Lucious's ribs and went back on the air announcing the cancellation of the Reverend Skaggs's Barbecue Crusade.

That was in late 1986 and Lucious had just opened a restaurant,

Ribs 'n Stuff. Less than a year later Lucious closed Ribs 'n Stuff and moved on. Cincinnati just didn't want his barbecue.

And now the Reverend Skaggs is back on the air, preaching against the local barbecue places.

(Lucious is out of the restaurant business, but he sells his dry rub by mail. For the address see the mail-order chapter at the end of the book.)

PORKLORE ○ The Barbecue Wisdom of Lucious "The King" Newsom

Lucious "The King" Newsom, 64, has been cooking barbecue since he was 14. If barbecue needed a missionary to spread the word, he would be the man to send.

Here is some of his accumulated wisdom on the topic:

On hot sauce: Some people believe they have to sweat when they eat barbecue.

On sauce: I believe sauce just covers up bad cooking anyway.

On giving up his city street corner trade and opening a restaurant: I got tired of moving from corner to corner. See I wouldn't buy a license. Eventually I ran out of corners.

On how he cooks his ribs: Let's just say there is smoke involved.

On barbecue people who boast about cooking their ribs all day: The reason they tell you they cooked their ribs eight hours is to keep you from cooking them at home. I cook mine about an hour and a half, an hour and forty-five minutes, on high heat. Ribs don't burn.

On barbecue beans: Baked beans don't go with barbecue. They knock your taste out. You need a white bean.

On boiling ribs before you barbecue them: Yeah, you can boil them. Let me tell you, if you do, also buy a pack of noodles. Then when you take the meat out, throw the noodles in so you'll at least have some noodles to eat because you just cooked the best part off the meat.

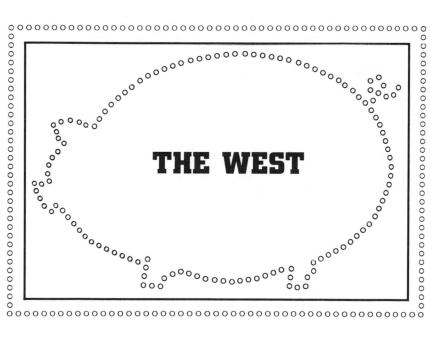

THE WEST

CALIFORNIA

Beverly Hills

RJ'S THE RIB JOINT

○ 252 N. Beverly Dr. ○ (213) 278-9044
○ Mon.–Thurs.: lunch, 11:30 A.M.–3 P.M.; dinner, 3 P.M.–10 P.M.;
   Fri.–Sat., 11:30 A.M.–11 P.M.; Sun.: brunch, 10:30 A.M.–3 P.M.;
   "ribs hour," 3 P.M.–4 P.M.; dinner, 4 P.M.–10 P.M.

"I wanted to create the Cadillac or Rolls-Royce of barbecue," says Bob Morris, the Robert J. who branded his initials on RJ's the Rib Joint. And in a sense he succeeded: He created the BMW of CaliforniQue.

CaliforniQue is barbecue for the privileged classes, for Gold Card carriers who entertain the same base passions as everyone else but need a safer place to park them. RJ's specializes in high-style culinary slumming, offering patrons the thrill of noshing on something a bit naughty without worrying about anything worse than spilling sauce on their Giorgio Armani suits.

"I wanted to do an upscale barbecue, with the feeling of Beverly Hills but the taste of Oklahoma, Kentucky, and Mesquite, Texas," Morris explains. He got the Beverly Hills feeling, all right, with a twenty-five-foot designer salad area, a two-story mirrored bar, stained glass, and antique ceiling fans, all tucked away beneath a discreet awning on Beverly Drive (on the same block as La Maison du Caviar). It's so classy that the eerily dirt-free sawdust on the floor is brought in fresh every day. But the barbecue? Well, it edges into the "pretty good" range by a nose, assisted perhaps by the heavenly Anchor Steam draft beer. The pork back ribs are lightly smoked over hickory and then flamed crisp on a broiler; they're not classics, but they are the best choice, even at $15.95 (and even though there was a $5 "sharing charge" to split them). If they're not the best, they may well be the most expensive ribs in America. RJ's "super-secret sauce recipe" is tomato-based, with splashes of Corona beer, fresh juices, and liquid smoke—but no hot pepper. This is not barbecue for people who have any intention of perspiring, ever. "We had to scale our tastes to local tastes," is the way Morris puts it. And it has worked well enough to foster the Dixie Manor Hickory House just two doors away. But though RJ's may be its ultimate expression, CaliforniQue isn't restricted to the tastes of Beverly Hills; it can be found up and down the West Coast.

In several locations, including Newport Beach, there are Tony Roma's A Place for Ribs restaurants, where Dom Perignon and tender, inoffensive baby back ribs coexist in plush comfort. In San Francisco, there's Hog Heaven, with meaty Memphis-style ribs, elaborate porker portraits of "Swine Lake" and "Alfred Einswine"—and sauce that's strictly off-the-shelf. Bull's Texas Cafe goes after the downtown San Francisco business crowd. Also in San Francisco is Firehouse No. 1, with less-determinedly upscale decor and perhaps the smokiest, best barbecue of the bunch, even though they did change their motto from "The Best Bar-B-Q in the Whole Damn Town" to "The Best Bar-B-Q in the Whole Darn Town." Finally, in the same city is MacArthur Park, where we can only hope the intense yuppie networking works better than the barbecueing does.

With these examples (and many others), California is just the tip of the iceberg. The basic concept of upscale CaliforniQue can be seen all across the country now, and many hard-core barbecue fiends consider it sacrilege, pure and simple, with its mild sauces, lightly smoked meat, and prissy surroundings. But we take a more optimistic view: CaliforniQue is the Trojan Horse of the barbecue world, looking respectable enough to attract the timid and then sending them home with sauce on their fingers and the nagging, persistent, inextinguishable urge to lick them. It's the first step on the road to ruin. These defenseless people may start out in their Porsches at RJ's, but they'll end up sitting on truck hoods at Sonny Bryan's or wiping their hands on their baggy overalls at Big Shoe's.

Rating: Pretty good.

Directions: To get to RJ's the Rib Joint, take the Santa Monica Freeway (I-405) to Santa Monica Blvd. and head northeast. When you get to Beverly Drive, turn right—and try not to bump any Ferraris when you park.

Encinitas

LAMONT'S

o 392 N. El Camino Real o (619) 753-1251
o Mon.–Fri.: lunch, 11:30 A.M.–2:30 P.M.; dinner: 5 P.M.–9 P.M.;
   Sat., 5 P.M.–9 P.M.; Sun., 4 P.M.–8 P.M.

When you stick your head into LaMont's suburban barbecue restaurant, you're looking at the future—at least the future according to

LaMont Burns, owner, operator, cookbook author, and barbecue prophet. Barbecue, he says, is just one example of "Southern regional cooking," which was originated and passed along by plantation blacks and is now poised to hit the great American upper middle class somewhere between its belly and its wallet.

LaMont plans to lead this resurgence of barbecue and true Old South cooking, and he's not wishy-washy about it. "This will be the next great movement in American cuisine," he states flatly, "and it will need a spokesman. You need someone's face to put on the jars of sauce and to appear on TV. Since I know something of the subject, it might as well be me. I'm not dreaming. I intend to be the Colonel Sanders or Famous Amos of Southern regional cuisine."

But LaMont Burns has plans that can send a chill through the heart of a barbecue purist. "Blacks have to develop the marketing and production skills to sell their products more widely," he says. "We have to get away from those old brick pits and slaving all night to get it just right." His solution? Gas ovens. Gas ovens! "There are gas ovens that work with wood chips to prepare the meat with great succulence in a shorter period of time."

Well, here's the bottom line: LaMont's barbecue is good, perhaps even outstanding for the state of California, but it's not as good as the guys' who stand next to those old brick pits, getting it just right. And it's not a question of black or white, but barbecue. Sometimes German-Americans tend the pits, like down in central Texas; and sometimes it's good old boys who sleep with their meat.

There's no denying that LaMont is a talented cook; one taste of his festive Creole Gumbo—filled with chicken and okra and peppery spice—will settle that. And his ribs are good, too, high-quality cuts marinated in herbs and spices and grilled over cherry or orange wood, and maybe a little mesquite. "By the time the meat goes on the grill, the flavor is set already," he says. But carefully mixed marinades and a fruity, spicy sauce can't make up for hours unspent in a smoke-stained pit. And these ribs stop a bit short of truly transcendental. It could well be that LaMont Burns is the future of barbecue; he's a thoughtful, knowledgeable man and a quiet orator who can be pretty darned convincing.

But we'll be out by the brick pit, just the same.

Rating: Pretty good.

Directions: To get to LaMont's, take I-5 south to the Encinitas Boulevard exit; make a left and go about a mile and a half, where you'll turn left onto El Camino Real. LaMont's is down in the Little Oaks Plaza.

Los Angeles

Barbecue Alley: To find good barbecue in Los Angeles, simply listen for the sound of the surf. Then head the other way. Good barbecue isn't to be found where the yachts dock in Marina Del Rey, and it isn't sold where the statuesque roller skaters cruise Venice Beach. Instead, barbecue joints are scattered throughout the vast interior of the city—from Hungry Al's and its Louisiana hot sauce to Benny's Bar-B-Que and its homemade sausage. We recommend a run down Slauson Avenue in the Hyde Park district, a short drive so rich with good barbecue that we call it Barbecue Alley.

MR. JIM'S

o 5403 S. Vermont Ave. o (213) 778-6070
o Sun.–Thurs., 10 A.M.–midnight; Fri.–Sat., 10 A.M.–2 A.M.

"You need no teeth to eat Mr. Jim's beef" is a slogan dear to the hearts of L.A. barbecue lovers. The various Mr. Jim's take-out places around town still sell the slow-smoked meat Mr. Jim Harding introduced at his first spot thirty-one years ago. This particular take-out location has a big parking lot, a little waiting room, and a menu full of delights. "We marinate the meat in a cooler overnight in our own special seasoning," Mr. Jim explains. The chopped beef is fall-apart famous, but the pork ribs are just as terrifically tender, smoked a sunset pink down to the bone. The hot links are intensely spiced, almost like Cajun *andouille,* and are a perspiration-popping thrill when dipped in Mr. Jim's excellent sauce, a seemingly middle-of-the-road number with a cleverly concealed kick. Service is snappy at Mr. Jim's, which is a shame because occupying about a quarter of the tiny waiting room is a terrific jukebox with stuff like "Recess in Heaven" by Bobby Bland and "I Better Not Look Down" by B. B. King. Maybe you'll luck out when you visit; maybe there'll be a line.

Rating: Real good.

Directions: Mr. Jim's is at the intersection of Slauson Avenue and Vermont Ave.; head north on Vermont about four blocks. There are other locations at 10303 S. Avalon, 1958 W. Florence, and 3809 S. Vermont Ave.

THE PIT

o 5309 S. Vermont Ave. o (213) 750-0254
o Sun.–Thurs., 11 A.M.–midnight; Fri.–Sat., 11 A.M.–2 A.M.

Tucked between a shoe repair shop and a cabinetmaker's place, the Pit's storefront proudly proclaims BAR-B-Q AT ITS BEST in letters larger than the restaurant's name itself. They could rephrase that slogan a bit if they wanted to, perhaps along the lines of "Bar-B-Q at Its Paint-Peeling Hottest." The hot links in hot sauce here are among the most incendiary in Los Angeles, or anywhere west of the Mississippi—the sort of skull-cracking sausage-and-sauce combo that inspires instant investigation of theories such as "A piece of white bread will put out a fire on your tongue faster than water." The fact that they're served with a plop of tasty mashed potato salad on top does little to quiet the general screaming and running around that accompanies eating them. When you taste the smoky hot sauce, slightly gritty with spices, you have about three quarters of a second to get your affairs in order. Then you'll be running to wrap your lips around the nearest fire hydrant. To be fair, a mild version is available, too, and it would let more of the nice smokiness of the ribs shine through. And there are sweet potato pies to make peace with your palate. By the way, the Pit does have indoor seating at stools, Formica tables, and pewlike benches. The latter will come in handy as you pray for your tongue to grow back.

Rating: Good.

Directions: The Pit is just a half block from Mr. Jim's.

WOODY'S BAR-B-Q

o 3446 W. Slauson Ave. o (213) 294-9443
o Mon.–Thurs., 11 A.M.–12:30 A.M.; Fri.–Sat., 11 A.M.–3 A.M.;
   Sun., noon–midnight

The luscious hot links at Woody's give you a neon grin when the spice kicks in, no matter which kind you get—the kind they make themselves or the kind they import from Louisiana Pete's, back in owner Woody Phillips's home state. Dipped in some of Woody's deep, dark, and mysterious hot sauce, the coarsely chopped chunks of sausage crank up the temperature gradually until it's hissing-radiator hot. It's a subtle and satisfying effect, the work of a man who has been a pro for fourteen years. "I always had a feel for cooking," says Phillips. "I been playing around with sauces since I was twelve years old." And it's not just the sauce, either. The ribs, beef, and links are slow-smoked over oak with care. "I designed my own pit," Phillips says, "and it's similar to an old-time pit." In fact, it's so authentic that it's built two feet below the concrete floor of this take-out operation. Phillips is proud of California's barbecue, calling it "better than most of the states' I've visited." And he's proud of his staff, which works two shifts seven days a week. "We are in demand," is how he puts it.

And, to be fair, it's hard to drive past a place with a snarling cartoon bulldog that grins threateningly and says, "I think y'all ought to buy some BAR-B-Q!"

Rating: Real good.

Directions: To get to Woody's, take the Slauson exit from the Harbor Freeway (I-110) and drive west until you see the big bulldog.

Oakland

FLOYD & ILA'S OKLAHOMA STYLE HICKORY BAR-B-QUE

o 5830 Telegraph Ave. o (415) 653-4412
o Sun.–Thurs., 11:30 A.M.–midnight; Fri.–Sat., 11:30 A.M.–1 A.M.

"Of course," Ila Williams said, "I don't eat barbecue myself." She allowed herself a grandmotherly grin, appreciating the irony. Here she was, standing in the aisle of the liquor and convenience store where she heads the homiest, friendliest barbecue joint on the West Coast. She was holding a bottle of Floyd & Ila's Oklahoma Style Hickory Bar-B-Que and All-Purpose Sauce, a dusky, mouth-watering concoction developed by Ila herself, a sauce that may be the best thing to happen to California cuisine, even allowing for goat-cheese pizza. And she doesn't eat barbecue?

"Oh, I'll take a taste of it now and then."

Ila and her daughter Valerie are carrying on the barbecue business begun in 1975 by her late husband, Floyd, known as the Colonel, who designed the metal, safelike electric pit where the ribs are cooked. Ila said, "I told him, 'You fool with the meat and let me take care of the sauce.' " Take care of it she did. It is a lovely marriage of tastes, created from ketchup but with a subtle sense of balance and proportion that rescues it from being too sweet (although there's molasses sweetness in it) or too hot (although it's hot enough to make inhaling interesting) or too smoky (although hickory essence is in evidence). "You don't want to let any one thing take over," is how Ila put it. "This is like sauce you make at home," she said. "Other sauce you can buy, you have to take it home and *then* 'make it.' " Her sauce was ordered by a group home for the elderly because it was low enough in salt to be safe for the residents with hypertension. "I don't much like salt," Ila said, "so I didn't put it in."

Ila serves barbecue down a hall and up some stairs behind the liquor store, in a little family dining room with brown carpeting and a built-in wooden hutch. There are just three tables, all with checkered plastic tablecloths and folding chairs. How homey is it? There was Play-Doh on the counter, along with family china. How friendly was it? Ila's granddaughter brought back some thick washcloths that had been moistened with warm water, just in case the napkins weren't enough. How good was it? It was real good. It doesn't matter that electric smokers are frowned upon by purists; the Colonel's cooker was stacked with smoldering hickory, and it churned out ribs that were dark and delicious, just like Ila's sauce. Besides, they had to order a big shipment of hickory from back in the Colonel's home state of Oklahoma. It wasn't cheap; and it's so valuable to them that they take half-burnt logs from the cooker and douse them in water so they can be used again.

It's this sort of care that translates directly into good barbecue, and into little kindnesses such as passing out some hot ribs in sauce as a "sample" while you're waiting to order. And, as a final favor, Ila's daughter issued a warning, the kind that should be required by law: "You don't want to fall asleep with that sauce on your fingers," she said. "Or you might wake up gnawing them off."

Rating: Real good.

Directions: Telegraph Ave. is a major north-south street that's easy to hit off State Road 24, a little north of where I-80 comes across the Bay Bridge.

EVERETT & JONES

o 2676 Fruitvale Ave. o (415) 533-0900
o Sun.–Thurs., 11 A.M.–midnight; Fri.–Sat., 11 A.M.–2 A.M.

It's the sort of story Presidents like to mention at news conferences: *Why, here's a little, ol' dollar-an-hour maid who now has her hot sauce featured in the gourmet section at Macy's.* It's also a story that helps to keep alive the Barbecue Dream, dreamed during long, smoky nights by owners and cooks across America, and even admitted to by some: *One of these days, my family recipe is going to make me famous, and I'll be lighting my pit with hundred dollar bills.*

The difference is, Dorothy Turner Ellington didn't just dream it; she lived it.

In 1961, at the age of twenty-nine, Dorothy (then Dorothy Everett) broke up with the man she had been married to since she was fifteen.

She found herself with a few problems: no job, no training, little money, and eight daughters. She worked as a maid, and she got an after-hours job tending a pit in a barbecue restaurant. "I thought I would never earn more than two dollars an hour," Dorothy has said. But she prayed and thought and eventually gathered her daughters together and told them that two things were going to save them: family togetherness and barbecue. They would open a restaurant. "At least we'd never starve," she had thought. So in 1974, with a borrowed seven hundred dollars, credit from suppliers, and a pit built in a condemned East Oakland building, the first Everett & Jones barbecue restaurant became a reality. On the first day, they gave away free samples for publicity, and the place was packed. On the second day, nobody showed up.

There have been hard times and good times since—like the time the original location burnt down while the family was celebrating their third anniversary in the business. Everyone rushed from Dorothy's house in their party clothes, but all they could do was watch. Joined by her son Allan and James Jones (husband of her eldest daughter, the Jones in the name), Dorothy also watched her family pull together. They are still together now, partners in three celebrated barbecue restaurants in Oakland, Berkeley, and San Francisco—restaurants where you might see one of Dorothy's twenty-four (and counting) grandchildren. The sauce recipe she brought with her from Alabama is indeed sold in Macy's, and the daughters who were teased as the Barbecue Babies in school have helped Momma retire from the front lines. Daughter Shirley told a reporter, "It was miserable watching other girls go dancing on weekends while we toiled over the barbecue pit. But she knew what she was doing, and she welded a wonderful family from what she had to work with. We all respect Momma's toughness now. She taught us everything."

The story has a happy ending for hungry visitors, too, because the food that made E&J famous is still on hand. The ribs, cooked in open kettles over oak for four or five hours, are a crusty burgundy on the outside, pulling off the bone with a tugging, satisfying resistance. The hot links are crude and chunky and wonderful, flecked with spices and begging for a bath in the E&J "Super Q" sauce, which is best in its medium and hot varieties. The sauce is very sweet, almost fruity, and very smoky, with a persistent perspiration factor that builds with each bite. Similarly hot are the tremendous baked beans, spicy with a blizzard of black pepper flakes and studded with stray chunks of the links.

Various E&J locations have their fans, but we prefer the one on Fruitvale in Oakland, a storefront operation that recalls the early days. It has a tree outside on the sidewalk—along with a table, an umbrella, and a few chairs that offer an excellent view of the Chevron station across the street. With your feet up and a rib in your hand, it's easy to believe in legends.

Rating: Real good.

Directions: Fruitvale Ave. is an easy jaunt south from I-580 in Oakland. Other locations are in Berkeley at 1955 San Pablo Ave. and in San Francisco at 5230 Third St.

San Francisco

DO-CITY BAR-B-Q

o 553 Divisadero St. o (415) 921-0400
o Open daily, 11 A.M.–3 A.M.

The skinny blond guy sighed: "These are greens an Alabama boy would die for." It was unusual, perhaps, to find a blond man from Alabama eating greens on Divisadero Street in San Francisco, but no more unusual than finding a place like Do-City selling them. In a city where the word barbecue can mean anything from Oriental hibachi fare to a bland businessman's lunch, this is definitely down-home. "Soul food is soul food," says owner Jasper Brown. "Cornbread, beans, collard greens, and candy yams—everything I got 'corresponds.' All of it blends together with the barbecue." At Do-City, it's a beautiful blend. The homemade sauce is a refreshing one, with overtones of fresh vegetables as well as a sincere kick in the seat of the pants. "It's like daylight to dark," Brown says. "My sauce stands alone." His ribs stand up to comparison, too, tender and delicious and cooked in a six-by-four-foot stainless steel pit with glass windows. Brown says he can cook a hundred pounds of ribs every nineteen minutes by rotating them after ten to twelve minutes from the bottom rack to the top where "they steam in their own juices." He uses nutwood—hickory or oak—and apricot or peach. "The wood is high," he says, probably because all the wood in California is used for waterbeds. He has to buy it from a fellow he calls a "wood broker." But the results are there, drawing the famous—from Dick Gregory and Redd Foxx to Richard Pryor. "The white stars don't come in as much," he says, "but, you know, the brothers do."

Brown married into the barbecue business, wedding the late Earl Collins's daughter, of the Chicago barbecue Collinses (they still run a couple of places there). Earl came out to California in 1969 and helped set up Jasper in the take-out business. It's a business that has been good to him (to the tune of a customized burgundy-and-orange

Cadillac with DO-CITY plates). But it's a business that, at sixty-two, he wants out of. Do-City has a sign inside that says EVERYTHING FOR SALE, and it doesn't just refer to the menu; it means real estate, recipes, pit, and plexiglass "safety shield."

So here's your chance. Put down this book, get up, and give the place a call. If you're lucky, it'll still be on the market, and you can get into the business of selling great barbecue instead of just reading about it.

Rating: Good.

Directions: To get to Do-City just take the Divisadero exit from U.S. 101 by the Marina. Drive south until you see a wild, red-and-yellow striped storefront—or a Cadillac with personalized plates.

San Jose

HENRY'S HI-LIFE BAR-B-Q

o 301 W. St. John o (408) 295-5414
o Lunch: Mon.–Fri., 11:30 A.M.–2:30 P.M. (no lunch Sat. or Sun.)
o Dinner: Mon.–Tues., 5 P.M.–10 P.M.; Wed., Thurs., Sun., 4 P.M.–11 P.M.;
   Fri.–Sat., 4 P.M.–midnight

Lost in a wilderness of Interstate ramps and downtown dead end streets, Henry's is a neon oasis of beer and barbecue with a style all its own. When Henry Puckett started it in 1960, he adopted a straightforward credo: "Pour a good drink and serve plenty to eat." Henry died in 1986, but his widow, Doris, and daughter Lois Shockey make sure the Hi-Life still does both—and in a friendly, funky atmosphere that seems to flicker through a time warp.

The Hi-Life is located in what was originally the Torino Hotel, built in 1885, an earthquake or so ago. Back then, it offered inexpensive lodgings to Italian immigrants in the Bay Area. The hotel's restaurant (where the Hi-Life now operates) sold buckets of ravioli for fifty cents during the Depression, and some higher-octane stuff during Prohibition. The atmospheric bar and back bar are inlaid-wood beauties put in during the early thirties, just after the repeal of Prohibition. The hotel had been vacant for six years when Puckett took it over and began its barbecue renaissance.

Now as many as three hundred customers visit it on weekend nights, making it the hottest joint in town, and the reason is clear: The Hi-Life is a hoot. First of all, you take a number from one of those funny little take-a-number machines. Then you wait in the jostling bar under dusty chandeliers, leaning against a thoughtfully padded joist in the middle of the room. The jukebox is belting out classic tunes of the Forties from the private collection of a friend of Henry's. The clock over the bar has random numbers that read "2, 10, 6, 7, 4, 8, 1—Who Cares?" There's a brass spitoon, a collection of dusty trophies, even antique marble doorknobs on the men's room. The time warp settles in. You feel like you're out on the town in a black-and-white movie.

Eventually, your number is called, but don't get the idea you're about to eat. A waitress tracks you down and takes your order and first name. Later, when you hear your name hollered over the general hubbub, it's time to move to the big dining room. Most of what you eat—from the steak to the ribs to the fabulous toasted garlic bread—is prepared in a huge brick pit with open iron doors at one end of the dining room. The chef works in plain view, flipping steaks, squirting the oak fire with an occasional blast from a hose, rearranging ribs, and hanging chickens on a rack over the fire like passengers on a subway to hell. There are flames, jets of steam, and bursts of hissing; it's all very colorful and an important distraction because the actual eating at the Hi-Life falls a bit short of the fetching atmosphere. Ribs smoked for forty minutes while hanging over grilling steaks tend to taste like steaks, even though they're pork ribs. Grilled before they're delivered, they're meaty, all right, but possessed of a mysterious hybrid taste that isn't aided by the very ketchupy sauce. The garlic bread, however, is good enough to stuff in your suit coat when you leave.

When you leave, by the way, it will be very hard not to linger in the bar with the crowds of waiting people, order another drink, drop a couple quarters in the jukebox, and let the years roll back. Sometimes the world looks better in black-and-white.

Rating: Pretty good.

Directions: To get to Henry's Hi-Life, take I-280 to the Julian exit. Take a left on Julian, go two stoplights and take a left on Montgomery. Then take the next left, which is St. John.

Van Nuys

DR. HOGLY-WOGLY'S TYLER, TEXAS, BAR-B-QUE

o 8136 Sepulveda Blvd. o (818) 780-6701
o Open daily, noon–10 P.M. o Closed two weeks at Christmas

"Here in L.A.," says George Larrimore, "it takes a half hour just to get to the mailbox." George is a member of the Hollywood Hogs

Barbecue Experience, a team of fanatics who have gone as far as Memphis, Tenn., to enter cooking competitions. But leaving his backyard pit and heading across the Los Angeles basin is a different proposition. "If you've got to drive an hour to get barbecue," George laments, "it kind of takes the edge off." Which is why the Mercedes sedans and blacked-out BMWs in the parking lot at Dr. Hogly-Wogly's really mean something: This is barbecue that people are willing to drive for. Since they're coming on freeways full of metal-to-metal madmen, it's high praise indeed.

If you survive the drive, you can tell immediately from the seven prominent NO CHECKS ACCEPTED signs that this Valley barbecue joint is the real thing, silly name or not. And if you need convincing, consider this: They frost their beer mugs—plastic ones. And they light the dark-paneled restaurant with bare fluorescent tubes. And there is nothing on the menu *except* barbecue (as long as you consider chicken to be barbecue). Oh, a little fried shrimp snuck in there, but it gets lost in the stampede of smoked meat.

The barbecue is very good for California, and it wouldn't be out of place back in its founder's hometown of Tyler, Texas. John Wideman started the place in 1970, in what had been a coffee shop. He has passed on, but the place is being run in fine fashion by Vicki, his wife, and Abel Olmos, their longtime manager.

They cook the brisket pillowy plush, the sort of soft you could fall asleep on. Tender and juicy, it's cut in big chunks and served with a Texas-style barbecue sauce that's authentically long on tomatoey tartness and short on peppery heat. The ribs are good, too, but (befitting a place named after the Lone Star state), the brisket is king. Unless you count the hot link, which is the smokiest meat on the menu. It's a big-shouldered beef sausage, crammed with garlic and good juices, and cooked, like the rest of the meat, over a slow fire. A lot of barbecue joints slap TEXAS on their signs, but the Dr.'s earns the right. And if you want to see what they do to low-down varmints, just try paying with a check.

Rating: Real good.

Directions: Dr. Hogly-Wogly's is just down the street from Dewey Pest Control and Valley Cycles Repair, Tune Up, and Overhaul. Sepulveda Blvd. is easy to hit off I-405 in Van Nuys. Look for a stucco exterior and some well-worn Astroturf at the entrance.

COLORADO

Denver

DADDY BRUCE'S BAR-B-Q

- 1629 East 34th Ave. (Bruce Randolph Ave.) o (303) 295-9115
- Tues.–Sat., 11 A.M.–midnight; Sun., noon–9 P.M.
- Closed Monday

Daddy Bruce's is more than a barbecue joint; it's an institution. But unlike many of our institutions (the army, for instance), it serves good food. The food at Daddy Bruce's is masterly barbecue, cooked in a massive iron pit and served in an aging, bright orange building that is a classic of its kind. But even before you see the colorful, sign-bedecked exterior, you know Daddy Bruce's is something special; the first clue comes when you turn onto the street in front of it. It's called Bruce Randolph Avenue, named after Daddy himself. To understand why the city of Denver would do such a thing, you'd need to stop by on Thanksgiving.

On Thanksgiving, Daddy Bruce feeds the needy—100,000 of them, by his estimate. "I feed the people all over the city," he says. "They call me and tell me what they need, and Yellow Cab delivers the food." From small beginnings, the event has grown, attracting volunteers from all around Denver and donations from across the nation. "They sent me five hundred pounds of cheese from Chicago and a semi freight of potatoes from Texas," he says. "Somebody, I can't remember who, sent me a freight-car load of rice. I'm still giving away rice." In preparation for his big giveaway, he starts cooking and freezing ribs as early as mid-September.

Of course, Daddy Bruce cooks ribs and serves them hot, too. He serves them cooked dark and full of smokiness and bite. He has been serving them at his gaudy, friendly place for twenty-four years, and a couple of the people working there have been serving them with him all that time. Daddy came from a little Ozark town in Arkansas, and before making it to Denver, he cooked in Texas and Arizona. "Any-where I cooks, they like it," he says. The ribs are cooked over hard-wood on a custom-built pit of his own design, and he's a little tight with any tricks of his trade: "I put the wood in there, put the meat on it, and it'll go."

He's more than happy to share his Daddy Bruce's Bar-B-Q sauce, however, which he says has been handed down through three generations. A commercially bottled version is now available in stores across Colorado, and may even go national. Here's a little secret, though: In addition to the stuff that's put in bottles at the plant, there's a version cooked up only on Bruce Randolph Avenue that's sometimes available in hand-filled bottles at the front counter. From its slapped-on yellow label to its floating chunks of garlic and spice, it's the real thing. Rich with the flavors of ketchup and Worcestershire sauce, it takes the familar and transforms it. There's the pointed perkiness of lemon and vinegar, with a hint of sweetness and a glowing, sunny warmth that shines on your tonsils long after you wash it off your hands in the little porcelain sink in the waiting room. Daddy Bruce has served it to countless thousands—at his restaurant, from a special trailer, and from a couple of portable pits. ("I can put a couple of cows in 'em.") He has appeared on *Donahue, Good Morning America,* and once on the *Today* show, when it was in Denver. "Willard really loved those ribs," he said. "We had a lot of fun."

At eighty-seven years of age, he has to field occasional questions about retirement. He does have an occasion in mind for it: "When they say, 'Ashes to ashes and dust to dust.'" Until then, he plans to go on selling barbecue—and giving it away. More than just a great pitmaster, Daddy Bruce has turned cooking into a calling. As it says on the trunk of his car, GOD LOVES YOU, AND SO DOES DADDY BRUCE.

Rating: Real good.

Directions: In 1986 the city of Denver renamed the street in front of Daddy Bruce's as Bruce Randolph Avenue, but in other sections it's still known at 34th Ave. From Stapleton International Airport, it's a quick trip over on 32nd Ave.

Fort Collins

BROTHER MEL'S SOUTHERN STYLE B.B.Q.

o 1624 Lemay o (303) 484-7427
o Mon.–Sat., 11 A.M.–9 P.M. o Closed Sunday

If anyone ever asks you who fixes the best barbecue in High Plains country, the answer is simple: Mel Johnson. The answer is so easy because the only competition for Mel Johnson in Laramie (see Wyoming) is Mel Johnson—in Fort Collins, Colo. The two men aren't related and have never met. "Boy, I hope his wife's not named Helen," said the Mel Johnson from Brother Mel's, " 'cause I'd be in trouble!" Actually, the only trouble that Brother Mel has is getting his hands on hardwood, that most precious of cowboyque commodities. "I get my wood from Arkansas," he says. "Hickory and oak. A man hauls hay down there to the race tracks—I mean, lots of hay—and he has enough room to come back with eleven cords of hardwood on the return trip. He has a regular circuit of people who buy his wood, all the way down to Denver."

Wherever it comes from, Mel puts his wood to good use—at a soulful oasis of ribs and tender brisket tucked away in the "food court" of a small shopping center in Fort Collins, home of Colorado State University. The plastic setting, with its orange awnings and bolt-to-the-floor seating, may not adequately prepare you for Brother Mel's brisket, sliced so thin that the singed edges are almost crisp, yet with a plush center so tender that it surrenders under the pressure of a tongue. So rich that it's almost sweet, Mel's beef is moist enough that it tastes best with just an occasional dab of Mel's sauce, sweet and tomatoey in both its hot and mild versions. The pork is delicious, too, smoked lightly like the beef and almost as tender. It's worth riding the range for, cowboyque at its best.

Rating: Real good.

Directions: To get to Brother Mel's, take U.S. 287 (College Ave.) about halfway through town and turn left on Prospect Rd. Take that to Lemay and some great brisket.

OKLAHOMA

Davis

THE SOONER CAFE

o 207 N. Third o (405) 369-3526
o Tues.–Sat., 11 A.M.–7 P.M. o Closed Sunday and Monday

The paneling inside this friendly roadside restaurant has assumed a warm brown that's slightly greasy to the touch. The ceiling has slipped past ivory into gray. The chair cushions in the five-table back room and the vinyl booths up front have achieved an indefinable blackish brown (or vice versa).

The monotone color scheme is silent, smoky testimony to a singleminded dedication to barbecue, a dedication that pays off in quirky, delicious pork ribs and a fetchingly original brisket sandwich. That sandwich, served on a very fresh, very toasted bun, features beef that is buttery rich and tender without being at all flabby. It also features a sprinkling of pickle relish that seems pretty strange until you get down to devouring it. Then it turns out that the tart sweetness of the relish pairs up perfectly with the cafe's mild, tangy sauce. This is not a gourmet Concept Sandwich; this is swell, satisfying eating. The chipped tan Texas Ware plastic plates don't hurt the effect much—nor does the plush mashed-potato salad, served cold (with more relish mixed in), nor the creamy white celery-seed slaw.

Sooner Cafe ribs are distinctive, too, thanks to a dry rub that cooks up slightly sweet and charmingly chewy. The ribs themselves are toothsome and satisfying, smoked with the skins left on the back, where they can be gnawed on absentmindedly or left on the bone like little petticoats.

The woman who runs the Sooner is Billie Pickens. And every time she opens the pit door, a little cloud of smoke drifts out, further enriching the color of the interior decor.

The Sooner Cafe has been around for about forty years or so, long enough for some of its brown shingles to have succumbed to gravity along with its flaking white trim. The iron pit, which protrudes into the lawn from one end of the cafe, is covered with a rich patina of rust. Basically, the whole place is gradually turning a mysterious shade of dusky tan, inside and out, and you should eat there before it becomes completely invisible.

Rating: Real good.

Directions: There's not that much to Davis, Okla., in the south-central part of the state, but you don't have to drive far from I-35 to get there. The Sooner Cafe is on North Third, a block north of State Road 7, which intersects the Interstate.

Oklahoma City

LEO'S

o 3631 N. Kelley Ave. o (405) 427-3254
o Mon.–Thurs., 11 A.M.–8 P.M.; Fri.–Sat., 11 A.M.–9 P.M.;
   Sun., 11 A.M.–5 P.M.

When it's high noon in Oklahoma City, it's as dark as midnight in Leo's. Well, maybe not midnight. But ten P.M. anyway. With the windows covered up and the huge bright orange brick pits going full-blast and the guys with meat cleavers whanging away along one side of the dim dining room, Leo's is the sort of barbecue joint that central casting would send over. It's a classic, and a look at the jammed parking lot tells you that's no secret, either.

In accordance with one of the Great Laws of Barbecue, Leo's is located in a former something-or-other, in this case a former gas station. The restaurant and pits now occupy the bays where mechanics used to work, and the take-out counter is where they used to stack the washer fluid and candy bars. The men's room is still the men's room. The gas pumps outside are gone, but the concrete islands remain, lying in wait for an unwary Mercedes.

Inside, the joint definitely jumps. Around lunchtime, between the bus boys and businessmen, it's standing room only—without enough room to stand. TIPS ARE ENCOURAGED TO INSURE GOOD SERVICE a sign says, and it's something to think about. The pace is fast, egged on perhaps by the relentless staccato of blades hammering through juicy ribs.

All the hubbub could be a bit befuddling to a first-time visitor, but Leo's has solved one problem: what to order. Order the Leo's Special, which includes beef, ribs, hot links, bologna, baked beans, and potato salad. All you have to remember is to get your beer and your sugary, scrumptious Leo's Homemade Banana Strawberry Cake for dessert.

Nibble what you like from a Leo's Special; you absolutely cannot go wrong. The beans, for instance, are spectacular, among the very best in the nation, brimming with plump chunks of various smoked meats. And if the idea of barbecued bologna is a foreign one, Leo's funky, thick-sliced version makes a perfect introduction—nicely

PORKLORE ○ Wood You if You Could?

When the manufacturers of modern electric and gas cooking pits failed to win over barbecue purists, who consistently chided their product as "not barbecue," they tried a new tactic: They tried to get the definition of barbecue changed. In 1982, Smokaroma of Boley, Okla., makers of pressure "barbecue" cookers, petitioned the U.S. Dept. of Agriculture to change the regulations for barbecue. The purists swamped the agency with opposing comments, the nicest of which said, "If they've got a new method, let 'em come up with a new name, too." Five years later the USDA ruled, "There is not sufficient justification to propose a change to the current barbecue standard." The purists won. Barbecue is still barbecue.

seared and sensuously soft. The ribs are smoky pink in the middle and crusty from the cooker. The beef brisket is tender and mellow. And Leo's flamboyant hot link is a fully armed torpedo with a candy-apple red exterior surrounding chunky meat flecked with spices in red, orange, green, and black (there may have been other colors, too, but your correspondent's eyes were watering). Speaking of hot, Leo's hot sauce earns its moniker, a thick, vinegar-sour concoction, grainy with enough spice to light up your lips like one of Leo's neon signs. A suggestion: Order the special with the mild sauce (it's sweeter and thinner, an altogether different affair) and get the hot sauce on the side for dipping and thrill-seeking.

Owner Leo Smith has been in the business twelve years, inheriting the recipe for that smoldering sauce from his uncle in Tulsa. And he says that the secrets of good barbecue are simple: "Don't rush it. We get here on time—five-thirty every morning. We cook our beef eighteen hours." Oh, and one more thing: "I don't have any microwave in my business."

Mr. Smith also can take credit for what seems to be America's only golf tournament sponsored by a barbecue joint, the annual Leo's Barbecue Open Golf Tournament, first held in August 1985. A mouthful of Leo's hot sauce should be good for an extra ten yards off the tee.

Rating: As good as we've ever had.

Directions: In Oklahoma City, take I-44 West to the Lincoln Blvd. exit. Take Lincoln south to 36th St. and then turn left onto 36th St. until you hit Kelley Ave., which is Leo's original location. (Leo also has another place at 6816 N. Western.)

TEXAS

Austin

IRON WORKS OFFICIAL TEXAS B-B-Q

o 100 Red River o (512) 478-4855
o Mon.–Thurs., 11 A.M.–8 P.M.; Fri., 11 A.M.–9 P.M.
o Closed Saturday and Sunday

Austin isn't exactly a great barbecue town, maybe because you can easily drive a few miles out into the country and get some of the best barbecue in the world. But the city does have a pretty good version, sold right downtown in an atmospheric, corrugated steel building that was built in 1935 as the Fortunat Weigl Iron Works and is now a for-sure Historic Place.

Owners Charlotte and Jerry Finch took over the building a couple of years after the iron works quit working in 1976. Jerry had been with the state health department before opening his own barbecue joint; in this business, that's sort of like joining the other side. But he makes good barbecue for a health department man, cooking it for about seventeen hours in a big, temperature-controlled brick pit. Smoky beef ribs are the specialty—big, meaty, and delicious. The slightly dry brisket falls a bit short of true Texas Transcendental, and the sauce is a trifle ketchupy—but fishing a couple of "japs" out of the glass jar of complimentary jalapeño peppers will more than make up for any sass lacking in the sauce.

The interior of old wood is dotted with burnt-in custom brands that were once a specialty of the Iron Works (there are brands for Jack Benny, Bob Hope, and Lucille Ball, among others). One corner of the shop has been left alone, with its tin signs, wrought iron, and dusty cluttered shelves. There's a wooden deck out back where you can eat and watch the turtles cruising Waller Creek. With its scattered antiques and old photos, and its sometimes-Polo-shirted patrons, the Iron Works runs the risk of coming across as a theme restaurant, but it's too funky to be Friday's. There's no air conditioning, just screen doors and big floor fans. There's no table service, just do-it-yourself. If you get thirsty, you can get up and get another dripping cold bottle out of the antique ice coolers, one for beer and one for pop (the opener is mounted by the cash register, and the bottle caps fall into a coal bucket on the floor). There is better barbecue to be found in Texas, but while you're pouring back a Shiner Bock beer fresh from a pool of icy water and listening to the turtles gurgle, it's hard to get real fired up to go look for it.

Rating: Pretty good.

Directions: To get to the Iron Works, take I-35 south to the First Street and Holly exit; at the stop light take a right onto First St. The Iron Works will be on your left at the second light. There's a sign in the small lot that says ILLEGALLY PARKED CARS WILL BE TOWED, CRUSHED AND MELTED.

P.S.: Austin is a music town, if not always a barbecue one, and the two mix happily at **Stubb's Legendary Bar-B-Q and Restaurant**, a swell little spot tucked into one end of a discount motel next to I-35. C. B. "Stubbs" Stubblefield, who made his delicious West Texas barbecue famous in Lubbock, moved to Austin a few years ago. His restaurant is plastered with autographed posters and photos of musicians from B. B. King to Bobby Bare, from Los Lobos and the Fabulous Thunderbirds to Ponty Bone and the Squeezetones. The jukebox is a marvel, too, with songs by Little Milton, Joe Ely, John Lee Hooker, Big Mama Thornton, and "I'm Too Poor to Die" by Louisiana Red. There's also a small stage for performances at one end of Stubb's, but the barbecue is the sweetest song sung here. Cooked over oak and sometimes a little mesquite, it's the result of more than thirty years' experience, and you can taste every year in the tantalizing beef. Cooking real good barbecue comes from a feeling, a God-given talent you're born with, Stubbs says. He has given out his recipe "to individuals, not competitors" and had them call him on the phone and say, "Stubbs, I've got a mess over here." The smart thing to do is let Stubbs cook it himself. You eat it. The restaurant is at 4001 N.IH-35 (the access road that parallels the Interstate) in the Tru-Valu Inn, next to the U Haul place. It's open 10 A.M.–10 P.M. Monday through Saturday (till 1 A.M. on Friday or Saturday if there's a band). The hours Sunday are 10 A.M.–1 A.M. (512) 465-9177.

Dallas

SONNY BRYAN'S SMOKEHOUSE

o 2202 Inwood Rd. o (214) 357-7120
o Mon.–Fri., 10 A.M.–5 P.M.; Sat., 10 A.M.–3 P.M.;
   Sun., 11 A.M.–2 P.M.

What would it take to make a Texan in a three-piece, custom-tailored suit sit on the hood of his black Lincoln and drip sauce on his silk socks? There's only one thing that could inspire such behavior: an order of some of the best barbecue in America, served at one of the best barbecue joints, Sonny Bryan's Smokehouse.

This tiny barbecue shack sits a bit outside Dallas's central business district, and its limited seating (a couple of long wooden benches with grade school armrest writing desks) falls so far behind its popularity that crowds of people in the big parking lot spread out lunches on the hoods of their cars, or even sit on the hoods themselves, eating fresh-from-the-fire beef brisket before it cools.

Sonny Bryan's is a genuine phenomenon, churning out about eight hundred pounds of beef every day in a cement-block building the size of a double-wide mobile home. The sixty-two-year-old chef and master theoretician R. L. "Sonny" Bryan has said, "I saw how happy my father was when he had a little barbecue place, and I saw how unhappy he was when he built a big place." (See the **P.S.** note that follows.) So Sonny, who started out toasting bread in his dad's place when he was eight, has kept his quarters cramped ever since he opened in 1957.

At lunchtime, it's a cross between a barn dance and the floor of the New York stock exchange, with orders being hollered out, beer tabs popping, and the cement floor in front of the counter filling up with everything from ten-gallon hats to hundred-dollar hairpieces, from designer dresses to I'M WITH STUPID T-shirts. "I got the most varied customers in the world," Sonny brags, "from bottom to top."

Waitresses cruise the crowd, taking orders and bringing the waiting legions cans of beer to help them bear up under the heat and hullabaloo. The cashier announces when the orders are ready by shouting the customers' initials over the general din. By 12:33 P.M. on a summertime Friday, the hungry crowd already had run the place out of ribs. But there was plenty of brisket left, and brisket is the star of the show. It is mouth-wateringly moist, with a burnt crust and a haunting smokiness, chopped in chunks and piled high on a toasted bun. Scattered around the restaurant are square-sided glass bottles of sauce, some resting on a hot plate to keep them warm. The sauce inside is thin and tart, with tomatoey tang but no hot pepper at all. It's good sloshed on the beef sandwich, and it's even good on the monstrous onion rings.

A trip to Sonny's seems semimandatory for tourists in Dallas, judging by the cameras and out-of-state plates we saw. But it'd be worth making your way there for lunch if you're anywhere in the area, say within the confines of continental North America. For all of those whose dream of the perfect barbecue joint is delicious food served in a dump, Sonny cheerfully fills the bill: "I guess my dinky, greasy barbecue place is what people expect Texas to be."

Rating: As good as we've ever had.

Directions: Sonny Bryan's Smokehouse is a few blocks away from Dallas's Love Field airport. To get there, make your way to Harry Hines Blvd. (there's an exit off I-35E); at about 5700 north on Harry Hines Blvd., you'll run into Inwood Rd. Sonny's is just a little ways to the northeast on Inwood Rd.

P.S.: THE BEST BARBECUE IN THE WORLD, AND THAT'S NO BULL says the sign at **Red Bryan's Smokehouse,** 3383 Lombardy Lane, Dallas. This cafeteria-style barbecue restaurant was opened in 1965 by William J. "Red" Bryan, Sonny's dad, who had been operating at a string of locations since 1929. Red's father (and Sonny's grandfather), Elias

H. Bryan, started the family barbecuing in 1910, when he moved to Texas from Ohio and opened up a restaurant. Red took over from his dad and, since Red died in 1973, his wife Catharine has owned the restaurant. It's nowhere near as funky as Sonny's place, what with its real chairs and tables and air conditioning that actually works. But there is a Dallas contingent that votes "Better Red's Than Dead" and packs the place daily, along with the occasional visitor like guitarist Eric Clapton. Brisket is the main attraction; it goes in the rotisserie pit about five in the evening for the next day's meals, cooking about sixteen hours and coming out tender and not overly smoky, served with a tangy sauce that counts a shot of tart lemon juice as one of its ingredients. Red's is open 11 A.M.–8 P.M. Sunday through Thursday, and till 9 P.M. on Friday and Saturday. It's real good. (214) 357-2727.

P.P.S.: On the other side of town, and the other side of the tracks, from Red's and Sonny's is **Black-Man Bar-B-Que,** which serves good, juicy brisket in a pleasantly garish onetime drive-in. The place exceeds the required slogan quota by one, offering two nice versions painted across its cement-block exterior: TRY IT ONE TIME AND I GOTCHA is joined by ALL THE WAY FROM LOUISIANA BAREFOOTED. At 3503 E. Illinois Ave., Black-Man is a swift shot off the Interstate, just a few blocks east of I-45 as it passes through Dallas. (214) 375-6080.

Elgin

SOUTHSIDE MARKET

o 109 Central St. o (512) 285-3407
o Mon.–Sat., 7 A.M.–6 P.M., o Closed Sunday

Some folks will tell you that the Southside really started going downhill in 1983, after the big fire. That's when the place began to put out forks. "I never had anything in here but knives," owner Ernest Bracewell, Jr., told a reporter at the time. "But we had too many people coming in from the North who couldn't eat with their fingers."

For Bracewell, who took over the Southside in 1968, it was only one in a series of heresies affecting the specialty that had made the little meat market famous across much of Texas since 1882—its chunky sausage that old-timers called "Elgin hot guts." For instance, there was that business about the ladies' room. Bracewell put one in. And first thing you know, the ladies came, too, ruining what had been an otherwise fine place for a bunch of men to stand around and eat barbecue. There were other things. Bracewell cut back on the red pepper, again to go easy on the suffering Yankees, which he calls "imports." He took the pork out of the sausage and changed the recipe to all-beef. And to make matters worse, he pulled the switch in secret, and nobody noticed for three months, not even his staff.

But to be fair to Mr. Bracewell, he can't be doing everything wrong. He still cooks as much as 2,200 pounds of sausage a day, sometimes sending it out of town on buses. His bright orange hot sauce still sits around on the tables in old whiskey bottles. And his sausage and sublime beef brisket still show up on brown butcher paper without a hint of a plate. Crackers are all you get with your basic order, and the highest-powered drink is Big Red.

Most of the barbecue eating takes place behind the meat market at the Southside, back in a cheerful tomb of a room with a bare plywood ceiling and white glazed-block walls. It echoes with the orders of regular customers, an extremely varied bunch to be waiting in the same line. A black man in tattered overalls slaps a somewhat surprised businessman on the shoulder and says, "Hi, old fella! Was you buying lunch today or was I?" By the time they reach the cashier, they're both smiling—and the meals are on one tab. And what meals! The place may be famous for sausage, but the brisket is tender and flavorful, among the best in the state. The sausage itself is moist and meaty, no longer really all that hot, but it picks up some quick zing with a dash of the thin, vinegary sauce that's colored orange with cayenne and other spices.

The sausage here is made "straight," as Bracewell puts it, in one continuous rope, not sectioned off in links (except for special orders). When you cook several hundred pounds of sausage a day, Bracewell decided, turning all those little links just took up too much time. Now he stretches long tubes of sausage across his oak-fired grill and rotates them for about a half an hour to cook evenly. "We do it with pride," he says. "We've still got quality to it."

His newfangled notions make sense (except maybe the notion of a second, paneled dining room with ceiling fans and sawdust on the floor). The results taste great—and if you get a little wistful for the good old days, well, you can still stand up to eat, you can leave the ladies out on the sidewalk, and you sure don't have to use a fork.

Rating: Real good.

Directions: The Southside Market is on Central St. in Elgin, Texas. That's Elgin with a hard *g* as in "hot guts." You can't miss the place once you get to Elgin, which is not all that hard, either. The town of about 4,500 is just about twenty miles or so east of Austin on U.S. 290.

Fort Worth

ANGELO'S

o 2533 White Settlement Rd. o (817) 332-0357
o Mon.–Sat., 11 A.M.–10 P.M. o Closed Sunday

There are numerous barbecue joints in this great land that for one reason or another choose not to sell beer. Angelo's makes up for all of them. Angelo's sells beer in eighteen-ounce schooners the size of glass-bottom boats. Angelo's sells beer in "longnecks," chilled old-fashioned bottles the very mention of which can make Texans all misty-eyed. It's hard to tell if the place is a beer joint selling barbecue or a barbecue joint selling beer. But after a round or two of either, the distinction ceases to matter. The barbecue is first rate, the beer is cold, and the huge rooms are so ratty and raucous that you could howl like a coyote without being noticed. Especially by the people howling at the next table.

In fact, if you're going to argue about who makes the best barbecue in the nation, you really should come to Angelo's. It's not that the ribs and brisket are so good that they'd end all discussion of the matter. No, it's just that arguing at Angelo's is so much fun.

The first clue may be the stuffed bear in the camouflage Angelo's shirt that greets you when you enter. Then there's the crowd, waving and laughing and tearing into platters of meat, sort of like a huge pinball machine on full barbecue "tilt." The gangly dude in the YA-HOO! T-shirt and the stay-pressed slick wearing an Alfa Romeo hat look equally at home. And when the waitresses bellow, "Two large!" over all the other hollering, they're not criticizing your girth or your order. That's Angelo's code for "Two more horse troughs full of beer!"

But lest you think that Angelo's may not be a "family" place, consider owner Angelo George: He can prove you wrong with his own family. One daughter oversees the bar, one tends the books, and son Skeet helps him run the place. The night we visited, Skeet was helping by sitting at the bar and joshing with some customers; if you feel like saying hi, Skeet's the fellow who looks like the stuffed bear in the entrance, only bigger.

And lest you think that all the frivolity blunts the focus of the place, rest assured: The barbecue at Angelo's is excellent, good even for Texas, with seriously smoky pork ribs—crusty, chewy, pink to the bone and cooked so fresh they don't even go on sale until five in the afternoon. The beef brisket, chopped into hefty hunks, is shot with smoky perfume and tender as a kiss from a cowgirl. The sauce served with all this is typical Texan—not too thick, not at all hot, but lively with a tomato tang.

Angelo isn't much for giving away tricks of the trade. Ask what makes his barbecue so good, and he'll intone: "Buy the very best you can, and don't get in no hurry." Angelo also isn't much on giving credit to his rivals. What other Texas barbecue does he like? "I don't eat nobody else's."

But if you could eat at Angelo's every night, why would you?

Rating: Real good.

Directions: To get to Angelo's—a wood plank building—hit the University Dr. exit off of I-30 (on the west side of Fort Worth). Then drive north about four miles to White Settlement Rd. and turn right. It's about a half a mile up on your right. It's open Monday through Saturday, but closed on Sunday because if you've been hanging out at Angelo's all week you really *need* a day of rest.

Glen Rose

HAMMOND'S BAR-B-Q

o A. J.'s: Box 161, Coyote Strip o (817) 897-2324
o Fri., 5 P.M.–8 P.M.; Sat., 11 A.M.–8 P.M.; Sun., 11 A.M.–6 P.M.

o Tom's: U.S. 67 o (817) 897-3321
o Wed.–Thurs., 11 A.M.–7 P.M.; Fri.–Sat., 11 A.M.–8 P.M.;
   Sun., 11 A.M.–3 P.M.

If a person stands next to the longhorn skulls in the gravel parking lot of A. J. Hammond's, high atop the Coyote Strip in the rolling hills of central Texas, he can squint over the trees and see the Comanche Peak nuclear power plant they put in a few miles away. But it isn't stray neutrons that make the brisket at Hammond's so meltingly tender and suffused with an almost supernatural beef flavor. No, that responsibility lies solely with A. J. Hammond, and he chalks it up to one thing: "Patience. You've got to have it. If you don't have it, you'd better get it." A. J. should know; he has patience that would have convinced Job to get out of the barbecue business. That patience—and a special cut of brisket that is not trimmed as lean as some other Texas pitmen order it—leads him to slow-cook his beef in a big closed pit for thirty-five hours before he feels right about it.

Now, let's do some quick math: thirty-five hours is pushing two full days, and it's more than twice as long as most big-time Texas barbecue restaurants advertise cooking their brisket. "Aw, you can't get the blood out in fourteen hours," A. J. grumbles. "Those people who brag on cooking it eighteen hours, that's nothing." What A. J. gets for his thirty-five-hour investment is the best pit-cooked brisket in the state of Texas, which pretty much means the best brisket anywhere. So much juice has percolated through that meat in its day-and-a-half-day stay in the pit that it is absolutely supercharged with the opulent, buttery flavor of fine steak; and despite its thick cut and substantial heft, it is tender as a sigh. "I have a rule on tenderness," A. J. explains. "I look out over the tables. When I see somebody taking that first big bite, it should come away clean, not have pieces pulling out of the sandwich onto the plate." As a rule, the rule holds true. But one time a while back, A. J. did spot a customer with bits of his brisket pulling out of his sandwich. A concerned chef, he checked on it. "It turned out the man had just had major dental work."

The fact that a man who had just undergone major dental work would feel compelled to travel down the twisty ridge road that leads to Hammond's corrugated steel building and order a beef sandwich gives you some idea of how fanatical A. J.'s fans can be. And the ones who have grown complacent about the brisket probably come for a piece of his wife, Liz's, peanut butter pie and the Bob Wills music. Evidence of the place's many fans is to be found all over its interior of unfinished wood and particle board, which has been signed on every square inch by admirers from all over the world. "The autographs started with a couple visiting from Paris," says Liz. "They wanted to sign a guest book or something, and I said, 'Oh, just sign on the wall in the corner over there.' " Now the signatures run up the rafters, behind the ceiling fans, under the plastic tablecloths, even under the tables. "Back here," says A. J. from one end of the kitchen, "you can see James Michener's. He was through here researching a book. And here his wife signed in Japanese."

A. J. and Liz moved their barbecue place out in the country in 1974, leaving the in-town Glen Rose concession to son Tom and his wife Linda. Tom serves up a mean beef sandwich, one of the best around, but he still has a few things to learn from dad. A. J., meanwhile, says, "I don't know it all. No way do I know it all. I've been in it a long time, but I still don't know everything there is to know. 'Cause I learn something new every day."

Rating: As good as we've ever had.

Directions: The folks in Glen Rose call A. J.'s "the country Hammond's." Getting there means driving west of town on U.S. 67 a few miles, until you see the billboard that'll send you off onto the winding Coyote Strip. You'll know when you arrive at Hammond's because the sign on top of the corrugated roof says WHOA! HERE 'TIS! The "in-town"

Hammond's, run by Tom, is on U.S. 67 in the middle of town, next to a liquor store called the Galvanized Palace.

Houston

GOODE COMPANY

o 5109 Kirby Dr. o (713) 522-2530
o Mon.–Sat., 11 A.M.–10 P.M.; Sun., noon–10 P.M.

Fear of yuppies and dishonest "theme" barbecue has prejudiced some purists against Goode Company, which is only ten years old but was created to look about a hundred and fifty years older. Its location, down the street from the chic Hard Rock Cafe on one of Houston's prime restaurant rows, puts detractors off, too. They'll tell you that, despite its outdoor benches and its old-barn exterior, it's a "concept" restaurant, as planned out as Disneyland and just about as authentic. But you can't eat concepts, and the food served at Goode Company would shut up such critics in a hurry if they'd consent to shove some in their mouths. It's better than Goode; it's almost Greate.

One reason is the beer: It floats in deep, icy water in a row of coolers that lets you pop one open before you even hit the cafeteria line. Another reason is the side dishes. At most barbecue joints, side dishes are straightforward, slap-together stuff, but not here. The beans are jazzy jalapeño pintos; served with pieces of bacon and pepper bits, they are toes-to-the-fireplace hot and luscious. The Jambalaya Texana is a vivacious version of rice, with an avalanche of ham and pepper chunks. And then there's the Jalapeño Cheese Bread. In sandwiches or separately, it's dangerous. Cut thick and swirled with seductive, golden bands of cheese, it's plush and inviting—until Mr. Jalapeño jumps on your tongue with sharpened cleats. You may expect the sauce to be hot, but here you get blindsided by the bread.

The basic barbecue is straightforward and respectable, with tender brisket and chewy, smoky pork ribs that are blushing pink and accompanied by a sauce as unusual, in its own way, as the Attack Bread. The sauce is not hot, and not made from ketchup, either. It is filled with hunks of meat and onion, tomatoey and rich and homemade; dieters could eat it from the cup like soup. There's also another barbecue oddity: barbecued duck.

All this is evidence of an active imagination in the kitchen, and some it belongs to owner Jim Goode, a commercial artist who retired and went into barbecue, opening the place in 1977. "We bought a former fast-food barbecue restaurant," he said. "We got in here and tried to do things right." There's an active imagination in the design, too, with a mounted buffalo head, an antique jukebox, and display cases of memorabilia from his great-grandfather's tenure in the Texas Cavalry during the Civil War, along with cornball old signs that say things like WHAT THE——ARE YOU LOOKING UP HERE FOR. Seating indoors is limited, but the picnic tables outdoors are under a roof. We decided not to mention the thirty-five dollar "bull bags" for sale at the cash register. Not in a book about eating.

Rating: Real good.

Directions: There's an exit onto Kirby Dr. from the Southwest Freeway (U.S. 59) as it cuts across the middle of Houston. The restaurant is next to a place that bills itself as "The World's Largest Coin-Operated Washeteria." Jim Goode also runs a seafood place and hamburger-and-Mexican place, if you like that sort of thing.

OTTO'S

o 5502 Memorial Dr. o (713) 864-2573
o Mon.–Sat., 11 A.M.–9 P.M. o Closed Sunday

There's an old barbecue-hunter's axiom that holds: "If it says 'burgers' on the sign, don't waste your time." But what is such wisdom to do in the face of Otto's? Otto's sells hamburgers all right, but in *an entirely separate building!* The Hamburger Otto's faces the parking lot on Memorial Drive, out by the main BARBEQUE-AND-HAMBURGERS sign. It's what you see first, and if you were hungry for some of Houston's traditional favorite barbecue, you might walk right in. You wouldn't find any. But what you should have noticed was a big arrow painted above the windows that points around back; BAR-B-Q DINING ROOM the lettering says. But let's get this straight: It's not a "dining room." There's an entirely different building back there, different architecture, different street, different parking lot, different menu. It's the Barbecue Otto's, and it's good.

"We started in front," said Miss Annie Sofka, "then we added on another building. A lot of people were asking for barbecue." Miss Annie, the wife of the late founder, Otto Sofka, is the life and soul of the place, greeting and chatting with customers at the cafeteria-style serving bar with an unforced friendliness that once led the city to declare a "Miss Annie Day." She dishes up some delicious barbecue, so it's easy to smile back.

"People come from New York with briefcases," she says. "Then they fill them with ribs and take them back to New York." It's easy to believe. The brisket in the beef sandwich is fall-apart tender, spouting with juice, seared along the edges and simply begging for an application of the tart, apple butter–brown tomato sauce. To capture the maximum flavor, the meat isn't trimmed until *after* it's cooked. Ribs, hot links, and ham round out the menu.

The interior is pleasant and paneled, with a blizzard of witticisms plastered all over the place. There's the funny-monkey section, with photos of chimps in human clothing. A discreet distance away, in the back dining room, there's the George Bush section, with photos of George in human clothing, and a nice letter from the fellow.

Before any barbecue hunters get too distraught at seeing a perfectly fine rule about hamburgers go down the tubes at Otto's, let us reassure them: Otto's does confirm another Prime Theorum of good barbecue, the parking lot test. Simply stated, it's this: Look at the cars in the lot; the greater the range, the better the eating. And Otto's tested out with the best parking lot we visited. It didn't just go from a primered Pinto to a Jaguar and a Jeep Wagoneer; there also was a black stretch limousine that was idling at the curb while its driver waited for his charges to finish dinner and lick the sauce off their manicured fingers.

Rating: Good.

Directions: Otto's is not too far from the Hogg Bird Sanctuary in Houston. To get there, get off of I-10 and onto Durham Dr., then head south to Memorial Dr. Turn right on Memorial; Otto's is between the Heart's chicken place and a Gulf station.

La Grange

PRAUSE'S MARKET

o U.S. 77, on the town square o (409) 968-3259
o Mon.–Fri., 7 A.M.–5 P.M.; Sat., 5:30 A.M.–1 P.M. o Closed Sunday

"The Best Damn Butcher Shop in Texas" this market has been known to call itself, though the claim is open to more or less endless argument. But some poetic license should be allowed, since Prause's is located in the hometown of the former Chicken Ranch, popularized on stage and screen as *The Best Little Whorehouse in Texas*. A lot of folks in La Grange think the Chicken Ranch isn't exactly what they'd like to go down in history for, no matter how good a whorehouse it was. It's out east of town, but finding it is kind of tricky these days; there's no monument or anything, although a promoter supposedly sold off so much Chicken Ranch property mail-order (at eight dollars per square inch) that he can no longer get to the place without trespassing.

Still, the city fathers are doubtless glad to have a butcher shop making a claim for the spotlight instead of those more sprightly heifers, and Prause's makes a good claim indeed. In the back room tradition of Texas butcher shop barbecue, it features an excellent back room. It's tucked right behind the meat counter itself, where you also can order fresh cuts of meat. In back where the barbecue's sold, there's brisket and sausage.

It's served on long, red Formica tables with scuffed wooden benches on a cement floor. Along one wall is a clothesline for holding announcements. Every now and then along the tables are corked whiskey bottles full of indeterminate and intimidating ingredients. As with all Texas butcher-block barbecue, the meat in Prause's Market is served without benefit of the runny, tomatoey sauce that holds sway over so much of the state. Instead, you have these bottles of . . . stuff. The management is tight-lipped about their contents, but the one they call green-pepper sauce seems to consist of big chunks of onion and tiny green peppers floating in vinegar. It is sour and tart and mildly hot—and delicious on the brisket, which percolates with beef flavor and is served with a strip of fat along one edge. The other sort of bottle, the kind they call Louisiana sauce, is a similar composition using larger red peppers. It was a touch hotter, but possessed of a gentle simmer that went fetchingly well with the coarsely ground sausage. Juicy and flecked with pepper, the sausage wasn't really hot, and a shot of Louisiana sauce made the ideal complement. Could a mere whorehouse ever be this satisfying?

Rating: Real good.

Directions: La Grange can be found on U.S. 77, about halfway between San Antonio and Houston. Prause's Market is easy to spot; you can't see in the windows because they are stacked with huge bags of charcoal. The sign on the window gives the hours it is open each day, but for Sunday it says GONE TO FISH.

Lockhart

KREUZ MARKET

o 208 S. Commerce o (512) 398-2361
o Mon.–Fri., 7 A.M.–6 P.M.; Sat., 7 A.M.–6:30 P.M., o Closed Sunday

What kind of cowboy name is "Kreuz"? And why is a lot of the best barbecue in Texas to be found in the back rooms of butcher shops and meat markets? Well, there's a good reason: That's where it all began, at least on a commercial scale. Back in the late nineteenth century a tide of German and Czechoslovakian immigrants washed across the New Braunfels area of Texas, in the south-central part near San

Antonio. With them came a passel of butcher shops. Their owners had an Old World butcher's aversion to tossing out perfectly good meat—but a frontiersman's good sense to see what wasn't selling. So they took their scraps and turned them into sausage, and they took their tougher cuts and cooked them over slow wood fires to enhance their flavor and tenderness. It was a good idea then, and it's a good idea now. People are still lining up to eat it.

So when you spot the big brick smokestack with KREUZ (pronounced "Kritz") painted on it, you're not only looking at a slice of Texas history (it has been operating since 1900, in this building since 1924)—you're also looking at a slice of barbecued beef of the sort they'd serve in heaven (or maybe hell, where the cooking's better). The shoulders favored here are a slightly more expensive cut of meat than the usual Texas brisket, and they're cooked a different way: hot and fast. Well, fast for barbecue—about four and a half or five hours. The towering, thirty-five-foot brick chimney, which rises from the corner of the L-shaped pit, creates a strong draw that inhales heat and smoke from open fires set at each end, burning right out on the concrete floor of the two-story back room. "This is indirect heat," says Don Schmidt, who runs the place with his brother Rick (it has been in the Schmidt family since 1948). "But it gets hot in here. We put a thermometer in front of the pit, and it measured six hundred degrees."

A bare counter runs in front of all this fiery activity, and that's where you order your barbecue. It's served on brown butcher paper crumpled at each end to make a tray. Actually, there is no tray, as well as no plate, no fork, and no barbecue sauce. A plastic knife is included (they used to bolt knives to the tables), and you have your choice of bread or crackers. Choose crackers; everybody else does, and to serve them, a pitman pulls a plastic-wrapped stack of Saltines out of a box and cleaves them neatly with a very large, very sharp knife. Half the pack is yours.

PORKLORE ○ Just Married

How do you cook barbecue? Joey Sutphen of Sutphen's Bar-B-Q in Amarillo, Texas, says, "First you stick your face in the smoke and when all the hair's gone from your arm, that's how you know you're cooking good. When it's almost uninhabitable for human beings, that's when the smoke and the sauce get married to the rib."

The eating gets done away from the pit, in a two-story, tin-roofed room that's air conditioned enough to take the edge off the six hundred-degree fires, but completely ineffective against the jalapeño peppers served out of a big jar. Sitting on the long tables are bottles of Louisiana hot sauce and little cardboard trays of a salt-and-pepper mixture—but both are absolutely unnecessary. The shoulder is perfect as it sits, cooked just shy of dry, startlingly full of flavor and too tender for even a plastic knife. And the smoked sausage, tied with string into U-shaped links, may be the best in Texas. It's spicy and peppery and spilling with chunky meat that's moist and precisely cooked. The spice lives on in your mouth for minutes, and the memory should last for months.

Rating: As good as we've had.

Directions: Lockhart is a ways northeast of San Antonio. To get there, take U.S. 183 north about fifteen miles from I-10. The front of the market is on Commerce, across from Ralph's Hairstyling Cuts, but there's a big dirt parking lot out back, right on U.S. 183. Go in that way; it takes you past that amazing pit.

P.S.: Another nearby market with barbecue in back is the **Luling City Market,** 633 Davis St. in Luling, Texas. It's near I-10 on U.S. 183. This market is smaller and more seemly than Kreutz, without all the pyrotechnics. But the barbecue is real good, and it makes an interesting comparison. It's open 7 A.M.–8 P.M. Monday through Saturday, closed Sunday. (512) 875-9019.

Taylor

LOUIE MUELLER BARBEQUE

o 206 W. Second St. o (512) 352-6206
o Open daily 7 A.M.–7 P.M., but closes at 2 P.M. on Thurs. and
   1 P.M. on Sun.

Louie Mueller's looks the way a small-town Texas barbecue joint should. Its weathered brick exterior is dusty, its windows are boarded up, and its screen doors slam with a bang against aging frames. There's no air conditioning, just two big fans mounted at either end of a huge, barnlike room. The glass skylights high in the roof are stained with brown, and the peeling green walls show enough layers to interest archaeologists. The floor is made of worn wooden planks, and, two stories up, so is the ceiling.

Oh, they could have fixed it up; enough barbecue and beer have flowed out of the place. But they haven't, and they won't. "We'll keep

PORKLORE ○ Movieque

Barbecue has made an appearance or two in the movies over the years. Liz Taylor fainted over barbecued steer brain in *Giant*. Henry Gibson kicked off his political campaign with a celebrity barbecue in *Nashville*. Dan Aykroyd was delayed by a trip to Leon's in *Dr. Detroit*. And let's not forget the choice of meat for the barbecue in *Texas Chainsaw Massacre*. On second thought, let's do forget it.

But as best we can determine only one barbecue joint has ever made it big on the big screen, Hutchens Bar-B-Q of Benton, Ky. Okay, technically Huchens didn't make it. But a radio commercial for Hutchens was used in *Coal Miner's Daughter*, the big-screen biography of country singer Loretta Lynn. Loretta and her husband, Mooney, were making the rounds of radio stations, trying to get a little airplay for her self-produced first record, "Honky Tonk Girl." Their first stop was WCBL in Benton, Ky. The deejay was trying to shoo them out of the studio when his record ended and he had to do some announcing. "You're listening to Tri-State country with your deejay Bobby Day. Now here's a word from our friends down at Hutchens Hot Pig. Oink, oink, oink, oink. Tell 'em all about it Hutch and all them little piglets." While Day continued his argument with the Lynns, you could hear bits and pieces of the Hutchens's commercial in the background. "This is Hutch Hutchens down at Hutchens Hot Pig saying bring the whole family down for our mouthwatering ribs. . . ." That isn't the real Hutch Hutchens on the commercial. He died several years ago. And that isn't a real Hutchens commercial. But Hutchens Hot Pig is still operating in Benton, still serving up good barbecue six days a week. (They're closed Wednesday.)

it just like it is," says Bobby Mueller, Louie's son, who owns it now. The building was put up in 1907 and has done time as a grocery store, a typewriter repair shop, and even a basketball gym ("It must have been a short court," says Bobby). But now it's barbecue—brisket so tender that it's almost like pot roast and a loose, juicy sausage with a rosy ring of smoke surrounding a center of rich, beefy brown.

The brisket is different from most in Texas, having been smoked over oak for four to six hours and then wrapped in butcher paper to steep in its own juices. That's the way Louie did it when he started out in the mid-fifties in a little tin shed, and that's also the way Fred Fountaine did it for years at Mueller's as the chief cook. "When I started at Mueller's," Fred says, "they had two barbecue pits. One cook quit, and Mr. Mueller said I was the new cook. I didn't know how to build a fire; I thought I'd burn the place down." He didn't, and before he recently retired from Mueller's, he had accumulated nearly forty years of experience. "The most exciting day was in 1978, when The New York Times came in," Fred says. "There was four of 'em, and I gave 'em something to eat. They said, 'This is the best we found.'"

It is definitely good barbecue, especially the brisket, which is so tender it practically collapses from the effort of staying in one piece. It's served cafeteria-style on butcher paper on an ancient plastic tray, accompanied by a delicious homemade broth of a sauce that is watery but meaty, full of tomato flavor and dotted with pepper flakes and chunks of onion. It's a slow-to-anger sauce, but there's a big bottle of ill-tempered hot-pepper potion on each worn table, just in case.

On the other side of a big dirt parking lot from Mueller's is Rudy Mikeska's, a big red barn of a barbecue joint run by one of five brothers who operate barbecue restaurants in five different Texas towns. "He does his one way; we do ours another," is all Bobby Mueller will say about Rudy, who does score points for uniqueness by serving lamb ribs at his considerably fancier place. There seems to be enough business in this town of about ten thousand to keep them both going. But we preferred Mueller's, partly because it scored better on the calendar test. In general, the more local calendars you see stuck up in a place, the better it is; Mueller's had nine—seven in a row on one wall—and one was from the Taylor Meat Co., Inc. Besides, at Mueller's you can lean back in your creaky chair, listen to the roar of the fans, and imagine what it must have been like to play basketball in boots and spurs.

Rating: Real good.

Directions: To get to Louie Mueller's, take U.S. 79 east from Interstate 35, north of Austin.

P.S.: After Fred Fountaine retired from Mueller's, he unretired himself and started cooking weekends at the **East Street Dining and Social Club,** 111 East St., down the road a piece in Hutto, Texas, where he has friends. The club serves barbecue only for lunch and dinner and only on Thursdays, Fridays, and Saturdays, which sounds promising; but it also serves blackened catfish and stir-fry shrimp. What in the world has old Fred got himself into?

WYOMING

Laramie

PONY EXPRESS BAR-B-Q

o In the 1900 block of Jackson St. o (no phone)
o Tues.–Sun., 10:30 A.M.–7 P.M. o Closed Monday

Bringing barbecue to the high plains of Wyoming is not easy. The rugged, rolling landscape is covered with clumps of dry, tenacious grass and punctuated with outcroppings of rock worn smooth by winds that could loft a Conestoga wagon like a kite. Winter shows up early and stays late, and in the foothills there is barely time for the pine and aspen to push skyward before the rush of fall. The only hardwood growing is scrub oak, and it's a protected species. Cowboy barbecue may be the toughest game going.

But every morning during the summer, Mel Johnson drives the fifty miles from Rawlins to Laramie and parks his bright red trailer in a dusty, windswept parking lot on the west side of town. He does it without fail; he does it because he's the Pony Express, and the barbecue must go through. Johnson's setup is totally mobile, with a tiny trailer that is half sales office, half kitchen, and half living room—and behind that a drum smoker on wheels. He'll show up with the goods at rodeos or company picnics. And the goods are good indeed.

His ribs are hearty and meaty, and his beef is sit-around-the-campfire smoky. Adversity has taught Mel Johnson well. He imports his wood from Texas and manages it wisely. He can explain the techniques of mixing green hickory and dry hickory so that a fire will burn all day unattended. A tall figure in a white apron and cowboy hat, Mel brought his barbecue knowledge to the high plains from Houston. Under a piercing blue summer sky, as the wind whistles through the straw of his hat, it's easy to see why he came to Wyoming. Later on, when the snows have closed Interstate 25 again, it may be a little harder to remember.

Rating: Good.

Directions: You can find the Pony Express trailer on Jackson St. in Laramie, as long as it's not snowing. To get there, take the Snowy Range exit off I-80 West, then go west two blocks.

P.S.: The Cowboy Bar, 309 S. Third in Laramie, doesn't serve barbecue fit to mention in this book, but we're going to mention it anyway. You can grouse about the fact that the monstrous beef ribs are grilled over charcoal instead of being properly smoked; we, on the other hand, will sit beneath Amos, the Mexican steer mounted over the bar, sip a shot of red-eye, and sink our teeth into ribs grilled crunchy crisp on the outside and pink in the middle. "I make 'em the way I like 'em," says Mary Griffin, a towering gal in jeans and rolled-up sleeves. She cooks the ribs out back, and she makes her own sauce five gallons at a time. She'll pour you a beer and tell you so, and add that she helped to open the original Cowboy Bar, just after Prohibition. Prohibition seems far, far away from Laramie now, and if the numerous other places that Mary operates aren't proof enough, check out the Buckhorn Bar. Barbecue isn't even sold under the scores of stuffed and mounted critters, but there's a bullet hole through the mirror behind the bar, and the waitress will pour you a drink that looks like a pickled rat's brain floating in a shot glass—and that's just for sissies. We only mention these places because, if you go to Laramie for barbecue, you very likely may get snowed in and have to stay all winter. Which ends in June.

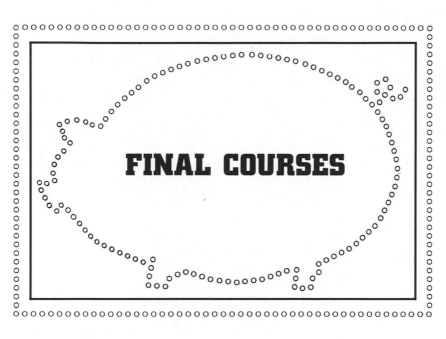

FINAL COURSES

THE NAME GAME

You can eat at Mom's in Los Angeles, Pop's in Nashville, and Unkie's in St. Louis. In Cleveland you can check out Baby Sister's and Mama's Boy. In Knoxville you can sample the fare at Brother Jack's. San Francisco has Bro-In-Law's, and Columbia, Mo., Cousin Bob's. In Indianapolis you'll find Pa and Ma's. In Jackson, Miss., it's Pappy's.

That is one of the best things about barbecue joints: their names. Because barbecue is one of the last bastions of individual enterprise, the naming process hasn't been taken over by ad agencies and public relations firms. Barbecue joints are named by their owners. They don't try to reflect the national mood or cash in on a craze. They don't commission market-research studies to determine optimum name recognition and consumer preferences. They just try to give their places good names. And they do.

The favored name for a barbecue joint is Old Hickory, which graces at least twenty-two towns from West Palm Beach, Fla., to El Dorado, Ark., and from Dayton, Ohio, to Clinton, Miss. Adding in all the variations on "Hickory"—Fred's Hickory Inn (Bentonville, Ark.), the Hickory House (Atlanta, Ga.), the Hickory Smokehouse (Hopkinsville, Ky.), Luchenbach's Hickory Hut (Birmingham, Ala.), Stubby's Hik'Ry Pit (Hot Springs, Ark.)—it is the runaway winner for most popular.

There are a lot of "Bubba's" out there, too. You could eat your way across the country if you knew Bubba. There are eleven barbecue joints operating under Bubba's moniker or a variation, including Bubber's in New Orleans and Big Bubba's in Louisville. In addition, Sikes Bar-B-Q in Eastover, S.C., is run by Bubber Sikes, and Sweatman's Bar-B-Que in Holly Hill, S.C., is owned by H. O. "Bub" Sweatman.

A good name is a good name, even if it doesn't seem to fit. Some good names are just in the wrong place. You can go to the Tennessee Pit in Jackson, Miss., the Tennessee Mountain in New York City, and Tennessee Andy's in Pompano Beach, Fla. There's the Texas Smokehouse in Dayton, Ohio; the Texas Cattle Co. in Baltimore; Bull's Texas Cafe in San Francisco; and the Texas State Line in Atlanta.

Other names seem more suited to a different cuisine. Miami has the Swiss Chalet Barbecue. ("Oh, Hans, I love your sauce.") Philadelphia has Mama Rosa's. (Barbecued spaghetti?) And New York City has The Pink Tea Cup, which sounds like a Fire Island tearoom but is really a soul-food place.

Some names are just plain bassackwards. Lamb's in Memphis

cooks pig, but Chicken Comer's in Phenix City, Ala., doesn't serve chicken. If you're in west Tennessee you can head over to Goat City Bar-B-Que in Milan, Tenn. Just don't go expecting to eat goat.

A good name is a good name, even if it no longer applies.

Big John's in Marble Falls, Texas, is now owned by a fellow named Henry. Brady and Lil's in Memphis is owned by Frank and Hazelteen. Jay's in Baton Rouge is run by Floyd LeBlanc. Mr. Allman has been dead for years but his name lives on in Allman's Barbecue in Fredericksburg.

In Lexington, N.C., John Wayne's Barbecue is not owned by John Wayne but by Mike Eller and Vaughn Miller. The same barbecue place has had a long and confused history. It was originally Stamey's, run by Warner Stamey. When Harold Craver and Paul Cope bought it in the fifties, they changed it to Old Hickory, the name of a restaurant they owned in Winston-Salem. It became Stamey's again in 1979, when Dan Stamey, no relation to original owner Warner Stamey, bought it. Dan was the son of Smiley Stamey, who owned Smiley's Barbecue, which is now Southern Barbecue. In 1981 Dan Stamey sold it to John Wayne Little, who changed it to John Wayne's before selling it to Eller and Miller. There is now a new Stamey's in town, owned by the same Dan Stamey, who had bought John Wayne's back when it was Old Hickory. Whew.

Big Bubba's in Middletown, Ky. is run by H. P. Stainback, who admits no one ever called him Big Bubba before he applied the name to his barbecue stand. "It could be Billy Bob's or something like that, but you've got to have a name . . . I'm two hundred ninety-five pounds and six four, and that's a pretty big Bubba, isn't it?"

Sometimes the name is better than a good name: It is a great name. Anyone who has seen the hard work required in cooking barbecue knows that there couldn't be a more appropriate name for a barbecue pit than Sweatman's Bar-B-Que in Holly Hill, S.C., or Sweat's in Soperton, Ga.

At some barbecue joints you can kill two birds with one stone: The Hickory Pit and Gift Shop in Dawson Springs, Ky. The Ace Taxi and Bar-B-Que Barn in Atlanta. The Bar-B-Que Inn and Donut Shop in Hopkinsville, Ky. Chavous Pit in Beech Island, S.C., is a barbecue joint and auto repair shop. At Paul's Place in Cave City, Ky., you can kill three birds with one bone: barbecue, country music, and square dancing. Our favorite in this category is the House of Prayer Bar-B-Que, Fort Lauderdale.

References to "pigs" are popular in barbecue joint names. A few of the best: Dr. Hogly-Wogly's Tyler, Texas, Bar-B-Que, in Van Nuys, Calif. The Pink Pig in Frankfort, Ky. The Red Pig in Fort Thomas, Ky.

The White Pig Inn in North Little Rock, Ark. The Flying Pig in Hapeville, Ga. The Whistlin' Pig in Fulton, Ky. The Pig Squeal in Waverly, Ala. Hog Heaven in San Francisco. Fat Willy's Hawg House in Rock Hill, S.C. And Maurice's Piggie Park in West Columbia, S.C.

Only Los Angeles would have a Flying Saucer Barbecue.

Here are a few of our other favorite names: Bangkok Bar-B-Que in Claremont, Cal. Barbecutie in Nashville, Tenn. Bar-B-Cuisine in Oakland, Calif. Big Shoe in Terre Haute, Ind. Bozo's in Mason, Tenn. Bubbalou's Bodacious Bar-B-Que in Orlando, Fla. Choo Choo Bar-B-Q in Waverly, Ga. Curtis' All American Ninth Wonder of the World Bar-B-Q in Putney, Vt. Do-City in San Francisco. Hoo Doo Barbecue in Boston. Mr. Boo Boo's Bar-B-Que in Vero Beach, Fla. Beasy's Back Porch Barbecue in Ashland, Ore. The Pits Barbecue in Edmonton, Ky. Radd Dew's Bar-B-Q in Conway, S.C. And Wrinkle Belly's in Atlanta.

Our favorite barbecue name comes from Corbin, Ky.: The Moo Moo Hut.

And finally there is Jehan's in Sanford, Fla. At least that's what the sign on top of the building said. The awning said Skip's. And it was listed in the phone book as Joe's.

BARBECUE FESTIVALS

There is no more serious gathering of serious barbecue cooks than at the Annual Memphis in May World Championship Barbecue Cooking Contest, held each spring on the third Saturday in May. The 1987 contest, the tenth annual, drew nearly two hundred serious cooks from as far away as California and Massachusetts, even Ireland and Scotland.

Because the teams are so serious about their cooking, they are very carefree about everything else. They treat the contest as a two-day party that gives grown men and women a chance to act juvenile again. The craziness starts months ahead when the teams pick their names. They use every imaginable play on pork nomenclature. The Best Little Boarhouse in Texas. Swine Lake Ballet. Capitalist Pigs. Dr. Smoke and the Professors of BBQ. ZZ Chop. Rib Ticklers.

The fun even extends to the barbecue cookers. These aren't your garden variety Weber kettles. Many of the grills have personalities of their own. Ray Green of Euless, Texas, had a whole tableful of trophies he had won at festivals around the country using Bubba, his five-foot-high armadillo-shaped cooker. Joe Amyx, another Texan out of water, brought along his six-foot-high rabbit-shaped cooker, complete with brass genitalia. The Diesel Powered Porkers, a Memphis cooking team, had converted a Detroit Diesel motor into a cooker. It reminded another contestant of the 1986 entrant who had converted his Nissan automobile into a cooker, with the fire in the engine compartment and the meat hanging where passengers usually hang out. The Federal Express team cooked in a four-foot-long, plane-shaped cooker that was so sharp and spiffy you would have thought it was the model the company used during some sort of corporate rally—that is, if you hadn't seen that eerie smoke pouring out of the fuselage. There was a locomotive-shaped cooker and a pig-shaped cooker and, in memory of Elvis, a guitar-shaped cooker.

These were all fine cookers, some of which presumably worked. But there was one barbecue team that stood out from all the rest when it came to cookers. Actually when it came to anything. They were the Leisure Brothers, five guys from Nashville who'd never put aside their leisure suits. In 1986 the Leisures used a card table covered with pig parts and a handmade sign reading SOLAR BAR-B-Q COOKER. They finished next to last and attributed their downfall to the rather leisurely approach they took to the judging process. When the judges arrived at their tent for the taste testing, they were too involved in partying. They served the judges on paper plates and when one judge asked about sauce, the brightest of the Leisures snapped his fingers, mumbled "Oh, yeah," and raced over to the Heinz tent to fetch a sample bottle. In 1987 they were back and more leisurely than ever. "We're here one part for the cooking and ninety-nine parts for the partying," said Larry B. Leisure, occasional spokesperson for the Leisures. The Leisures only spoke occasionally. They prefered to turn up their hi-fi and boogie. They made their cooking area as leisurely as possible, installing a waterbed and a portable bar and an Elvis-on-black-velvet tapestry on the wall. It sure seemed like home.

They had absolutely the most unique barbecue cooker at the festival. And very utilitarian, too. They had converted the dresser, the one that matched the waterbed, into a cooker. Meat in the top drawer, fire in the bottom drawer. They were cooking pig tails when we were there and invited us back for the tasting, but we declined. We don't much like Heinz sauce.

The Annual Memphis in May World Championship Barbecue Cooking Contest is but one of hundreds of barbecue cooking contests held each year. Barbecue festivals can make for a lively weekend outing. We've also found them to be great places for tasting great barbecue. At most festivals, once the judging is over, the contestants start passing out free meat. All you have to do is stand in line. At others you may need to make friends. But that's easy enough. One thing about barbecue cooks: They love to talk about their barbecue. Just pick out a contestant who looks interesting (or who has a large number of trophies displayed out front) and start talking to him (usually) or her. Next thing you know, you'll be gnawing away on barbecue that is as good as you've ever had.

Here is a list of some of the top barbecue festivals held each year. Call or write to make sure the event hasn't been rescheduled.

Newport Pig Cooking Contest, Newport, N.C., first weekend in April (except if it's Easter weekend; then it moves to the second weekend). For more information, write P.O. Box PIG, Newport, N.C. 28570.

Southaven Spring Festival Barbecue Cooking Contest, Southaven, Miss., April. Write P.O. Box 211, Southaven, Miss. 38671.

International Bar-B-Q Festival, Owensboro, Ky., second weekend in May. Write Owensboro Chamber of Commerce, 119 W. Second St., Owensboro, Ky. 42301.

Annual Memphis in May World Championship Barbecue Cooking Contest, Memphis, Tenn., third weekend in May. For more information, call (901) 525-4611.

Grain Valley Daze Cook Off, Grain Valley, Mo., May. For more information, call Carolyn Wells at (816) 763-8823.

Louisiana State Barbecue Championship, Shreveport, La., May. Write 239 Hanging Moss Trail, Shreveport, La. 71106.

Razorback State Championship Barbecue Cook-Off, Blytheville, Ark., May. Write to P.O. Box 1323, Blytheville, Ark. 72315.

Riverfront Barbecue Open, St. Louis, Mo., May. For information, call the National Kidney Foundation in St. Louis. (314) 863-5858. (It's a fundraiser for the Foundation.)

National Rib Cook-Off, Cleveland, Ohio, Memorial Day. Call (216) 241-3888.

Virginia State Barbecue Championship, Fairfax, Va., Father's Day. Write Clifton Gentleman's Club, Box 185, Clifton, Va. 22024.

Arkansas State Barbecue Championship, Fort Smith, Ark., June. Write P.O. Box 5211, Fort Smith, Ark. 72913.

Carolina Barbecue Championship Cook-Off, Raleigh, N.C., summer. Write to 156 Mine Lake Ct., Raleigh, N.C. 27615, or call (919) 846-9758.

One for the Bun Cookoff, Nashville, Tenn., June. Write P.O. Box 140693, Nashville, Tenn. 37214.

Great Lenexa Barbeque Battle, Lenexa, Kan., fourth weekend in June. Call (913) 541-8592. Kansas state championship.

Mississippi Championship Pork Barbecue, Clarksdale, Miss., June. Write Coahoma Co. Chamber of Commerce, P.O. Box 160, Clarksdale, Miss. 38614.

Show Me State Cook-Off, Kennett, Mo., June. Write: Frank Carter, Kennett Jaycees, P.O. Box 165, Kennett, Mo. 63857. One of two Missouri state championships.

Texas State Championship Barbecue Cook-Off, Smithville, Texas, July. Write P.O. Box 647, Smithville, Texas 78957.

Possum Town Pig Fest, Columbus, Miss., fourth weekend of August. Write P.O. Box 2099, Columbus, Miss. 39704. Mississippi state championship.

Taylor International Barbecue Cook-Off, Taylor, Texas, August. Write Taylor Chamber of Commerce, Box 231, Taylor, Texas 76574.

Blue Springs Barbeque Blaze Off, Blue Springs, Mo., September (weekend after Labor Day). Call (816) 228-0187.

Do Dat Barbecue, Nacogdoches, Texas, September. Write P.O. Box 68, Nacogdoches, Texas 75963-0068.

Ribfest, Chicago, September. Founded by columnist Mike Royko and sponsored by the *Chicago Tribune.* Write Ribfest, 435 N. Michigan Ave., Chicago, Ill. 60611.

Riverfeast, Knoxville, Tenn., September. Call (615) 523-7543.

Super Bowl of Brisket, Abilene, Texas, September. Write Box 3452, Abilene, Texas 79604.

World Championship Barbecue Beef Cook-Off, Pecos, Texas, September. Write Pecos Chamber of Commerce, Box 27, Pecos, Texas 79772.

American Royal Barbecue Contest, Kansas City, Mo., fall. Write to 1701 American Royal Court, Kansas City, Mo. 64102, or call (816) 221-9800.

Diddy-Wa-Diddy National Barbecue Sauce Contest, Shawnee Mission, Kan., October. Write P.O. Box 2292, Shawnee Mission, Kan. 66205.

International Barbecue Society Tournament of Champions, Grand Prairie, Texas, October. Write Doug Beich, Traders Village, 2602 Mayfield Rd., Grand Prairie, Texas 75051.

Lexington Barbecue Festival, Lexington, N.C., October. Call (704) 243-2629.

Slosheye Trail Big Pig Jig, Vienna, Ga., second weekend in October. Write P.O. Box 436, Vienna, Ga. 31092.

Livestock and Rodeo Show Barbecue Cook-Off, Houston, Texas, February. Call (713) 791-9000.

PORKLORE ○ Barbecue in Other Countries

Phil Fisher travels all over the world for the Brown & Williamson Tobacco Co., teaching farmers in other countries how to grow tobacco. And when dinnertime arrives the locals usually invite him to their favorite eating establishment. Oftentimes that establishment serves barbecue. And that suits Fisher just fine because he is a barbecue fanatic. "I've eaten barbecue all over this country, all over the world." He has tasted the local cuisine in fifty-five countries and eaten barbecue in many of them.

One of his most memorable barbecue eating experiences came in Spain. "We were in Jarandilla, Spain, my boss and me. It's in the back country. We were staying in a castle turned into a resort hotel. The locals said, 'How'd you like to sample the local cuisine?' I always believe 'when in Rome.' So we walked down the hill to this place." This place was called La Cueva Puta, which translates as Cave of Bad Women. That's right, a combination barbecue joint and whorehouse. That beats the hell out of Ace's—Atlanta's combination barbecue joint and taxi stand—and out of Cafe Tattoo, Baltimore's combination barbecue joint and tattoo parlor. "We walked in and the owner chased the girls out. Then he put what looked like a door across two nail kegs and brought out the food. There was octopus cooked in black ink, raw squirrel, and barbecued goat. Because it was the only thing really cooked, I ate it. It was good, really saucy. And it was an experience."

The story of Spanish barbecue reminds him of the time he had barbecue in Turkey. "We were in a small village and

Continued, next page

Continued from previous page

they took us to the mayor's house to eat. They had a whole
lamb there that they were cooking over a spit barbecue.
They told me that because I was the honored guest I got the
choice part of the lamb. Then they reached over and stuck
a toothpick through the eyeball and handed it to me. Now,
in a situation like that, you can't turn your hosts down. So
I ate it." And what does a barbecued lamb's eyeball taste
like? "I don't rightly know because I swallowed it whole."

YOU'RE ONLY AS GOOD AS YOUR GRILL

Hey, you there.

Yes, you in the backyard with the apron and the funny hat.

The time has come to face an awful Truth about Life: Maybe you
can't judge a book by its cover, but you can tell a heck of a lot about
a cook by his barbecue grill.

A dedication to the never-ending quest for perfect barbecue
means searching for the ultimate apparatus. So a tricked-out grill is
a sure measure of madness—and method.

Yes, it is possible to cook barbecue on the most rudimentary of
grills, darned good barbecue, and we'll even tell you how—but that is
missing the point. Barbecue may be the melding of meat and hot air,
but all of the latter doesn't come from the coals. Boasting and basting
go hand-in-hand, and the war of words over the best backyard barbecue has its own arms race of barrels, dials, drip pans, and smokestacks.

A novice needn't worry unduly about such matters, however. Barbecue fanaticism isn't something one needs to cultivate; it simply
takes over. One day a guy may be perfectly happy with his hibachi and
then, in an instant, he'll find himself eyeing the specs for something
different, something imposing, perhaps even something intimidating,
like a runaway freight train screaming full-throttle down on quiver-
ing tables of innocent diners—something like . . . Big Baby.

But we'll get to that soon enough.

BASIC-GRILL BASICS

There's no shame in using a simple hardware store grill to cook barbecue. Well, maybe there's a little shame. But there's no reason you can't go ahead and do it anyway. The fact is, you can produce delicious meat using such a grill; it's just that some recipes will be out of your grasp due to space limitations or the difficulty of maintaining the right sort of slow fire. The price of admission to the backyard barbecue world, however, is a grill with a lid that closes.

The whole idea behind barbecue is to cook meat slowly in hot air and smoke. With a basic grill, you use charcoal for heat and a few wood chunks for smokiness; that's why you can't get by with an uncovered design. Leaving the top open would be a waste of that precious wood smoke. Also, a covered grill takes advantage of convection cooking (hot air blowing around the food), and that keeps meat much more moist and evenly cooked. The air vents in a covered grill allow a chef to control the coals better, too, damping them down to make for longer cooking times. It's theoretically possible to simulate a covered grill by making a tent of aluminum foil over a hibachi or an open grill; but such a jerry-rigged contraption, especially in a bit of a breeze, is a lot better way to learn new curse words than to cook food.

Step one in barbecuing on a hardware store special is to grab yourself by the throat (you may use either hand for this) and shake until you have sufficiently reminded yourself: "I am barbecuing; I am not grilling. I am barbecuing; I am not grilling." Grilling is what takes place when your neighbor's backyard burgers nuke themselves to cinders in a burst of flame: It's quick cooking over hot coals, designed to sear the meat to hold in juices that would otherwise be boiled out by hot coals. It's fine for hamburgers, hot dogs, and chicken. It is not barbecuing.

Barbecuing is a different proposition, gentle by comparison, that uses lower temperatures and no direct flames. Hot smoke does the cooking, gradually adding its own flavors to the meat, which remains naturally moist.

Starting a charcoal fire: All charcoal is not created equal. Sometimes you can find charcoal *au naturel,* with all the twigs and uneven chunks that come from the real wood used to produce it; that's good stuff. Other good stuff, available in both national and local brands, is made by smoldering hardwoods or mesquite into charcoal and then pressing the pieces together into briquettes. It is possible that some sort of binder may be used to hold the briquettes together, and in "off brands" this can be something as unappetizing as recycled petroleum products. You usually can spot these by sniffing, however, so avoid them. Instant-light briquettes, which are pre-impregnated with starting fluid, are OK for grilling or fire-starting, but not genuine, long-haul barbecuing—because they are consumed too fast, and adding new ones supplies new chemical fumes.

Wood chips and chunks of various varieties, available in stores and by mail order, are not intended to be burnt like charcoal. Instead, they are usually soaked in water for at least an hour (to keep them from burning up immediately) and then added to hot coals to provide true wood smoke.

To start a charcoal fire in a basic grill, the most important requirement is patience. There are a multitude of theories on the best way to light charcoal, from arranging the briquettes over tight twists of newspaper to just tossing on some fuel and standing back. Feel free to argue about these techniques, as well as everything else that has to do with barbecue. The fact is, almost any method will work, as long as you allow enough time for the coals to mature. Usually this will be at least thirty to forty minutes, although a stopwatch isn't a good guide for charcoal. The right time to start cooking is when the hot coals are almost completely coated with gray ash, with just an occasional flicker of blue flame.

However you did it, short of using a tactical nuclear device, let's figure you got your charcoal going. For most basic-grill barbecuing, you're going to want to shove the coals off toward the sides and stick a drip pan (cake pan, iron skillet, whatever fits) in the middle. As the meat cooks over this pan, the drippings are caught; they help to preserve the moisture inside the closed grill and send their sizzling flavor wafting back up to the meat.

FANCIER GRILLS

The popularity of backyard barbecuing has brought a boom in all sorts of charcoal grills better suited to serving up the gen-you-wine article. Once available only by mail order, these also turn up now in hardware stores and wood-stove outlets.

o **The Water Smoker.** These are the cookers that look like R2D2, squatty cylinders with rounded tops. They first became popular with outdoor types who used them to smoke game, but they work quite well for barbecue, too. A pan to hold liquids is mounted inside the closed smoker between the coals (or electric coils) below and the meat above. When making barbecue (as opposed to smoking a turkey), it's good to go easy on the liquid in the pan, as it tends to keep the meat soft instead of letting it get crispy. Some barbecuers complain that the temptation to dump anything, from the rest of your beer to Aunt Olive's rosewater, into the pan means you're likely to end up with meat that tastes like anything but what the Good Lord intended. And it's also true that you add at least fifteen minutes to your cooking time every time you peek at the meat, because raising the lid lets out a considerable amount of heat, and the relatively small charcoal fire takes a while to build it back up. Soaked wood chips can be used with water smokers, tossed in among the coals, just as with a standard closed grill. Some water smokers even have little doors in the side to make adding chips, or more charcoal, easier to do without letting heat escape. (Always add hot charcoal that has been started in a hibachi or pan off to the side.) Most water smokers have simple, semiuseful thermometer dials mounted in the lid.

o **The Chinese Kettle or Japanese Kamado.** These smoking ovens look a bit like decorative vases, the Japanese version being vaguely egg-shaped and the Chinese more barrel-shaped. They are made of ceramic, which is rugged and a good insulator. The coals rest in a firebox at the bottom, which can be pulled out to add more charcoal and which includes an adjustable air vent. Meanwhile, the meat sits in the middle. With the lid off, these Oriental cookers can work like a grill for burgers; closed up, they will contain the smoke for good barbecue. Again, wood chips may be added for extra smoky flavor.

o **The Gas Grill.** Gas grills are easy to light, compact, portable, and nice to roll around the deck. They also are kind of a prissy way to make barbecue. It is possible to buy accessories to convert such a grill, which was basically designed to cook steaks and burgers, into something that will sort of cook barbecue. For twenty bucks or so, you can buy a ventilated metal box in which to put wood chips for smoking (it sits directly on the fire bricks). There even are variations that include a water pan for moist heat. But let's face facts: A gas grill is good for a spur-of-the-moment sirloin, but makes a lot less sense when you're talking about cooking beef brisket for five hours or so. Gas grills can maintain an even heat for long periods of time, but their compact size makes it difficult to fit drip pans in there anywhere or to keep the meat away from the fire bricks. Plus, gas grills are seriously short on soul.

o **The Gas or Electric Smoker.** This isn't the same thing as the more familiar backyard patio grill; these often look like little metal shacks with doors on them. Inside, these smokers use a heating element at the bottom, then a pan or tray for wood chunks, and finally some racks for the meat to recline upon. Like water smokers, these were originally used mainly by hunters to smoke game. But they come with a thermostat and can be cranked up to produce barbecue, too. In many ways, they are like miniature versions of the commercial gas or electric equipment used by Brave New Barbecue restaurants that seem to be in too much of a rush to mess with a traditional pit.

○ **The Backyard Brick Barbecue Grill.** Across America, suburban houses of the proper postwar vintage are possessed of a giant brick edifice in the backyard, a Sphinx of a grill, a superstructure suitable for feeding the masses at a state park. Unfortunately, it is entirely unsuitable for cooking barbecue. Burgers yes, barbecue no. To put this in a more optimistic light, just think of what wonderful planters these brick grills would make! Or fountains! Why, with a little plumbing and some water lillies, it could be just beautiful.

THE GRILL OF YOUR DREAMS

This is the heavy artillery.

When ordinary backyard smokers have lost their charm, and money is no object, do what the Pentagon does: Go shopping for big guns. This selection of barbecue monsters will give you an idea of what's out there. They may be designed principally for caterers and churches, but nobody's going to be checking your ID when you plunk down your cash. Tell them you're with the Church of the SubGenius. Tell them anything. Then pay your money and your shipping charges and wait to see the look on your neighbors' faces. Who cares if you have to park your Pinto at the curb just to make space? This is barbecue, Bubba. And the heavy hitters have to be ready to step up to the plate.

○○○

PORKLORE ○ First Barbecue

The first mention of the word *barbecue* in this country was in the Acts of the Virginia Burgesses in 1610, according to Jerry Simpson, who spent a summer researching it. The Burgesses passed a law "forbidding the shooting of firearms for sport at barbecues, else how shall we know when the Indians are coming."

○○○

o **The CB940.** It has a four-position hanging fire basket. It has cast iron cooking grates and a professional-quality thermometer. It's made of 16-gauge steel, with aluminum end plates, chrome legs, locking caster wheels, and hardwood side shelves. It looks like what you'd get if a gas-grill manufacturer got serious about making something for the backyard charcoal chef. Which is exactly what it is, made by Char-Broil, 1037 Front Ave., P.O. Box 1300, Columbus, Ga. 31993. Complete with a five-year guarantee against burn-through or rust-out, it sells for about $300, plus shipping. The Char-Broil folks are ready for you with a toll-free number, even: 1-800-241-8981.

o **The M & A Mobile Oven.** When your barbecue oven has thirteen-inch tires and fenders, people pretty much know you mean business. This black boxlike affair features a fifty-by-thirty-four-inch cooking area, adjustable cooking heights from four to nineteen inches, and a tongue jack to connect it all to a trailer hitch. The basic charcoal version goes for a mere $690 or so, plus shipping charges and other such details. The price does not include visits to an analyst or the services of a lawyer in the event of possible divorce action. It's available from the M & A Manufacturing Co., Inc., Ashley Bellamy, president. The address is Route 2, Box 359, Loris, S.C. 29569. The company also makes the M & A Patio Oven, which has a petite thirty-four-by-twenty-two-inch cooking area and rolls around like a pushcart on eight-inch rubber wheels. The gas version goes for about $490, the charcoal one for about $295.

o **The Texas Smoker.** If you think a three-by-four foot grill with wooden longhorns for handles might look a little out of place in the "epicurean" section of a department store, you obviously haven't been to Neiman-Marcus in Dallas, where such an item probably is sitting at this very moment, with a discreet $1,650 price tag dangling from it. The Texas Smoker is made by partners Larry Boyd and Charlie Braswell, who have termed it "a piece of furniture that cooks." It cooks meat directly over the coals, on two grate levels, and it displays the shape of the Lone Star state on the end when it's closed. It comes equipped with wheels, although shipping by motor freight is recommended if you live farther than two blocks away (the shipping charge is $200). Allow about ten days for delivery from Neiman-Marcus, P.O. Box 2968, Dallas, Texas 75221-2968.

o **The Grill Doctor's Standard Grill.** The "standard" $1,250 grill from the Doctor ought to be good for what ails bad barbecue. It features an offset firebox at one end of a twenty-four-by-thirty-six-inch cylinder and a smokestack at the other, and the Doctor prescribes a steady temperature of about two hundred degrees in the crossflow between the two. A whole hog will squeeze onto its twenty-by-thirty-inch main grid, and there's a ten-by-thirty-inch upper rack, too. The steel-and-stainless-steel affair rolls around on its own wheels and stands forty-eight inches tall. The Doctor makes house calls, promising to ship a grill within two weeks of receiving an order (shipping is extra and varies depending on how far from Dallas you have been unwise enough to live). It's available from the Grill Doctor, 8311 Westchester Dr., Dallas, Texas 75225. Other versions are available, from $650 to $6,000.

o **The Pitt's and Spitt's Grill.** Wayne Whitworth and his brothers, after honing their designs in barbecue competitions in Texas, began selling grills to the general public, and are now up to about four hundred a year. He sells a $2,950 grill mounted on a trailer, among others. Its design features a separate firebox (to keep direct heat from drying the meat) as well as two cooking areas—a thirty-by-sixty-inch main chamber that chugs along at two hundred degrees, and a twenty-four-by-twenty-four-inch upright smoker on one end that purrs along at a pleasant one hundred forty degrees for slow cooking. The folks at Pitt's and Spitt's don't have a lot of truck with questions such as, "Is that the deluxe model?" "All the grills we sell are deluxe models," they say. The company sells them for as little as $650, and has built one-of-a-kind mobile rigs that price out at $50,000. Some of these they'd ship to you without complaint; others they'd recommend picking up in person. That'd be at Pitt's and Spitt's, 14221 Eastex Freeway, Houston, Texas 77032.

o **The WHAM Turbo Cooker.** It's always risky to call anything "the best," but what the heck. This is the best barbecue oven that plain folks like us will ever be able to buy. And that's not just because it costs $3,500 in all its custom-built, stainless steel glory. This is a cooker with a concept, indeed, a whole philosophy, behind it—courtesy of inventor, restaurant owner, and champeen barbecue chef John H. Willingham of Memphis, Tenn. His basic theory of barbecuing goes against the grain of a lot of traditional wisdom: Barbecue isn't flavored by "smoke," he says. Rather, it absorbs its pink color and distinctive smoky overtones from the "essence" of the wood, the unburned gases that rise along with the smoke from the fire. "Smoke is nothing but ash suspended in a column of hot air," Willingham says. "How is ash going to penetrate meat? Ash would just land on the surface. You can't poke your finger into a piece of meat, and that has a lot more force behind it than ash." Operating on the theory that smoke is just a smokescreen when it comes to good barbecue, Willingham designed his Turbo Cooker to burn clean, with almost no smoke at all—and then locked it up for six years until his patents came through. In its "backyard" version, it's a cartlike affair with a glass-enclosed greenhouse that accepts numerous racks of ribs, hanging and rotating in the hot "essence." There's a water pan beneath that directs drippings over toward the firewall, where they sizzle up and re-enter the whole cycle. The cookers are built in groups of four, whenever Willingham accumulates four orders. "It could be a year," he said. Each is constructed of stainless steel and arrives with a brass plaque with the owner's name and date of construction. "This is built so you can pass it on to your grandchildren," Willingham said, and allowed as how each buyer will be asked to sign a confidentiality agreement not to use the cooker commercially. It seems silly to talk about skimping in this rarified price range, but there's a black-iron version available for just $1,750. Write Willingham at 2707 S. Perkins, Memphis, Tenn. 38118.

HOMELY AND HOMEMADE

Homemade barbecue is the way all barbecue started out, and there's still something noble and uplifting about an ungainly, flat-black contraption smoking away out in the yard, producing delicious barbecue according to its inventor's intentions. It sort of makes you wonder where the Wright Brothers might have ended up if they hadn't gotten off on that whole aviation thing.

o **The Covered Pit.** The simplest homemade cooker to construct, of course, is the pit. All you need is a shovel, a pretty good pile of hard rocks, some gunny sacks, and chicken wire—and the sage advice of Pat and Bill Martin at the Elk Mountain Hotel in Wyoming, where they barbecue four hundred pounds of meat at a time on their own customized spit. And a hog, of course.

First, dig a craterlike hole in the ground a few inches wider than the hog in question (let's take an eighty-pounder as an example), making it about twice as deep, about three or four feet. Once you have put away your shovel, the real work begins: Cover the bottom of the pit with a layer of hard rocks (the rocks are there to absorb heat, not just to give you a terrific backache). Then build a healthy fire of wood or charcoal and let it burn way down until you have a thick bed of hot coals lining the pit.

Next, haul out a piece of chicken wire big enough to poke out of opposite sides of the pit; this will help you lower the pig in and lift it out again. It'll also keep the pig out of the coals, and to help it do that, lay down some aluminum foil on top of the chicken wire where the pig will rest.

Now, a short digression on the pig itself: After it's been dressed by your friendly butcher (don't have the pig skinned and don't poke holes in it), wrap it in gunny sacks soaked with water and a mixture of spices—like sage, thyme, garlic, bay, salt, and pepper—or else soak the gunny sacks in barbecue sauce. Put the pig on the foil-covered chicken wire and lug it over to the pit, lowering it onto the hot coals and rocks. Cover it with more rocks until the pit is sort of leveled off, and then build another fire on top of those rocks. Let that burn down to coals and then go have a beer; you've earned it. For the really fun jobs, like lifting and removing hot rocks and chicken wire, be sure to wear all the protective clothing and gloves your mother would want you to. As a bonus during such back-breaking work, you'll have plenty of time to wonder if maybe you shouldn't have put in a flower bed instead.

Eight hours later, pull the top layer of rocks off the pig with a rake or shovel, grab the chicken wire, and lift up a juicy, flavorful main course, adequate for feeding six to eight people. One of them may point out that the pig is technically not "barbecue," since it cooked in moist heat and not a stream of hot smoke. That person, while correct, should go home hungry.

○ **The Open Pit.** An open pit is a lot like the pit described above, except you go for a deep bed of coals (a foot deep, say) and steel yourself to turning the pig (or side of beef) while it cooks, basting it more or less continuously. Classic whole-hog open-pit barbecue is a bit hard to find, and even harder to do at home, since it requires a hefty spit arrangement that can be turned, in addition to a bucket brigade of basters willing to keep at it for twelve hours or more at a stretch. We're not trying to discourage you, but forget it, OK?

○ **The Cement-Block Pit.** Many big-volume barbecuers, like church groups or contest entrants, use what is basically an above-ground pit made of cement blocks stacked up in a rectangle on some hard surface like a street or driveway (mind the asphalt, now). The blocks are stacked from two to five high, making walls on all four sides. The wood goes in the middle, and we're talking about a lot of wood here, in trip-to-the-sawmill-type volumes. At the International Barbecue Festival in Owensboro, Ky., monstrous versions of these cement-block pits send flames hundreds of feet in the air as they burn down to the requisite coals. Cooking this way requires a lot of tending and turning of meat, with a water hose handy to squirt on outbreaks of flames and somebody strong enough to yank a couple of cement blocks out of the wall when wood needs to be added. At Owensboro, most of the competitors use rough-cut planks of hickory, with a few other hardwoods tossed in for spice. Aside from the actual work of tending one of these, which will continue from the late evening of one day until the afternoon of the next, the hardest thing about cement-block pits may be scrounging for the big metal grids that lie across the blocks and support the meat. You can try looking in scrapyards for big hunks of expanded steel. But with all the scrounging, lugging, lifting, and tending, the cement-block barbecue tends to be the province of teams, usually of men, and frequently of men who can forget about how tired they are tending the fire at 3 A.M. if they just have another beer.

o **Drum Smokers.** The smaller scale of many homemade smokers doesn't lessen the ingenuity involved in building them. You will see smokers made out of segments of oil pipeline, out of refrigerators and stand-up freezers, out of welded sheet metal, and out of the favorite of the barbecuer on a budget, the 55-gallon drum.

God must have loved the 55-gallon drum; He made so many of them. Forget for a moment that most of them seem to turn up on the news surrounded by guys in white protective suits looking for toxic waste. Good, healthy, wholesome drums exist, and they can form the core of an impressive barbecue smoker that a reasonably stupid person can put together with an electric drill, a saber saw, a few hand tools, some bolts and rods, and angle iron. One of your reasonably stupid authors has done it.

First, get the right sort of drum, a drum that won't have you and your loved ones worrying about growing extra arms. Some fairly benign stuff comes in drums that can be found at your average factory, like soaps and other cleaning compounds. Such drums are available in reconditioned form at drum supply places, too. A good washing should whip one of these babies into line. But the best drum, even better than a new drum, is one from a farm supply store, should you be lucky enough to live near one. In many parts of the country, farmers will add bulk molasses to their livestock feed, and this sticky, sweet-scented stuff comes in, that's right, 55-gallon drums. A drum like that you don't even *want* to wash out, and the last couple your authors have bought have had a little puddle of rich-scented residue still inside.

Once you have your drum, try your best to scrape away or sand off any loose paint. If you don't, the heat of the fire will make it peel off later. After you make sure such loose paint is gone, repaint the thing with some high-temperature paint, either the type sold at hardware or discount stores labeled BAR-B-Q BLACK, or else the stuff they sell at auto stores that's made to paint headers and exhaust pipes. In this latter variety, you'll find reds and bright yellows, suitable for adding flames or other painted designs to your stoic black grill.

Next, decide whether you want a single-drum smoker or want to go all the way to full-bore double-barreled barbecue.

A horizontal single-drum smoker is simple to construct: You cut a drum in half lengthwise, add some hinges at the back, and a rack for the meat to rest on across the middle. Getting it up off the ground is really the trickiest part, but you can make legs by welding or bolting together angle iron; you also can just set it atop properly spaced columns of cement blocks for a quick but rather inelegant apparatus. With the lid open, this sort of horizontal smoker can be used as a grill by cooking directly over a fire made in the bottom; to use it as a smoker, build the fire at one end and cook the meat at the other, placing it over a drip pan if so desired, and closing the lid.

A vertical single-drum smoker won't grill; it just smokes stuff, but it's probably the simplest drum smoker to make, because it requires no legs to stand on. The fire is built in a separate pan set on blocks, and the drum (with one end removed) and its rack of meat are simply lowered onto the coals.

These are both fine ways to cook, but your authors admit to a fondness for what we term "double-barreled barbecue" and a grill we call Big Baby. It may not be the ultimate drum smoker, but with both its smokestacks sending forth clouds of hickory and fire roaring out the front, it'll sure scare off your neighbor's dog. And that's nothing compared to what it'll do to your neighbor, who may in the past have harbored a few faint doubts about your cooking ability.

BIG BABY AND DOUBLE-BARRELED BARBECUE

The basic plans for Big Baby are on page 206. Memorize them and eat them (perhaps with a Kansas City-style sauce) before your friends see them. It is incalculably cool to be the first barbecuer on your block with a belching Big Baby in your backyard; however, showing up with the second one falls a bit short of overwhelming. Building one, if not exactly a breeze, is at least not one of those projects that requires the mythical "handyman." Basically, the Big Baby philosophy is to take stuff that's more or less lying around and turn it into a smoker that works on the same principles as the $1,600 jobbies that the pros sell.

The essential function of a top-notch barbecue smoker is to keep the meat entrusted to it comfortably separated from flames and direct heat and yet in the path of the hot air and smoke that give it its flavor. Big Baby does this by burning a hardwood fire in her bottom barrel and using the top barrel to contain the meat and direct the smoke.

The top barrel also serves as a big, self-contained drip pan that catches meat juices. And the vents and dampers located all along the air path mean that the fire can be precisely controlled, keeping it from dying or flaring up.

Besides two 55-gallon drums, the "trick" to the smoker is in making use of wood-stove kits designed to convert such drums into cheap stoves for heating storage sheds and such. The kits come with a cast-iron fire door, cast-iron legs on which to mount the smoker, cast-iron supports to connect the bottom drum to the one above it, plus flues to connect the two drums. From a hardware store or wood-stove shop, you toss in some dampers and a couple of neat little smokestacks for each end to let the smoke escape from the top drum.

BIG BABY

The way Casey Jones would have cooked

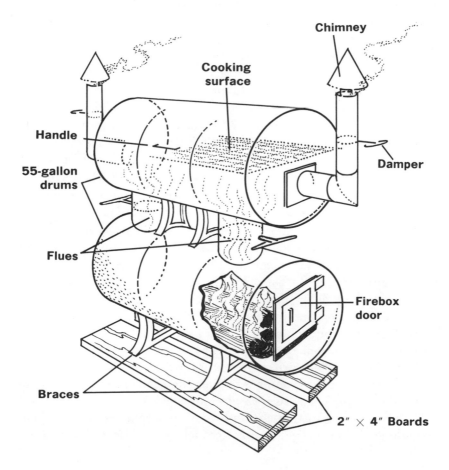

Building Big Baby: Before you get started, make sure you have the stuff you'll need. The drums you should be able to find for about ten or twenty dollars; the stove kits (it takes two) are available at hardware and wood-stove stores or by mail order from Northern Hydraulics, 801 E. Cliff Rd., P.O. Box 1219, Burnsville, Me. 55337, for less than forty or fifty dollars. The two twenty-two-by-fifteen-inch grill surfaces can be had at a barbecue supply house for twenty-five dollars or so. Add some bolts, brackets, hinges, smokestacks, fire bricks, paint and such, and you're up to a total expense of about a hundred and fifty dollars, more than the price of a simple covered grill but considerably less than the cost of a B1 bomber, which, by the way, does a simply horrible job on a rack of ribs.

The steps are simple: Paint the barrels first, then start cutting them with your saber saw. Use a fresh metal-cutting blade (ask the guy at the hardware store or tool rental place for one), and prepare yourself for a violently annoying noise roughly akin to five hundred colicky babies with the croup. Cutting through a hollow drum with a buzzing saber saw makes enough racket that you may want to consider earplugs. Or suicide. But persevere, and cut a hole for the fire door at one end of the bottom barrel and matching holes in both barrels for the flues that connect them. Cut the top barrel in half horizontally, setting the top half aside. Then do your drilling and mounting and bolting, referring to the directions in the wood-stove kit whenever appropriate. Basically, you want to mount the bottom barrel on its legs (and we recommend connecting these to a couple of two-by-fours for a sturdier base), and then mount the fire door to it, followed by the connecting supports and the two flues (remember to insert the dampers before you bolt on the top barrel). Then you add the top barrel, bolting together the supports and flues between the two. At this point, lay the top half of the top barrel in place and mark holes for the hinges and handles. After the lid is in place, you can drill holes and bolt in place a small chain to keep the lid from falling over backwards. About now you can use the saber saw one last time to cut holes in either end of the bottom half of the top barrel and mount the two smokestacks (again, don't forget those dampers). Drill a hole for your thermometer (an inexpensive dial-type candy thermometer works fine, and even includes a clip that will hold it in place). Line the bottom of the bottom barrel with fire bricks, which keep it from burning through. Then drill and mount the brackets that support the grill surfaces, slap those puppies in place, and call one of those fellows who delivers wood. You're ready to barbecue!

It's best to operate this smoker over a nonflammable surface, from something as basic as packed dirt to concrete. The Babe sits a bit low to the ground, and her firebox gets more than a mite hot, so she will send any grass in the area to Turf Heaven almost immediately. For a neater look, you could put down gravel and even border the area with bricks.

Cooking with Big Baby: Big Baby is designed to burn real wood, not charcoal. She'll be happy with just about any hardwood—hickory, oak, mesquite, whatever—but stay away from soft stuff like pine. Build a good-sized fire in the bottom barrel and let it go for a while, maybe an hour or more, until it has formed a healthy pile of hot coals. Avoid cooking over a "fresh" fire, since such fires send up a lot of soot and creosotelike goo. Go for a hot bed of coals onto which you can toss the occasional log, keeping the temperature as even as possible. Barbecue is not set-it-and-forget-it food; cooking it requires almost constant tinkering and tending to keep the heat even over a period of hours. But with a big base of coals for consistency and the proper combination of damper settings for the wind and outdoor temperature, the Babe will chug along at a constant heat for an hour at a time, certainly time enough to go out for more beer or cassette tapes.

There will be very little in the way of barbecue that Big Baby can't handle, from a suckling pig to three twelve-quart stockpots of smoky chili. But she's more than a simple smoker.

Big Baby is a sculpture in basic black, a life-style statement, a conversation piece, a badge of honor, and a joy forever. And on a hot summer day, even when you're not cooking anything, it still smells like barbecue.

BACKYARD BARBECUE
Mysteries of the Meat

Barbecue is Horatio Alger cuisine.

The big names of barbecue have grown almost without exception to fame and (infrequently) fortune from a hole in the ground or a sliced-open 55-gallon drum in the backyard. That makes cooking up a batch of BBQ in your own yard a spicier proposition; you never know when your latest experimental technique or sauce might turn out something truly transcendental, catapulting you into the ranks of the masters and perhaps even the next edition of this book.

After all, if you're not expecting some bragging-good barbecue, what are you doing out in the lawn with your eyes full of smoke? You can get mediocre barbecue at the local Spee-D-Shop or Dairy Dollop; you can get it a lot quicker and you won't smell like a Boy Scout Camporee when you're through. The only reason to cook backyard barbecue is to do it right. Here's how.

GO AHEAD AND USE THE GOOD STUFF

Good barbecue comes from good meat. Though its origins connect it with wild game and its reputation with less desirable cuts, barbecue cooking properly done is a process that can enhance anything from the lowly brisket to the lordly tenderloin. In the competitive world of barbecue joints, owners don't skimp on the meat. Even less-celebrated cuts can vary considerably, and a good butcher can be invaluable in getting you the best basis for your barbecue. Get to know one. Tell him about your smoker, about the big weekend you have planned, and he'll usually be happy to keep his eye out for a particularly good cut. Remember that lots of finicky customers never really talk to butchers, probably because they're afraid they might have to shake hands with them. If you treat your butcher like an actual human being, he'll appreciate it. Don't give him the cold shoulder if you want him to give you a good one.

BE GENTLE

Despite the fact that the finished product may taste hot enough to strip the chrome off a '55 Chevy, barbecuing itself is a gentle process. That means it's best done over fairly long periods of time, without abrupt changes that will "shock" the meat.

Remember: Barbecue is your friend, even if it's your dinner, too. And you should treat it in a friendly fashion. Don't whip a hunk of meat out of a chilly refrigerator and toss it directly over a hot fire; wouldn't you complain if something like that happened to you? Besides, cold meat can attract condensation in a smoker, resulting in a bitter, smoky liquid.

So take it easy. Relax. Make your friend comfortable on the countertop, sit back, pop open a brew, and get to know each other. Start a conversation: "Been puttin' on a little fat there, bub?" It's OK to be a little familiar; after all, you're friends. Besides, later on you'll probably want to trim some of that fat and position the rest so that it "cooks through" the body of the meat when it's on the grill. Or you may decide to carve the cut into chunks of a particular size to even out your cooking time. Also, countertop time is prime time for marinating or dry-rubbing. In general, time spent getting to know your meat won't be wasted.

Keep your little buddy bundled up in freezer paper or plastic wrap so he won't catch a bug while he gets the chill out of his bones, and continue your chat while he does his best to hit room temperature. Perhaps he seems a bit nervous; there's a certain stage fright that comes from being the main course. But if he's been marinating overnight, keeping him tender shouldn't be a problem, unless you've been marinating overnight, too.

TO MARINADE OR NOT TO MARINADE?

Soaking meat in an exotic concoction of liquids and spices is one of those things that just seems like fun, whether or not it does much good. Actually, the process of pit barbecuing is very effective at tenderizing, so that marinades aren't really needed for the reason most people use them—to soften up a tough piece of meat.

It's true that many marinades do have this effect, since the acid in them breaks down fibers and tissue. (Common acid ingredients in marinades include, in descending order of intensity, vinegar, citrus juices, dry wine, sweet wine or vermouth, and apple juice.) A number of professional pitmen, especially in Texas, will have nothing to do with marinading, however, or even basting, because they maintain that a marinade (especially a vinegar-based one) actually draws natural moisture out of the meat in the cooking process, leaving it with somewhat of a chalky texture and sometimes even a bit of a slimy feel.

When some chefs want to add flavor to the meat (the second reason to use a marinade), they tend to go with a "dry rub," a mixture of spices that coats the outside of the cut. Actually, if you like to marinade there's no real reason not to. Just figure to marinade for flavor, not tenderness, and make sure to cut any vinegar in the recipe with something less acid to lessen its effect.

You can marinate for a couple of hours at room temperature or overnight in your refrigerator, but if you're having much in the way of barbecue, finding room to accomplish this can be a pain in the old Boston butt. Fitting odd-shaped cuts like a slab of ribs in any known pot or pan is difficult, and if you can find one, it's likely to be much too awkward to cram in the fridge. OK—great chance to run down to the local discount emporium and get one of those stupid Gadgets You Can't Live Without: the Dazy Seal-a-Meal. For about thirty dollars this apparatus (or one of its cousins) will heat-seal many cuts of meat in a custom-sized freezer bag along with the marinade of your choice. A Seal-a-Mealed rack of marinating ribs fits nicely atop a couple of six-packs. You can stand them up or stack them with no fear of leaks. And you can carry them in their little plastic wrappers out to the grill under one arm, pitching the plastic after they're on the grill. And there are no pans to wash. It's great. Really. Just because you're cooking the old-fashioned way doesn't mean you have to live in the Stone Age.

Barbecue sauces make a flavorful base for marinades, especially with pork, and you can use your favorite. Some commercial vinegar-based sauces can be used as is, or cut with a little beer or cider to dilute their vinegary effect. Thicker tomato-based sauces require a little tinkering:

2 cups apple cider vinegar	**1 tablespoon dry mustard**
1 cup ketchupy barbecue sauce	**1 tablespoon cayenne pepper**
2 tablespoons lemon juice	

Combine all the ingredients in a saucepan. Bring to a boil, reduce the heat, and simmer just long enough to make sure the flavors are mixed. Cool it down before using it as a marinade. If the strong vinegar flavor is not to your liking, substitute a couple cans of beer or even dilute lemonade for the apple cider vinegar. You can let the meat marinate for up to a day in the refrigerator.

A less store-bought approach is to take something that softens you up and use it to marinate the meat. Wine and beer are common bases for marinades, sometimes used straight, though you can find recipes that use gin and even bourbon (which may sound strange, but it beats the socks off wasting the stuff on a mint julep). There's really no need to follow a recipe; just start with a bottle of wine (light for pork, red for beef), some oil, vinegar (flavored or otherwise), and an available spice rack. To a bottle of wine, you can add in the neighborhood of a cup of vinegar, a half cup or so of oil, and pinches and teaspoons of spices, plus any garlic, Worcestershire sauce, or dry mustard that the moment demands. Trial and error is fun, and the errors are never so serious that a little fiddling can't fix them.

AYE, HERE'S THE RUB

Massaging spices into a hunk of meat before barbecuing is an excellent way to add flavor or an undercurrent of heat. Some cooks maintain that a dry rub seals pores in the meat, making it retain its juices; and some even theorize that a rub attracts moisture from the air and

PORKLORE ○ The Battle of the Bozos

If you ate at Bozo's Pit Bar-B-Q in Mason, Tennessee, any time before 1982, would you please give owner Helen Williams a call? Williams, daughter of Thomas "Bozo" Williams, who opened the place in 1923, is involved in a squabble with another Bozo, Bozo the Clown, of Chicago's WGN-TV.

It seems the clown thinks he owns the name.

Bozo the Clown recognizes that Bozo the barbecuer has been in business longer. But he is still fighting Bozo the barbecuer's trademark application. So Bozo's is trying to establish that it has a long history in interstate commerce.

If you took Bozo's barbecue across state lines, call the restaurant at (901) 294-3400. The mailing address is P.O. Box 475, Mason, TN 38049.

Better still, go there and sign Bozo's petition.

Bozo's is thirty miles east of Memphis. To get there, take exit 35 off I-40; then 80 north four miles on Highway 59 to U.S. Highway 70 and east on 70 for three miles. Bozo's is on the left.

After you've signed the Bozo petition, order a "brown pig" sandwich. You won't be disappointed because when it comes to barbecue, this Bozo is no clown.

actually adds it to the meat. Whatever the explanation, the results speak for themselves: Dry rubs and smokers were made for each other. For the most part, rubs are simple mixtures of spices eminently suited to tinkering with, although some pitmen say that salt (although a frequent item in recipes) should be avoided because it tends to draw moisture out of the meat. But other ingredients can be used according to divine inspiration: chili powder, garlic powder, paprika, all types of pepper, mustard seed, sugar, even that bottled "barbecue seasoning." And increasing numbers of commercial rubs are becoming available as people realize that you don't need to soak meat in a marinade if you have the right kind of grill.

A fresh cut of meat at about room temperature should bask in its spices for at least a half an hour before hitting the smoker. Frozen meat can be rubbed down when it's removed from the freezer; by the time it reaches room temperature, it will have absorbed sufficient spices. Also, you can rub meat, wrap it tightly, and stick it back in the fridge for a day or two.

Kansas City chefs often seem to like some sweetness in their rubs. Here's a basic formula from barbecue guru Dr. Rich Davis, the man behind K.C. Masterpiece sauce:

½ **cup brown sugar**	½ **cup paprika**
½ **cup black pepper, coarsely**	¼ **cup chili powder**
ground	2 **tablespoons garlic powder**

Combine all the ingredients in a bowl.

Down in Cajun country, there's more of a tendency to go for the jugular. The following red-white-and-black rub is nothing but hot and is based on a common cooks' aphorism in bayou country: Black pepper gives you the aroma, red pepper gives you the burn, and white pepper gives you the bite. This mixture bites your head off.

¼ **cup black pepper, freshly**	¼ **cup white pepper, freshly**
ground	**ground**
	¼ **cup dried red pepper flakes**

Combine all the ingredients in a bowl.

ACME ATOMIC OIL

A classic technique in grilling meats is to coat them with oil, which tends to keep them moist and seal in juices. It works in barbecuing, too. Olive oil is excellent for this, since it doesn't burn easily. But in the midst of all the excitement attending a barbecue, using plain old olive oil (even the mild, expensive stuff) seems a tad boring. Luckily, olive oil is more than happy to take on the characteristics of various flavorings and spices dropped into it. Try rubbing and basting beef or pork cuts with the following recipe; for better effect, remove the label from the olive oil bottle. The resulting flask full of mysterious ingredients will amaze and astound.

1 **(16-oz.) bottle mild olive oil**	2 **tablespoons cracked**
(about ½ litre)	**peppercorns (white)**
1 **clove garlic, crushed**	1 **tablespoon tarragon**
3 **hot red peppers, dried**	**Cayenne pepper (to taste)**
2 **tablespoons cracked**	
peppercorns (black)	

Drop all the ingredients into the olive oil bottle and let the mixture sit at room temperature for a couple of days. It keeps for quite a while.

SOPPING AND MOPPING

Some barbecue cooks absolutely swear by basting; some won't be caught with a mop in their hands. Both sides can produce delicious meat to defend their positions. Hey, we don't care. If you do it, it won't make you go blind. Actually, basting is just a pleasant bit of cooking procedure; it's fun to peek at the progress of the meat while you dab it with your little cotton mop (available at most restaurant supply stores). Done properly, it can add spicy heat and flavor to a mild meat like pork. But every time you open the lid of your smoker, you're letting hot smoke escape and wrecking the ovenlike conditions you worked so hard to create.

If you do baste, use a basting sauce (one without sugar or tomato, which burns easily). And keep your fire a little hotter to compensate for all the heat you're letting escape. Basting partisans baste a lot when it's hot, while the meat is open to suggestions. Also, adjust your basting recipes to conditions; a sauce like Frank's Sop (see the recipe that follows) has a lot of oil—not appropriate for a cut of meat with lots of fat already. To lighten up on oil, add water or vinegar as part of the liquid. For hotter basting sauces, add hot Hungarian paprika, Tabasco sauce, Louisiana hot sauce, jalapeño peppers, black pepper, or cayenne pepper.

FRANK'S TEXAS-STYLE BAR-B-QUE SOP

Frank Volkmer started out roughnecking on a drilling rig in Texas, but about twenty years ago he decided his fortune lay in barbecue. "I was going to semiretire," he says. "I thought I'd found a gold mine." Aside from nearly going broke three or four times, he was more or less right. At the nuclear plant's open house in his hometown of Bay City, Texas, Frank served 20,000 people, including demonstrators. At the Exxon Day picnic he served 12,500. Then he moved to Denver, where he saw a city just waiting for some good Bay City barbecue. He opened up a catering business and a restaurant and kept expanding until darned if he didn't nearly go broke again. But he still runs Frank's Catering in Denver, and he still slings south Texas barbecue to happy crowds. He has resisted the clamor of Coloradans for a sauce hotter than the mild Texas version he prefers. "Hot is not good," he says. "Hot is to be put on the table and added." So when you dab this all-purpose sopping sauce on a slab of ribs, you won't be turning your pork into plutonium; it's meant to enhance the meat, not explode it.

"It gives you distinctively flavored barbecue," he says. "It has a wonderful aroma."

1 stick	1 large onion, chopped
1 clean rag, torn	thumbnail-size
1 length of string	2 tablespoons vinegar
1 quart cooking oil	2 tablespoons salt
1 quart water	1 teaspoon ground black pepper
2 lemons, sliced or quartered	¼ teaspoon garlic powder

"First, take a stick off a tree," says Frank. "Tie a rag around it with string. This is your sop stick." Then, he says, combine the remaining ingredients, bring them to a boil, reduce the heat, and let them simmer for fifteen minutes. "Don't cook it," he cautions, "just let it boil about a minute. Then keep it warm all day while you cook your barbecue." When your meat is about three-fourths done, start sopping. Keep doing it every fifteen minutes until the meat's done. Frank lists options for this sauce, and the first one is "nine sixteenths imagination." With a caution ("In recipes, if a little is good, more is not better") Frank will accept any of the following added to the sauce: 1 can Coors beer, 1 small bottle ketchup, 2 tablespoons Worcestershire sauce, 2 or 3 chopped jalapeño peppers, 2 tablespoons Tabasco sauce, or 1 medium bell pepper.

"Now, you can add Worcestershire sauce or beer or anything you want," Frank adds, "but the problem with that is, you like it and the neighbors maybe can't take it. A lot of guys put beer in it, get real drunk, and then say, 'It was in the sop!' I say, 'Keep it simple.'"

BARBECUE HONEY

In Kansas City you'll find chefs who like to baste their slow-smoked pork and beef with honey, beginning a couple of hours before the end of its cooking time. Yes, it tastes a little sweet, they'll tell you. And, yes, it tends to burn a little—but who doesn't like slightly burnt barbecue? Indeed, "burnt ends," little snippets of beef from the end of the brisket, are a Kansas City staple. Just as with olive oil, however, it's possible to take a jar of honey into the lab and come out with something frightening: barbecue honey. Add pinches of cayenne pepper or hot Hungarian paprika, even prepared horseradish. The combination of hot, sweet, and burnt is intriguing and unusual, the sort of thing that can set your barbecue apart from the pack.

PORKLORE ○ The Case of the Saucy Thief

The year: 1957. The time: after midnight. The place: Scott's Famous Barbecue in Goldsboro, N.C. A neighbor spots a thief climbing in the window and alerts police. But when officers arrive, nothing. No burglar, only a broken window. They are ready to leave when they hear a thud in the storeroom. They ease open the door and peer in. Two eyes are peering back. There, hunkered down in Scott's sauce barrel, is the burglar. He had almost evaded capture, but now he is stirring because he is very uncomfortable.

"He was in the hot sauce barrel," laughs Jim Scott, grandson of the restaurant's founder, "and that hot sauce is hot. It'll blister your hands if you work in it very long without rubber gloves." Police roll the man out of the barrel and cart him downtown to spend the night in jail. The next morning owner Martell Scott drops by. He isn't going to press charges, he says. He asks only that his broken window be replaced. The man is released. There is no prosecution. But the crime doesn't go unpunished. Police have handed out their own, albeit unintentional, punishment. All night they had refused to let the barbecue burglar shower. He spent his night in jail marinating in Scott's Famous Hot Barbecue Sauce.

BACKYARD BARBECUE
Making the Cut

TENDERLOIN

At the top of the list of backyard cuts is the tenderloin, a lean, tender, and boneless core of meat that runs along either side of the backbone in Mr. Cow and Mr. Hog. If you've ever been to a Southeast-style "pig-pickin'," in which guests help themselves to their meat of choice from a whole roast pig, you know about the tenderloin: It's what was already gone by the time you arrived. And beef tenderloin is familiar to diners in a variety of cuts that usually show up at the expense account end of the menu, like filet mignon (from the head of the tenderloin), Chateaubriand (from the center section), and tournedos (from the tail).

Tenderloin makes impressive, fast barbecue, although we're including it here as a sort of *nouvelle* version because it's served less than well done. It's not cheap, but it can be cooked relatively quickly into a spectacular main dish that is smoky and spicy on the outside but, when sliced, feathers into a plush, rosy pink in the center that is delicate, beautiful, and delicious.

Once you decide on a tenderloin, don't skimp; get a prime or choice cut. And ask the butcher to remove the sheath that encases the meat. It's possible to barbecue an entire tenderloin; the cut tapers at each end, providing a range of "doneness" at any given cooking time. For less meat, consider buying just the part of the tenderloin from the sirloin area of the beef; it's a thick cut that should feed about six to eight people.

○ ○ ○ COUNTY LINE SMOKED ○ ○ ○ TENDERLOIN

Time: 45 minutes to an hour
Grill types: Any enclosed grill

This simple but spectacular recipe comes from Texas's County Line restaurants, which have grown from a single spot into a chain of eleven and counting. In a world of slow-cooked barbecue, this is a relatively fast recipe. The County Line folks may spend eighteen to twenty hours smoking their brisket, but this recipe for tenderloin will deliver a tender, spicy piece of the very best beef in less than an hour. Naturally, it's best on a smoker like Big Baby; but it also can be cooked on a standard covered grill.

1 whole peeled beef tenderloin, graded choice, about 5–6 pounds
Lemon-pepper seasoning

Dab baste (melted butter, fresh lime juice, freshly pressed garlic)

With the meat at room temperature, cover all sides of the tenderloin heavily with lemon-pepper seasoning. Place the meat on the rack in your smoker. (This meat can be prepared on a standard barbecue grill that has a lid; if the meat is to be close to the coals, you may want to place it in a foil "boat," which lessens the grilled effect but helps preserve juiciness. To a hot charcoal fire, add several chunks of hardwood that have been soaking in water for at least a half hour.)

Cook at a grill temperature of 225 degrees. After 20 minutes, begin to check the tenderloin's internal temperature with a meat thermometer. Check it every 10 to 15 minutes; at this heat, it can overcook quickly. Since you're going to be opening the lid anyway, take the opportunity to baste the meat with a mixture of freshly squeezed lime juice, melted butter, and freshly pressed garlic (the exact proportions can vary according to taste; prepare it in advance).

When the meat thermometer registers 150 degrees, you will have arrived at a medium-done tenderloin, with the center a blushing pink. The meat can be served immediately, of course, but it also can be held at a reduced grill temperature of 120 degrees until your guests show up, as long as they're not coming from Fairbanks.

Variations: Like every barbecue recipe ever written, this one can be fiddled with. If the lemon-pepper flavoring isn't to your liking, try rubbing the meat with a fine coating of cayenne pepper; this will produce a slow, manageable glow in the mouth that goes well with barbecue sauces. Or try coating the cut with Acme Atomic Oil instead of a dry rub.

BRISKET: THE TOAST OF TEXAS

What happens between brisket and a barbecue smoker is something akin to true love. The two simply were made for each other. Brisket is cut from the breast of a steer, just behind the foreleg, and it's made up of two main pieces of meat, surrounded and separated by seams of fat. It's this fat, which bastes the meat during a long, slow barbecue, that gives it such a rich, luxurious flavor—not as obviously smoky as pork, but moist and meaty, with a whisper of wood. Brisket is graded prime, choice, and select; any will do, but better is better. Often supermarkets will sell two versions of the wedge-shaped cut, one of them trimmed by the store to eliminate some fat (and sold at a higher price). Many pitmen recommend brisket with a maximum of one-half inch of fat on the outside. A ten-pound brisket can feed ten to twelve people; the meat will lose about half its weight while cooking. Actually, six-to-eight-pound briskets are more common; also, smaller cuts are available, with the second cut (farther away from the shoulder) having fewer fibrous layers.

Time: 9 hours
Grill types: Larger enclosed grill

At Beasy's Back Porch Barbecue in Ashland, Ore., the outdoor pit and the picnic tables overlook Lithia Creek. "We have one of the most beautiful summers you've ever seen," says Beasy McMillan, a happy refugee from the heat of Texas hill country. When he headed north, he took his Texas-style brisket with him and gave Oregonians a taste of something besides fish. Here's his recipe; with it, you can come close to Lone Star-level brisket on any backyard smoker big enough to burn a little wood and close a lid over it.

<table>
<tr><td align="center">DRY RUB:</td><td align="center">BARBECUE:</td></tr>
<tr><td>Cayenne pepper</td><td>Beef brisket, 8- to 9-pound cut</td></tr>
<tr><td>Black pepper</td><td>Oak or hickory wood, pieces</td></tr>
<tr><td>Salt</td><td></td></tr>
<tr><td>Chili powder</td><td></td></tr>
</table>

Combine the dry rub ingredients using proportions to suit your taste. Rub the meat with the dry-rub mix. "Rub it in there good," Beasy says. While you let the meat hit room temperature, build your fire of pieces of oak or hickory, as big as you can and still leave room for the meat to sit off to the side of the grill. When the wood has burnt to hot coals, put your meat on the grill. ("Just as long as you can put it where the fire doesn't touch it, you're okay.") Keep the grill thermometer between 230 and 250 degrees. Make sure the fatty side of the brisket is on top. Cook for four hours, adding wood as necessary to maintain a constant temperature. After four hours, take the brisket out, wrap it in foil, and cook it for four more hours. Then remove the foil ("Save the juice; it'll come in handy in other cooking") and put the brisket back in for hour No. 9. ("That hour gives it its crispness on the outside.") After that final hour, take out the brisket and separate its halves "like a surgeon." The top half is used for chopped brisket. ("This is also known as the outside cut," Beasy says, and can be shredded. "When you go to a barbecue restaurant, you can ask for the outside cut; it's like burnt ends.") The bottom half should be cut across the grain of the meat at a diagonal. This gives you one-and-a-half-by-six-inch slices, completely lean, with a beautiful red ring of smokiness around the outside. Serve with the Texas-style sauce (page 225).

RIBS: BONING UP ON GOOD BARBECUE

Ribs and backyard cookouts are an American tradition, but the few ribs prepared according to the immutable laws of Real Barbecue get lost in all the hordes of sorry, smoking cinders that are either burnt black on a grill or else boiled in a pot of water first. This is not barbecue; this is meat abuse. Avoid it. First, get a good rib—loin ribs (from the back) or classic spareribs from the chest. We prefer spareribs, for philosophical reasons: Ribs should be eaten by hand, by people who don't care that they've just ruined their wardrobe; and country-style "ribs" will tempt weaker souls to use a fork. No one, not even royal personages, can eat a sparerib with a fork. Small loin ribs, weighing less than two pounds, are favored by some pitmen as the meatiest and tenderest cut (they're often called "baby back ribs"). But others prefer spareribs, since real barbecuing works its wonders on them, making them plenty tender. (If they are trimmed of the flap of bone and brisket along one side, they're called St. Louis style.) The best weight for spareribs is generally agreed to be under three pounds—"three-down" they're sometimes called. Stay away from ribs that weigh much more than that; the bigger the rib, the older the hog and (usually) the tougher the meat. Also, stay away from ribs the "right" weight that have been heavily trimmed; they're probably bigger, tougher ribs that have been chopped to sell.

∘ ∘ ∘ FLOYD LEBLANC'S ∘ ∘ ∘
BATON ROUGE RIBS

Time: 1 hour or more
Grill types: Any enclosed grill

Jay's Barbecue in Baton Rouge, La., is one of the best barbecue joints in America (see listings), and owner Floyd LeBlanc can be found there most days turning out delectable meat in his pit. Even on holidays, he doesn't exactly take a holiday—on Mother's Day he cooks barbecue in the backyard for his wife; on Father's Day she does the same for him. And when Floyd cooks ribs in the backyard, this is how he does it:

Pork spareribs, 3-pound racks	Wood pieces (hickory, oak, or
Salt (to taste)	pecan)
Pepper (to taste)	Barbecue sauce (your favorite)
Garlic powder (to taste)	Fresh white onions (1 per rack),
Charcoal (not quick lighting)	sliced

Wash the ribs in cold water, then remove the tough skin from the back using a knife. Salt and pepper to taste and add a little garlic powder. Then go light the charcoal (being sure to use a closed grill) while the ribs sit at room temperature. After the charcoal turns white, put your wood chunks on it. ("I don't soak my wood," Floyd says, "because it kills the fire.") The smoke will start 10 to 15 seconds later. Cover the grill and get the temperature to about 200 degrees (or, if you have a lot of meat, 350 degrees). When you put the ribs on, the charcoal should just smoke, not flame up. If it flares, dampen it with water. Then close the grill again. "The slower you cook it, the better it is," says Floyd. "Don't cook it any faster than an hour. Do it so you can really enjoy it and don't have to rush." Sometime later on in the cooking process, when the spirit moves you, you can add a little more garlic powder. ("Garlic powder gives pork a real good flavor; it kicks out the meanness in the meat.")

Your meat will be ready when you can mash it in the seams between the ribs with your fingers ("Your fingers will sink right through it. If you can, hold the meat with your fingers and squeeze it to test it.") As you approach that point, when your ribs are about three-quarters ready, put them in a pan and put barbecue sauce on them. ("Don't baste em: You loose too much sauce.") Put foil on top of the pan and let the ribs and sauce steam on the coals for a while. "I'm one of the few Frenchmen who doesn't like a lot of spice," Floyd admits, "but if you do, after you're done, slice up a fresh onion and spread the slices on the ribs. The juices will sink into that hot meat." Remove the onions before serving the ribs with additional warmed barbecue sauce on the side.

PORK SHOULDER: SUPERIOR SANDWICH STUFFING

Around Lexington, N.C., if it isn't chopped pork shoulder on a bun, it isn't barbecue. Although it isn't required by law, it's also the favored cut of many other places in the Deep South. Pork is graded differently from beef and lamb, but on the same grounds of flavor, tenderness, juiciness, and cutability (how much meat it has on its bones). For pork, a grade of "U.S. No. 1" corresponds to "prime," and "U.S. No. 2" equals "choice." You can get by with "U.S. No. 3," a grade that corresponds to "select" (and usually the lowest grade sold in supermarkets), but if you're going to spend the next nine hours of your life cooking it to amaze your friends, you might as well spring for the good stuff, which has more fat running through the meat and makes juicier, tastier barbecue. Pork shoulder comes from about where you'd expect on a pig, and it's often cut and sold as arm roasts or picnic hams. But you want the whole thing, bone and all. Look for light pink or white meat and fresh red-tinged bones, not dark ones. A shoulder of about sixteen pounds, even though it will cook down by about half, will feed about fifteen to eighteen people.

Time: At least 6 hours
Grill types: 55-gallon barrel smokers work best; but as long as you can fit the shoulder in a closed grill and get the meat 12 to 16 inches above the coals, you'll probably be okay.

Buddy Halsell runs the Dixie Pig in Blytheville, Ark., where they barbecue nothing but pork shoulder. No ribs. Just shoulder. Buddy's brother Johnny, who runs a different Dixie Pig in Little Rock, always says, "We cook the flavor in; we don't pour it on." So when Buddy's son Bob explains how to cook good shoulder, he doesn't mention marinades or basting sauces. You could follow this basic procedure and baste your heart out, though. Just don't tell Bob about it. Or Johnny or Buddy.

1 pork shoulder	**Hot coals**

First, start your fire (either with wood or charcoal); don't cook until it's glowing evenly. "Keep a side grill going," Bob says, "so you can add coals that are already hot." While the coals are getting ready, trim most of the fat off one side of the shoulder, leaving a little bit. "You want to leave some fat," Bob says. "It's good for smokin' and drippin'. Don't trim the knuckle skin off." (There's a bone joint that sticks out of a shoulder cut which has membrane attached.) Put the shoulder on the grill, trimmed side down first, 12 to 16 inches above the coals. Cook at least 3 hours—and as many as 4 or 5 hours. Now turn it. "You got to be very careful," Bob cautions. "You're going to turn it one time only." (If you turn it more often, the meat gets tough.) "Edge it up, or you'll pull the crispy pieces off. Jiggle it." Then let it cook maybe 3 or 4 more hours, maintaining a good bed of glowing coals underneath. To tell if it's tender enough to be done, take a fork and lift the shank end of the bone; it'll just come apart at the muscle. Then slice or chop it immediately, dabbing it with a rag or paper towel to soak up some of the grease.

SECRETS OF THE SECRET SAUCES

Yes, we're revealing the recipes to some prize-winning sauces here, but we're also urging you to ignore them—or at least experiment with them. Good barbecue sauce is so completely a matter of personal taste that there simply isn't one that can't be "improved."

Half of the fun of whipping up sauces from scratch is the Mr.

Wizard business of pouring in ingredients not covered in any written recipe. An eerie glow fills the room as you burst forth with a mad laugh, "Nyah, hah, hah!" and hold the beaker aloft, filled with a secret formula known to no one else. As the organ music rises, you impulsively take a sip and . . . if you don't turn into a werewolf, you've probably got a tasty little sauce there, friend.

In fact, it's almost a matter of honor to add a hidden element to your homemade sauce. Face it: What's worse than having a secret sauce that's someone else's secret?

One technique is just to fiddle around with the proportions in these recipes; a little more cayenne pepper and you can bring out the sweat beads on your guests' foreheads, a little more honey and you can lull them into a false sense of security. But more fun is to adopt a trademark secret ingredient that will add a distinctive character to the sauce you concoct, sort of a signature effect. A little imported hot Hungarian paprika will raise some eyebrows when dropped into the right recipe. An unexpected dash of balsamic vinegar or maple syrup can work some strange transformations, too. Just keep track of what you add as you add it, or it'll be a secret even to you.

PORKLORE ○ More Barbecue Insults

"Somehow during that great human migration that flooded south after Jamestown, Georgians, an otherwise agreeable race, simply never mastered the art of barbecuing a pig like their cousins from North Carolina. It may have been that all that hard journeying, coupled with the assorted perils of passing through South Carolina, caused them simply to forget the procedure by the time they got down here. Maybe as a people they were just forgetful."—Jim Dodson, native North Carolinian now living in Maine.

"Texans tend to talk louder with their mouth than with their meat. . . . The meat itself is about as much real barbecue as an oak toilet seat."—Dodson

"Shakespeare wrote *Much Ado About Nothing* after sopping his white bread through a batch of Georgia pork sauce."—Caleb Pirtle III

At this point, the authors will reveal a favorite secret ingredient: single-malt Scotch whiskey, especially a pungent brand called Laphroaig. Its intense, peaty flavor will add an air of mystery to a sauce, and you don't need to add much (which is a good thing because it costs more than a college education). But if Scotch is not for you, plenty of alternatives exist. The main thing is the quest. The only perfect barbecue sauce is the next one.

○ ○ ○ MEMPHIS-STYLE SAUCE ○ ○ ○

In Memphis, if your ribs aren't "dry," they're served with a sauce basically like this. Used full strength, it's a typical table sauce. For a basting sauce, mix one cup of the recipe below with one cup of vinegar and one cup of water.

1 cup tomato sauce
1 cup vinegar
5 tablespoons Worcestershire
   sauce
1 tablespoon butter
1/2 small onion, chopped

Dash black pepper (more if you
   want it hotter)
Dash cayenne pepper
1 1/2 teaspoons salt
1/2 cup water

Mix all ingredients together in large sauce pan, bring to a quick boil, reduce heat, and let simmer for 10 minutes. Figure out your own secret ingredient and dump it into the mix.

PORKLORE ○ More Barbecue Insults

"In eastern Kentucky you can ask for barbecue and you are apt to get roast beef," says Bill Powell, a retired newspaperman who just happens to live in Paducah, Ky., in the western part of the state. "That silly bunch up there in Owensboro, they don't know what they're doing. They're kidding themselves. And Texas doesn't even have barbecue."

"In Wisconsin, they think a Sloppy Joe is barbecue."— Bill Schuetze, a Wisconsin native who now lives in Louisville, Ky.

∘ ∘ ∘ WESTERN KENTUCKY–STYLE ∘ ∘ ∘
SAUCE

Belinda Kirby, who works for Falsoft, Inc., a computer magazine company in Prospect, Ky., is a native of Franklin, Ky. and offers this recipe:

½ cup brown sugar
½ cup ketchup
1 teaspoon garlic powder
1 teaspoon onion powder
3 or 4 dashes cracked black
    pepper
2 teaspoons soy sauce

3 tablespoons Worcestershire
    sauce
Pinch of oregano
1 tablespoon lemon juice
½ teaspoon black pepper
2 or 3 dashes paprika
2 or 3 dashes chili powder

Combine all ingredients until blended. Marinate meat in the stuff overnight. Remove the meat from the sauce and grill. Baste the meat only during the last 20 minutes of cooking time. Save the rest of the mixture, bring to a boil, simmer 20 minutes, then use as a table sauce.

∘ ∘ ∘ KENTUCKY COLONEL SAUCE ∘ ∘ ∘

This recipe for a pork basting sauce comes from the Kentucky Home Pork Producers Association, which has been preparing barbecue for the Kentucky Colonels Derby barbecue since 1977.

2½ cups water
1 tablespoon sugar
3 tablespoons black pepper
2 tablespoons butter
¼ cup vinegar
1 tablespoon salt
¼ cup chopped onion

1 clove garlic, minced
1 teaspoon cayenne pepper
2 teaspoons chili powder
1 teaspoon hot red pepper sauce
1 teaspoon dry mustard powder
3 tablespoons Worcestershire
    sauce

Combine all ingredients in a sauce pan and bring to a boil. Reduce heat and simmer 5 minutes. Cool. Refrigerate overnight. Warm before using. Start basting meat at beginning of cooking and continue until pork registers 170 degrees on meat thermometer. For ribs this should take about 20 minutes.

∘ ∘ ∘ OWENSBORO BLACK DIP ∘ ∘ ∘

This is the original recipe for mutton dip used by the Moonlite Bar-B-Q Inn in the mutton capital of the world, Ownesboro, Ky. The barbecue restaurant no longer uses this recipe. But you can. It even goes with beef.

1 gallon water
1⅔ cup Worcestershire sauce
2½ tablespoons black pepper
⅓ cup brown sugar
1 teaspoon MSG
1 teaspoon ground allspice

1 teaspoon onion salt
1 teaspoon garlic powder
2 tablespoons salt
2 tablespoons lemon juice
1⅔ cup vinegar

Combine all the ingredients in a saucepan and bring to a boil. Remove from heat and use some to baste meat. Use the rest as a dip for chopped or sliced mutton.

◦ ◦ ◦ TEXAS-STYLE SAUCE ◦ ◦ ◦

President Lyndon B. Johnson had a reputation as a man who was particular about his barbecue. It had to be like they had in Texas. This is a variation on the sauce that Lady Bird used when making barbecue sauce for LBJ.

½ cup butter
¼ cup lemon juice
¼ cup vinegar
¼ cup ketchup
¼ cup Worcestershire sauce

Dash salt
Dash pepper
2 teaspoons Tabasco
Dash cayenne pepper

Melt butter in saucepan. Add lemon juice, vinegar, ketchup, and Worcestershire sauce. Bring to boil, then add seasonings. Remove from heat, cool, and refrigerate one to two days. Serve as table sauce.

◦ ◦ ◦ DOWN EAST–STYLE SAUCE ◦ ◦ ◦

In eastern North Carolina, they don't cotton to tomatoes. They don't think they're poisonous anymore, but they still don't use them.

1 gallon vinegar
¾ cup salt
2 tablespoons cayenne pepper

3 tablespoons dried red pepper flakes
½ cup molasses (or 1 cup brown sugar)

Combine all ingredients. Allow to stand four hours. Serve as table sauce.

○ ○ ○ WESTERN NORTH CAROLINA–STYLE ○ ○ ○
SAUCE

The meat of choice in western North Carolina is pork shoulder. The sauce of choice goes something like this:

⅓ cup apple cider vinegar
1 teaspoon salt
1 teaspoon celery seed
½ teaspoon cinnamon
½ cup ketchup

½ teaspoon chili powder
⅛ teaspoon nutmeg
½ teaspoon brown sugar
1 cup water

Mix all ingredients together in a saucepan, bring to a boil, and remove from heat. Pour over meat. Use some as a baste and save the rest to serve on the side.

○ ○ ○ BLONDELL'S BARBEQUE SAUCE ○ ○ ○

Joan Blondell (who died in 1979) was a city gal, born and bred in New York City, but as a teenager she worked with a stock company in Texas, and once was named Miss Dallas. Our bet is that's where she picked up her BBQ recipe. Hollywood Studio *magazine said, "The dynamite lady was a gourmet cook before that phrase was invented and loved to entertain friends and family at home. She was devoted to her grand-kids and a great lover of animals. On weekend barbecues, Joan would entertain the likes of pals such as Barbara Stanwyck, Nancy Sinatra, Sr., Orry Kelly, Clark Gable, Bette Davis, Mary Astor, Ross Hunter, and Jacques Mapes and dear friends and former restauranteurs Jerry Jerome and Cecil Hedrick. . . . She often jumped into the kitchen of their famous La Cienega Blvd. boîte, 'Ceejee Upstairs,' to join in the cooking."*

½ cup chopped onions
1 tablespoon bacon drippings
  (or vegetable oil)
½ cup apple juice
2 tablespoons wine vinegar
¼ cup lemon juice

¼ cup molasses
1 cup chili sauce
1 teaspoon ground pepper
1 teaspoon French-style
  mustard
¼ cup ketchup

Sauté the onions in the drippings or oil until brown. Add the rest of the ingredients, bring to a boil, reduce the heat, and simmer for 20 minutes. To use, baste on meats or chicken to be barbequed (during their last 15 minutes of cooking).

I was mixing up some barbecue sauce, trying once again to capture that elusive taste, to create a sauce that would stand the test of time and thwart duplication. I had been playing around with a Lexington-style base, vinegar-thin with spices and herbs to enhance the natural flavor of the meat, but with a hint of tomato and sugar to add a distinction. I wanted something delicate enough to seep through the meat but stout enough not to soggy up the bun. In short, the perfect sauce.

No matter what I did, every concoction seemed to just miss. If it had the right consistency, it lacked something in flavor. And when the flavor seemed close, everything else was wrong. I needed a secret ingredient. Every barbecue cook worth his salt pork has a secret ingredient. I was digging around in the cupboard when I spotted it on the shelf above the sink. No one was looking, so I sneaked it down, measured out a half teaspoon, and stirred it in.

I tasted it, and it was there; it was what I had been searching for.

A few days later I entered it, quietly, in a sauce contest. None of the thirty judges knew it was my sauce. In fact, they had no idea where any of the sauces came from. My Hacking Sauce didn't win—that honor went to Zarda's from Blue Springs, Mo. But it did respectably and finished ahead of such well-known sauces as Maurice's of West Columbia, S.C.; Ollie's of Birmingham, Ala.; and Demetri's of Homewood, Ala.

And it was the only sauce in the contest—or in America—that would tinge your palate while soothing your throat. You see, my secret ingredient is cough syrup.

⅓ cup apple cider vinegar
1 teaspoon salt
1 teaspoon celery seed
½ teaspoon cinnamon
½ cup ketchup
½ teaspoon cayenne pepper

1 teaspoon chili powder
⅛ teaspoon nutmeg
½ teaspoon brown sugar
1 cup water
½ teaspoon cough syrup*

Mix all ingredients together in a saucepan, bring to a boil, and remove from heat. Let sit in the refrigerator covered for five days to allow the flavors to wed.

*but not just any cough syrup. Most of them will make your sauce taste mediciney. The only one I found that works well in a sauce is a clear generic: elixir terpin hydrate with D-Metherphan; hydrate 40 percent alcohol. (Just ask your pharmacist for Terpin hydrate-D-M.)

○ ○ ○ BAY OF PIGS SAUCE ○ ○ ○

This sauce was one of the winners in the 1985 Annual Memphis in May World Championship Barbecue Cooking Contest, concocted by the Memphis Ad Ribbers team. It uses a little of this and that. If you don't have this, use that.

1/2 pound (2 sticks) butter
2 bottles (8-ounce) Griffin's
    Hot-Sweet Mustard or other
    hot mustard
24 ounces tomato sauce
1 (32-ounce) bottle Heinz
    ketchup
1 quart Regina red wine
    vinegar
40 ounces French's
    Worcestershire sauce

2 teaspoons Tabasco sauce
8 teaspoons brown sugar
4 teaspoons paprika
2 teaspoons garlic powder
4 teaspoons Lowry's seasoning
    salt
4 teaspoons lemon juice
1/2 teaspoon chili powder
1/2 teaspoon black pepper
1/2 teaspoon cayenne pepper
1/4 cup Coluin's liquid smoke

Melt butter in saucepan set over medium heat. Add mustard, tomato sauce, and ketchup. Stir constantly. Add vinegar and Worcestershire sauce. Stir constantly, then add remaining ingredients. Bring to a boil, reduce heat, and simmer for 30 minutes. Brush on ribs at end of cooking time, then serve alongside.

○ ○ ○ TWO-SHOT SCRATCH SAUCE ○ ○ ○

A lot of barbecue sauce recipes consist of taking other sauces and combining them in deeply mysterious ways. There's no doubt that such tinkering is loads of fun: If you have a commercial sauce with a flavor you like but no horsepower, mixing in various hot elements can give you a new creation altogether. And if you can get lost in arguments over whether to add Heinz (wrong) or Brooks (right) when a recipe calls for ketchup, then you won't be missing the fun in assembling sauces from other people's bottles.

Still, it's possible to yearn for a sauce that starts at square one, with no Worcestershire, no ketchup, no Thousand Island dressing. This is such a sauce, based in the distant past on a Texas sauce recipe in a Time-Life cookbook. It has experienced the usual number of mutations, including a couple shots of unblended Scotch whiskey, but it retains the characteristics that make it distinctive: It is chunky and rich with flavor that seems straight from the garden. It is thick to the point of being stubborn, thick enough to cling tenaciously to a rack of ribs (be sure to apply it only in the last 15 minutes or so of cooking, or it will turn black and crusty). And finally, it has the characteristic that hardcore barbecue fiends insist upon: It is hotter than bare legs on black vinyl.

3 cups chopped onions
½ cup vegetable oil
1 tablespoon chopped garlic
1 (1-pound) can tomatoes,
    drained and chopped
1½ cups tomato puree
2 tablespoons dried red pepper
    flakes
2 tablespoons chili powder
1 teaspoon ground cumin

2 tablespoons dry mustard
2 tablespoons sugar
3 tablespoons white vinegar
1 teaspoon salt
½ teaspoon hot Hungarian
    paprika
1 tablespoon pure Vermont
    maple syrup
2 shots Laphroaig unblended
    Scotch whiskey
Cayenne pepper, to taste

Sauté onions in oil until soft. Add garlic and cook two minutes. Add tomatoes, tomato puree, dried red pepper, chili powder, cumin, dry mustard, sugar, vinegar, salt, paprika, maple syrup, and Laphroaig. Cook over low heat for about an hour. Add cayenne pepper to taste. Cool and puree until smooth.

SIDE DISHES

Man cannot live by smoked meat alone.

But some dishes are better than others to serve alongside home-made barbecue. These can range from a sharp slaw that rejuvenates the old taste buds to the funky smokiness of Trixie's Baked Beans, which conspire rather than compete with a slab of ribs.

PORKLORE ○ Big Pig

The grand marshal of the 1986 Lexington Barbecue Festival Parade was Norma Jean, a two-year-old, 600-pound, house-broken Duroc pig, who lives in a room in the home of Dr. and Mrs. Norman Sattler of Lumberton, N.C. Norma Jean got so large by pigging out on her favorite foods—Godiva chocolates and champagne.

Some sections of the country practically insist that certain side dishes be served alongside barbecue, dishes with traditions almost as long as those of the main course. If you haven't whomped up a pot of Brunswick stew or burgoo, ladled any hash over rice, or stuffed down a second helping of sweet potato pie, then you're missing a treat. Keep reading, though; your days of deprivation are about to end.

Most of the recipes included here are family recipes, with family-size proportions that serve a dozen or so semistarving, semipolite people without starting too many fights in the serving line. For your nutrition-conscious guests, we have included a number of incredibly sweet or unconscionably unhealthy dishes and desserts that should serve to make them feel much better about eating the barbecue itself.

∘ ∘ ∘ TRIXIE'S BAKED BEANS ∘ ∘ ∘

Trixie is a party animal, and these are party beans made to be eaten outdoors under a blue sky with hot barbecue and cold beer. The recipe makes a few concessions to modern life, like using canned instead of dried beans; such shortcuts keep the things from being such a chore that you shy away from making a mess on fairly short notice.

There's chopped (or pulled) pork in the recipe, which you'll have to cook or buy in advance, so there's a little bit of planning. And part of getting the taste right involves letting the beans simmer for a while as you tamper with the precise formula on the stovetop. Start cooking 'em early on the day of a party; the pungent perfume from the kitchen will keep you in the right mood. You also can stick a stockpot full of Trixie's finest on a 55-gallon drum barbecue smoker; they'll cook up with an extra suffusion of smoke, which you can increase by gently stirring the beans frequently.

2 (15½-ounce) cans white beans
2 (40-ounce) cans pork and
 beans
6 ounces smoked pork, chopped
 or pulled
3 medium white onions, cored
 and quartered
2 tablespoons spicy mustard
2 tablespoons white vinegar
½ cup Brooks (or very tangy)

ketchup
¼ cup dark brown sugar
¼ cup pure Vermont maple
 syrup
1 teaspoon horseradish
1 shot unblended Scotch
 whiskey
¾ cup hot barbecue sauce
Generous splash of hot red
 pepper sauce (to taste)

Drain beans. Place into a pot with the rest of the ingredients. Mix as gently and as little as possible to combine. Taste and adjust seasonings—hotter or sweeter—to taste. May be cooked in a crock pot, on a stove, or in a smoker. As the beans cook, gently stir periodically. Simmer, covered, for two hours, then uncovered for one hour.

○ ○ ○ THE RIB JOINT ROADHOUSE'S ○ ○ ○ BLACK BEANS AND RICE

The Rib Joint Roadhouse Restaurant is a 1930s log cabin built into a hill along State Road 1 in Dana Point, Calif. The rough-hewn interior is dotted with license plates from Samoa to Ontario, from Tasmania to São Paulo. Sam Ibreighith, who has been running the restaurant for about nine years, came from South Jerusalem himself; and his unique perspective resulted in this excellent side dish for anyone a little bored with baked beans. This mixture is tasty, funky, and just fine with ribs.

1 gallon raw rice
½ gallon dried black beans, soaked in cold water overnight
½ pound bacon, chopped
2 onions, chopped
2 stalks of celery, chopped
2 tablespoons black pepper

2 tablespoons ground cumin
1 tablespoon crushed garlic
1 tablespoon ham base (or bouillon)
1 tablespoon beef base (or bouillon)
1 tablespoon Mexican oregano
10 crushed bay leaves

Bring 2 gallons of water to a boil, add the rice, cover, reduce the heat, and cook 20 minutes or until all liquid is absorbed. Set aside. Next, begin cooking the beans in 2½ gallons of boiling water; cook for 1½ hours or until beans are soft when squeezed between your fingers. While the beans are cooking, heat the bacon in a pan until it releases its fat. Add the onions and celery, and sauté until soft. Set aside. After the beans are cooked, drain them, add the rice, the sautéed bacon mixture, and the remaining ingredients. Mix well, bring to a boil, and let cook one minute. Bake covered in preheated 350-degree oven for 20 to 30 minutes. Serves a hungry crowd. (If you want to cut the size of the recipe, keep the ratio of rice to beans the same and reduce the spices accordingly.)

◦ ◦ ◦ LEO & SUSIE'S ◦ ◦ ◦
FAMOUS BAKED BEANS

This recipe comes from Leo & Susie's Famous Green Top Barbecue Cafe in Dora, Ala.

6 slices bacon
½ medium onion, chopped
Chopped Bell peppers, to taste
¼ cup barbecue sauce (Green

Top, if you've got it)
1 (32 ounce) can of pork and
beans

Preston Headrick, Leo & Susie's Famous Son, says, "Sauté the bacon, then add the onions, bell peppers, and sauce. Put all this in a big pot, add the beans, and cook them real slow on the stove until they're tender. Don't bake them."

◦ ◦ ◦ MAMMY'S GREEN BEANS ◦ ◦ ◦

Her real name is Herbert Shankel, but you can call her Mammy. "No one would ever believe that Herb was my name," she says. Herb acquired the unusual name because she was the seventh girl born in her family. "My mama and papa wanted a boy so bad that they hadn't even bothered to pick out a girl's name."

She picked the nickname Mammy. "All the kids in the neighborhood were always coming over to my house and I'd give them a popskull—that's what we always called Pepsis—and they'd thank me and every one of them would have trouble with my name. They'd call me Hobbie and Hubie. So I just told them all to call me Mammy, I was just like their mammies. They're all grown with children of their own now. But a lot of them'll drop in ever once in a while and say, 'Mammy, I brought my kids, I wanted them to meet you.' And I'll get the young 'uns a popskull out of the refrigerator and maybe put on a pot of beans."

It is those beans that Mammy's young 'uns haven't forgotten— guaranteed to be the best green beans you've ever tried, juicy and greasy and so full of flavor. Here is her recipe.

3 pounds green beans
2-inch cube ham fat
½ cup cooking oil
1 tablespoon sugar

Dash pepper
Dash salt
Water

"Take and wash the beans and break 'em in small pieces. Then throw 'em in a pot with the ham fat. Add your oil and sugar and salt and pepper. Cover them with water and cook it for about 3 hours. The beans should come out almost shiny."

○ ○ ○ JOHNNY CAKES ○ ○ ○

This recipe may be about as old as barbecue itself. The name is a corruption of "Shawnee cakes," and the Indians would whip them up on hot flat rocks. It's okay if you use a stove.

2 cups white cornmeal	3 cups boiling water
1 teaspoon salt	Shortening for frying

Mix cornmeal and salt in deep earthenware bowl. Slowly pour boiling water into it, stirring constantly to scald all of meal. This may take a little more or a little less than 3 cups of water, depending on the texture of the meal. When mixture is well stirred, allow to set for 10 to 15 minutes, with bowl covered. Then meal should be so stiff it has to be pushed off the spoon onto the hot greased griddle. With pancake turner, pat the meal into flat cakes, about three-eighths of an inch thick. When one side is a rich brown, beginning to turn darker, turn and cook other side. The two sides should have a thick, nutty crust, and the inside should be cooked through. Butter, honey, and maple syrup have been known to associate with Johnny cakes.

○ ○ ○ CHEESY CORNBREAD ○ ○ ○

This is a bridal shower recipe, which means two things: (1) It's good enough to give as a gift, and (2) it's hard to louse up. Although blank white Wonder Bread is served alongside much of the great barbecue at joints across America, cornbread makes a good accompaniment, too. Yes, you can eat it by the wedge, hot and steaming with a pat of butter. But you also can shove the leftover crumbs around on the plate where the sauce is and pick up a sloppy fingerful of spicy, cheesy cornbread that doesn't need butter to send you back for more.

1½ cups yellow cornmeal	2 canned jalapeño peppers,
1 tablespoon baking powder	finely chopped
1 teaspoon salt	2 tablespoons minced green bell
1 (14½-ounce) can cream-style	pepper
corn	2 tablespoons minced onion
⅔ cup salad oil	1 cup grated sharp cheddar
1 cup sour cream	cheese

Stir the cornmeal, baking powder, and salt together in a bowl. Add everything except cheese. Mix. Pour ½ mixture into hot, greased 10½-inch-round iron skillet or pie pan. Sprinkle half of the cheese over this—add remaining mixture and cover with the other ½ cup cheese. Bake at 350 degrees for 35–40 minutes. Serves six.

○ ○ ○ **MOONLITE BURGOO** ○ ○ ○

Owensboro's Moonlite Bar-B-Q Inn is run by Ken Bosley, along with his two brothers and sister. "And we have the third generation working here for us now," he says proudly. Three generations of Bosleys have specialized in cooking mutton: "We take hickory wood and build a fire in our pits and keep it under the meat at all times," explains Ken. "We cook mutton about sixteen hours, basting it a little after it's turned."

For side dishes, Ken suggests serving potato salad, cole slaw, barbecue beans, or burgoo. Burgoo is a native Kentucky stew, not unlike the Brunswick stew favored in the Carolinas and Georgia. Here is the Moonlite's burgoo recipe, which yields three gallons.

4 pounds mutton, on the bone	¾ cup ketchup
1 to 3 pounds chicken	Juice of one lemon
5 pounds potatoes, peeled and diced	2½ tablespoons salt
¾ pound cabbage, ground or chopped fine	2 tablespoons black pepper
	1 teaspoon cayenne pepper
¾ pound onion, ground or chopped fine	½ cup Worcestershire sauce
	¾ cup vinegar
2 cups fresh corn (or 2 [17-oz.] cans corn)	3 (10¾-ounce) cans tomato puree

Gently boil mutton in enough water to cover. Cook until tender, about 2 to 3 hours. Throw out broth and bones. Chop meat fine. Set aside. Gently simmer chicken in two gallons of water in a large kettle until tender. Remove chicken. Add potatoes, cabbage, onion, corn, ketchup, and one gallon of water to chicken broth. Meanwhile, chop chicken meat. Discard bones and skin. When potatoes are tender, add chicken, mutton, lemon, salt, pepper, cayenne pepper, Worcestershire sauce, vinegar, and tomato puree. Let this simmer for two hours or longer, stirring occasionally as it thickens.

The Moonlite is one of the few barbecue restaurants that sells its own cookbook. You can order the *Moonlite Bar-B-Que Inn Cookbook* by sending a check or money order for $5.95 to: Moonlite Bar-B-Que Inn Cookbook, Moonlite Bar-B-Q Inn, Inc., 2708 Parrish Ave., Owensboro, Ky. 42301.

○ ○ ○ **BARBECUE COLE SLAW** ○ ○ ○

This is cole slaw made with the same stuff that's used to baste barbecue in western North Carolina. The amounts aren't real exact; experiment a bit.

1 medium head white cabbage	barbecue sauce
¼ head red cabbage	½ cup water
3 tablespoons granulated sugar	¼ teaspoon cayenne pepper
1 cup cider vinegar	Freshly ground pepper, salt,
1 tablespoon grated onion	and hot pepper sauce, to
⅔ cup catsup or thick	taste

Grate the cabbages and combine. May be stored in refrigerator in cold water for several hours before using. Drain before mixing with other ingredients.

Cook sugar and vinegar in saucepan until the sugar dissolves. Add remaining ingredients and simmer for 10 minutes. Pour over cabbage, toss, and drain well. Chill and serve.

○ ○ ○ **MAPLE SYRUP PIE** ○ ○ ○

There's no particular reason for this subtle, luxurious pie to show up in a book about barbecue, but it's so good that the recipe ought to appear in every book published, including new editions of War and Peace. *The recipe (actually for* Tarte au Sirop d'Erable*) comes from Aux Anciens Canadiens, a restaurant in old Quebec that specializes in down-home up–North Canadian cuisine. Since the eastern provinces seem to be constitutionally unable to produce good barbecue, this recipe is sort of a consolation prize for our neighbors to the north. And some consoling! This pie is simple, but simply divine, rich enough to make you beg for more and light enough to let you eat it. The recipe makes three pies, which will barely be enough.*

1 cup pure maple syrup	2 tablespoons soft butter
1½ pound brown sugar	4 eggs
1½ cups whipping or heavy	3 unbaked 9-inch pie shells
cream	

Beat together the syrup, sugar, cream, butter, and eggs. Pour into the pie shells. Bake 40 minutes at 350 degrees or until a knife inserted near the center comes out clean. Serve with additional warmed cream poured over each slice.

○ ○ ○ **MAMA'S HOT AND GREASY** ○ ○ ○
FRIED PIES

One accoutrement that seems to cross barbecue-style lines is the lowly fried pie. We found it, or commercial versions of it, on sale in barbecue places from North Carolina to California and from New England to south Florida. The first fried pie we ever had hooked us. It came right off the top of a pot of boiling grease. It was made by Jerry Woods's grandmother, Mama (that's what Jerry called her). Mama lugged out a skillet as big as she was, dumped in enough grease to keep Elvis's hair in place for a year, fired it up to the boiling point, and dropped in half-moon-shaped pieces of dough with apple filling inside. She fried them until they turned the color of red clay, then fished them out, dabbed the grease off with a paper towel, and handed each of us one. That was thirty years ago. We tracked Mama down in southern California. She says the weather's fine, stays the same all the time, bores her to death, and makes her wish she were back in east Tennessee where they have seasons.

To make her famous pies, she starts with the fruit.

1–3 pounds dried apples (dried apricots or dried peaches	can be substituted—or mix all 3 fruits together)
	Sugar

"Wash the fruit real good. Soak it in water overnight. Put it in a large pot and cook it in a small amount of water on low heat until it's tender. Stir it occasionally and don't let it stick. Add sugar to your taste. Continue to cook it until it begins to thicken. Keep stirring. When it gets thick, remove it from the stove. When it cools down enough, mash it with your hands or through a sieve. Let it stand until it's cool. Any extra you can freeze."

Now for the crust.

1 cup sweet milk (whole milk)	1 tablespoon vinegar
2 cups flour	½ teaspoon baking powder
½ teaspoon salt	2 tablespoons Crisco shortening
½ teaspoon baking soda	

Mix the milk, flour, salt, baking soda, vinegar, and baking powder until there are no lumps. Gently work in the Crisco. Put in the refrigerator until chilled. Pinch off in little balls and roll them out on a floured board. Put one tablespoon of fruit on each piece of dough, then roll the dough over and seal the edges.

Fry in a skillet filled with hot melted Crisco until golden brown.

∘ ∘ ∘ **WILBER'S BANANA PUDDING** ∘ ∘ ∘

Wilber's in Goldsboro, N.C., is famous in the Down East Barbecue Belt for its barbecue and its banana pudding. Wilber Shirley, the owner, won't give away his secret sauce recipe. But he agreed to part with the banana pudding secret. "People think it's a complicated recipe, and I don't tell them otherwise," says Wilber. "There ain't nothing to it. My granddaughter could make it if she didn't eat all the cookies first." Here it is:

1 package vanilla pudding   Box of vanilla wafers
4 medium bananas

"Mix up the vanilla pudding according to the directions on the box. Then slice the bananas and stir in along with vanilla wafers to taste. We like to use a lot of wafers to give it a kind of cakey taste."

∘ ∘ ∘ **AUNT ESTHER'S** ∘ ∘ ∘
SWEET POTATO PIE

Vince's Aunt Esther Shanks, who lives in Leesburg, Tenn., says, "My people all come from over around Shelby, N.C. They raise a lot of sweet potatoes over there. Too many sweet potatoes. They got to figure out ways to eat them." Here's a good way, the sweet potato pie recipe passed down through four generations of the Sutherland family of Shelby, N.C.

2 9-in. unbaked pastry shells   2 cups sugar
5 or 6 medium sweet potatoes,   2 tablespoons cornstarch
    peeled and sliced thin. ("I   ¼ pound (1 stick) margarine
    like the white sweet   Dash nutmeg
    potato.")   1½ cups water

Use one pastry shell to line a 13-by-9-inch pan (or a circular pan). Then place the sliced sweet potatoes in shell. Mix sugar and cornstarch together and sprinkle over sweet potatoes. Arrange margarine pats on top, and sprinkle lightly with nutmeg. Add water. Now put on the top crust. Bake at 350 degrees for 45 minutes or until sweet potatoes are tender.

Vince's mother, Margie Staten, is the finest pie chef in east Tennessee. At least that's what Vince says.

Let's let him describe her speciality:

My most vivid childhood memory is of sitting on the kitchen floor, playing with my cowboy figures while my mother baked. She was always cooking sweets—cream puffs, coconut pies, pumpkin pies, jam cakes, sheet cakes—and passing the beaters down to me to lick.

She ran a catering business for a number of years but is now retired. Her pecan and coconut pies are both outstanding contributions to a barbecue meal. Here are her secret recipes.

○ ○ ○ MOTHER'S PECAN PIE ○ ○ ○

I've eaten pecan pie at innumerable barbecue stands, and it is all wonderful. But none can stand up to Mother's.

¼ cup (½ stick) margarine
4 eggs
¾ cup white sugar
1¼ cup white Karo syrup

1 tablespoon vanilla
1 cup pecans (cut up)
Unbaked 9-inch pie shell

Melt margarine. Beat eggs, add sugar and syrup. Add melted margarine, vanilla, and nuts. Mix well. Pour into pie shell. Bake in 325-degree oven for 25–30 minutes or until a knife inserted in the center comes out clean.

○ ○ ○ MOTHER'S CHOCOLATE ○ ○ ○ MERINGUE PIE

This pie will stand the test of time. But what I like best of all is Mother's meringue. I think it is better than Mary's meringue at the Family Pie Shop in DeVall's Bluff, Arkansas, and many people think Mary's is the best in the world.

2½ cups milk
3 tablespoons flour
1¼ cups sugar
2 tablespoons cocoa

3 eggs, separated
2 tablespoons butter
1 teaspoon vanilla
Baked 9-inch pie shell

Scald milk. Combine flour, sugar, and cocoa. Set egg whites aside for the meringue. Beat egg yolks until thick and lemon colored. Add flour, sugar, and cocoa mixture, and combine. Add some scalded milk and mix. Pour into the remaining milk and cook, while stirring, until thick. Remove from heat and mix in butter and vanilla. Cool. Pour into baked crust.

Now make the meringue:

1 tablespoon cornstarch	6 tablespoons sugar (½ cup)
2 tablespoons cold water	1 teaspoon vanilla
½ cup water	Dash of salt
3 egg whites	

Blend cornstarch and cold water in a bowl. Bring water to a boil in a saucepan. Add cornstarch mixture and cook, stirring constantly, until clear and thickened. Let stand until cool. With electric mixer at high speed, beat egg whites until stiff. Add sugar and continue beating at low speed. Add vanilla and salt. Gradually beat in cold cornstarch mixture until stiff and shiny. Spread over the chocolate pie filling and to the edges of the crust to seal it. Bake in 400-degree oven for 10 minutes.

○ ○ ○ MOTHER'S COCONUT ○ ○ ○ MERINGUE PIE

It's easy to turn the chocolate meringue pie recipe into a recipe for coconut meringue pie. Just omit the cocoa. Then fold in 1 cup flaked or shredded sweetened coconut after you have added the butter and vanilla. The rest is the same.

Also add coconut to the meringue. After you have slathered the meringue on the pie filling, sprinkle ¼ cup flaked or shredded sweetened coconut on top. The rest is the same.

PORKLORE ○ The Big Fix

Only in Cleveland would a barbecue cook-off contestant claim the fix was on. That's what Calhoun's, a Knoxville restaurant, did in 1985 when it failed in its bid to repeat as national champion. Michael Chase, owner of Calhoun's, had a bone to pick with contest organizer Gary Jacob. Chase charged that Jacob, who also tabulated the ballots, had worked as a consultant to the winner prior to the event and that one of the thirty judges was negotiating a limited partnership with the winner. Both charges were true, but Jacob said neither affected the final results. Calhoun's threatened legal action, but thus far no case has been filed. Jacob says that all the smoke has only given him a bad reputation. "People think I'm the Al Capone of ribs."

COLLECTOR'S ITEMS
Mail-Order Masterpieces

The day may come when you and your buddies finally have finished battling over the best ribs in town. And popular acclaim is the worst thing that can happen to a barbecue joint, transforming a lovely secret into a boring certainty. Worse still is uncontested local dominance; it's a barbecue fanatic's nightmare—no more sticky-fingered arguments, no more sudden Saturday trips to settle the issue beside a smoking pit, nothing but succulent, perfect barbecue, day after day, night after night, forever.

Should you find yourself trapped in such epicurean ennui or, worse still, in a blighted area of our great nation that's shy on smokers altogether, don't despair. There's an exciting cure for the barbecue blahs: Start a sauce collection. To do that properly, you've either got to do a lot of traveling, or else you've got to start licking a few stamps in with the spareribs. Short of bringing the stuff home with you after a barbecue safari (still the recommended way to acquire sauces), mail order is the best bet.

It's true that there are barbecue sauces sold in the grocery store, and it's also true that some of these are starting to go beyond the ketchupy predictability of supermarket sauces past. (The mass-marketing of what once had been a good regional sauce, K.C. Masterpiece, is an example of how the store shelves are showing signs of shaping up. There's even Kraft Kansas City style.) Still, any sane grocer won't be filling up his valuable shelf space with a smorgasbord of sauces for you and your finger-licking friends. For true variety you'll have to go elsewhere.

Luckily, a crowd of chefs stands ready and eager to send you sauces through the U.S. mails or via various package-delivery outfits. You can mail order what is arguably the best sauce made in Missouri, as well as a mustard-based masterpiece from Georgia that's arguably better.

Note that the operative word here is "arguably." The magic of mail order can plunge you back into the fray of the barbecue wars, clashing with your compatriots over the merits of a clingy, ketchupy sauce from Texas versus a vinegar-based concoction from the Carolinas. Your acclaimed local (or backyard) barbecue may be the reigning champeen, but it becomes merely the arena for Round Two: namely, the battle over the Best Sauce in America. And that, we confidently predict, is a mighty struggle with no peace treaty in sight.

CARE AND FEEDING AND ONE-UPMANSHIP

Barbecue sauce is not tender stuff, but it ought to be refrigerated after you open it. Sauce left to sit out indefinitely undergoes some, shall we say, "interesting" transformations (check out the prehistoric, sedimentary stuff in the windows at Arthur Bryant's, for instance), but while it may acquire a certain cachet as an *objet d'art,* it loses a lot in subtleties of flavor and good, old-fashioned, Home Ec-approved safety.

A minor problem with chilling your condiments is that cold barbecue sauce is in an unnatural state and must be brought to room temperature before it's served (actually, for the proper temperature, just match whatever the thermometer read at four in the afternoon on last Aug. 12 wherever you live).

On the plus side, refrigerated sauces are the best justification imaginable for the little shelves that refrigerator-door manufacturers put in refrigerator doors. There is absolutely nothing like the sight of row upon row of secret sauces revealing themselves when that door slowly swings open, any of them ready for a curious sniff or fingertip. It's a poetic vision that simply crushes the nearest social climber who has invested all of his stock certificates in an expensive, effete wine cellar stocked with wines that have to "rest" for another seven years before they may be delicately decanted.

Of course, it's perhaps a bit unfair for a member in good standing of the Carnivore Club to lay such a shot of one-upmanship on a feeble, undernourished sort whose passions are restricted to fermented *grape juice,* for God's sake. The only truly worthy victims of a sauce collection shutdown are alleged barbecue connoisseurs unfortunate enough

---

PORKLORE ○ Sheep Dip

Harold P. "Big Bubba" Stainback of Jeffersontown, Ky., on barbecued mutton: "The only way I'd have sheep in my pit is if one happened to fall in there. I thought we must have eaten up all the sheep in World War II but there must have been two left someplace."

---

to have disagreed with one of your considered opinions on the subject.

There is a literally delicious moment that comes when you casually swing open the door to the fridge and inquire, "By the way, what do you think of that new three-alarm Firehouse No. 1?" You will watch as your slack-jawed acquaintance stares in miserable awe at your assemblage of sauces, salivating slightly in spite of himself. Try that with a dusty bottle of Bordeaux.

Naturally, there's a friendly side to all of this, too. A sort of Christmas-morning excitement attends the arrival of a new carton of mail-order sauce. Since many are sold in twelve-bottle cases, it helps to have some similarly afflicted friends to share the cost—and the sauce. And there are those wonderful surprise phone calls, too: "My Willingham's came in today; want to come over for ribs?"

MAIL-ORDER MANIA

The available variety of mail-order sauces is staggering—and ordering them can be habit forming. After you've been at it for a while, you may find yourself wondering about maybe getting a hold of a second refrigerator, just a plain white job down in the basement or out in the garage, just big enough to contain the collection. At least that way there might be room enough for your children to have milk again.

Here are some of the best sauces available through the mail. Shipping charges vary, and the sauce prices themselves may change, of course. But this is no time to start worrying about money. You can make car payments later; we're talking *sauce* here.

MAIL-ORDER SAUCE

o **Brazos Beef Emporium 2-Pot Bar-B-Que Sauce** Craig Conlee wants to put his hometown of Tabor, Texas, on the map, and his sauce is part of the plan. It's inspired by his grandmother's Brazos Valley cooking, much of which was done for jail inmates (because Grandfather Conlee was the county sheriff). The sauce is called "two-pot" because of the way it's made, in "two seperate pots, combined at just the right moment." A ketchup-based sauce with definite overtones of Worcestershire, it tingles with spices that are sunny but not sizzling. It's available in Thick, Lite, and mesquite-flavored Smokey, at $4.95, including shipping, for a 12-ounce bottle. The company also sells a couple of hot sauces, Caliente and Cowboy Cayenne, and a Red Meat Rub, as well as Fajitas Sop and Chicken Sop, two marinades or basting sauces, and even the little wooden-handled mops with which to sop them. It also sells mail-order barbecued brisket (see the next section on mail-order barbecue). The Emporium is at 700 S. Bryan St., Bryan, Texas 77803-3928. They will take credit card orders at (409) 776-0298.

o **Cattlebaron** This stuff has the classiest labels in the business—evocative cowpuncher paintings of real folks on real ranches by Fort Worth Western artist Bill Hall. The Cattlebaron folks like to think of their sauce as a work of art, too. Three varieties are available—Traditional, Mesquite, and Jalapeño Hot. Each is made with "nothing but the freshest ingredients" and is cooked right in the container you buy it in, a traditional home-canning jar. The sauce is marketed aggressively, which means you may find it in a gourmet food store in your area; it's even exported to Paris (France, not Texas). But it's also available by mail order for $23 per case of twelve 17-ounce jars, not including the UPS shipping charges. The Mesquite variety is a pleasant open-range recipe with a double-barreled dose of mesquite, but otherwise middle-of-the-road in terms of sweetness and sting. Order them all from Cattlebaron Foods Inc., Post Office Drawer 800037, Dallas, Texas 75380 (that's in the United States, for you folks in Paris).

o **Craig's Original Barbecue Sauce** The steamboat on the gold label isn't just there for looks. The sauce's inventor, Lawrence Craig, developed the sauce while working on a riverboat on the mighty Mississippi, before he opened up his family restaurant in DeValls Bluff, Ark. "It's not a sweet sauce, it's a pour-on-the-table sauce," says John Thomas, who works up the road in Brinkley, where the stuff is made. "It has no additives or water," Thomas brags, "and it has good things in it like oranges and apples." The sauce itself boasts an insinuating sting, with a smoky touch and a lot of tiny, tasty unidentified floating objects (shake well). It's available in Hot, Medium, and Mild, in a case of twelve of the 12.7-ounce bottles, all one variety or mixed-and-matched, for $15.60, plus shipping. Order from Cache River Bayou Deview Enterprises, Box 272, Brinkley, Ark. 72021.

o **Curley's** This stuff is the lava flow of barbecue sauces, dark, oozing, seriously smoky and molasses-sweet. People who consider chicken to be barbecue have been known to eat Curley's on it. If you're searching for a sauce with about as much smoke as Mt. Saint Helens, Curley's has Smoky, Hickory, and Mesquite versions. There's also a hot-and-spicy style that sends in its zing after a brief grace period, and it even has enough liquid smoke to set off your home alarm. You can get Curley's in cases of twelve 22-ounce bottles, with styles mixed and matched as you please. The price is $30, plus UPS shipping charges. Orders (and checks) are welcome at Curley's Famous Hickory Burgers

Inc., 915 S. Main St., P.O. Box 1244, Hutchinson, Kan. 67501. The hickory style also is available in a case of four one-gallon containers for those who really like to show off; it's $57.50, plus shipping.

o **Demetri's "America's Best" Gourmet Barbecue Sauce** "It's a Cadillac product; it's perfect," says Helen Nakos, whose husband, Demetri, developed the sauce twenty-eight years ago. "It's not a hot sauce, it's not sweet, not faked or gooped up. It has pure ingredients, no stuffers." Those ingredients include a little tomato, a little Worcestershire sauce, a little mustard, and some vinegar, lemon juice, and margarine. The result is a concoction that's long on flavor and short on singe, good enough to have been carted back to Sweden by traveling barbecue lovers. When you receive a bottle, it arrives with a half-hour barbecued chicken recipe that involves Coca-Cola and a frying pan. Bottles come in pint ($2) and quart ($3.50) sizes, shipping extra, no minimum order. You can order it from Demetri's Barbecue Sauce, 3560 Spring Valley Rd., Birmingham, Ala. 35223.

o **Everett & Jones "Super Q" Barbecue Sauce** Contrary to what you read in the papers, California is not just a land of sprouts and shark soup. There is Real Barbecue there, too. This sauce has won praises for its sweet but zingingly hot taste, as well as its luxuriously thick texture, suitable for slapping on ribs (at the last minute, please). It comes in Mild, Medium, and Hot. The Medium is mildly hot, so the Hot should be mildly amazing. Forget that it's available in Macy's. Forget that people in Volvos like it. Order a case of twelve 12-ounce jars for $35.40 (or two half-gallon jugs for $19.90), plus shipping, from Everett & Jones Barbecue, 2676 Fruitvale Ave., Oakland, Calif. 94602. Don't worry that it's too upscale to be good. Just keep telling yourself, "It's only from Oakland; it's only from Oakland."

o **Firehouse No. 1 Bar-B-Que Sauce** This sauce had its origins a couple of generations ago on a pushcart in Leavenworth, Kan. Now it's sold by a company in the foggy climes of San Francisco. A favorite of specialty food stores, the tomato-based sauce is available in three degrees of fieriness, from one-alarm to three-alarm. The beginner's grade is almost as bland as some of the ubiquitous grocery store stuff, but by the two-alarm level, you're starting to get into some interesting territory. And the triple-bell variety is just enough to tweak your tonsils without doing permanent damage; its kick is balanced with a robust roster of flavors, which include brown sugar, red wine vinegar, lemon juice, and garlic powder. It's available by the case for $36, plus shipping, from the Firehouse Bar-B-Q Sauce Co., 563 Castro St., San Francisco, Calif. 94114.

o **Gates & Son's Bar-B-Q Sauce** In Kansas City's pedigreed barbecue scene, there is Arthur Bryant's, which won't send out sauce mail order, and there is Gates & Son's, which will. Bryant's may have garnered more ink in the press, but Ollie Gates's sauce has soaked its share of napkins at several locations around the city. The stuff is packed with a balanced flavor that incorporates tomatoes, spices, a touch of vinegar, and a lot of hot. There are three versions available— regular, mild, and a newer no-salt recipe. It's sold by the case of twelve 18-ounce bottles for $31.63, including shipping and handling. Order from Gates & Son's Bar-B-Q, 4707 Paseo, Kansas City, Mo. 64110.

o **Hans Barbecue Sauce** You've got to love a sauce that says, "Made From a Famous Old Norwegian Recipe," especially when it comes from Oklahoma City. The sauce is bottled Hot or Medium Hot, and both varieties use nothing but fresh ingredients, following the recipe that Norwegian immigrant Hans Abrahamsen devised for his restaurant in 1929. Though not intensely incendiary, it has an unusual combination of sharp vinegar, mustard, and biting spice that makes it much more interesting than just a full-bore flame-out. You can get a bottle from Hans Barbecue, Inc., 4101 Northwest 10th St., Oklahoma City, Okla. 73107. An 8-ounce bottle goes for $2.50, plus $3.50 for shipping and handling. They stand ready to ship anything from one bottle (for the timid) to a truckload (for the true believer).

o **Johnny Harris Famous Barbecue Sauce** This peach of a Georgia sauce has something for everybody—a little shot of smoke, a splash of Worcestershire, a dab of ketchup, and a mouthful of down-home flavor in a sauce that splits the difference between a mustard recipe and the traditional ketchup style. Slapped on near the end of smoking time, it cooks up a pretty golden color. A little on the side at the table gives a tang that cuts through the smokiness of barbecued pork or chicken, the meats of choice. It would be derelict not to mention that this stuff won the 1985 Diddy-Wa-Diddy Barbecue Sauce Contest in Olathe, Kan. The sauce also is available in a Hickory Smoke version, but the regular is the preferred item. It is sold, appropriately enough, by Johnny Harris Famous Barbecue Sauce Co., 2801 Wicklow St., Savannah, Ga. 31404. It'll run you $14 for a sturdy cardboard "gift carton" of six 12-ounce bottles, including shipping. (It's $2 more when shipped west of the Mississippi River. And worth it.)

o **Hayward's Pit Bar-B-Que Sauce** One of the semi-innumerable sauces duking it out in the Kansas City area, Hayward's comes in pints ($1.75 each or $18 for a case of 12) and gallons ($12.10 each).

There's only one flavor, the one that Hayward Spears started cooking up about eighteen years ago, now served in one of the fanciest barbecue joints anywhere, complete with etched glass and a professionally tended lawn. The sauce itself is sweet and very tomatoey, containing both ketchup and tomato paste, but it has a delicate zap at the end. Hayward's is at 11051 Antioch, Overland Park, Kan. 66212.

o **D. L. Jardine's Chuck Wagon Recipe Barbecue Sauce** This very liquid concoction will add a little smoke, a little spice, and a shot of juicy flavor to your beef barbecue. It's mixed thin, so you can get away with slapping some on over the fire, but it's also suitable for pouring at the table. You can get it in Original, Hot, and Mesquite versions in various combinations. For $15.80 there's a four-pack of 13-ounce bottles of Original or a mixed version at the same price. For $10.75 you can order "Texas in a Box," which includes an 8-ounce bottle of Original, a packet of Texas chili fixings, and a bottle of Texas Champagne hot sauce. It's all available from D. L. Jardine's Texas Foods, Box 18868, Austin, Tex. 78760. Shipping charges are extra.

o **Lucious "The King" Newsom's Dry Rub** Lucious "The King" Newsom has a dry rub that works well on ribs. The mail-order address is Lucious The King's Southern Seasonings, 428 McCallie Ave., Chattanooga, Tenn. 37402. The price is $1.75 for a 2½ oz. pack or $16.68 for a dozen 2½ oz. packs. In both cases add $2.50 for shipping and handling.

o **M & S Meats Barbecue Sauce** This place sells a Montana Ranch Land Bar-B-Q Sauce that's like sucking on a sagebrush. The vinegary sauce has a dash of sweetness and an unusual flavor that will make you say, "Boy, I bet this stuff'd go great on an order of buffalo boneless roast." Which is convenient, since M & S sells that, too, as well as frozen buffalo chili in quarts. The company will pony express you an 8-ounce plastic squeeze bottle of sauce ($1) or a glass pint ($1.69) container, no minimum order, from M & S Meats, Highway 93 South, Rollins, Mont. 59931. Shipping is extra. You're on your own with the buffalo.

o **Maurice's Gourmet Barbecue Sauce** Maurice Bessinger probably wouldn't mind being the Ronald McDonald of barbecue. He'll not only air-express you his mustardy, greenish-gold "heirloom recipe" sauce in a variety of varieties, but also send packages of microwave-ready chopped pork barbeque, seven-at-once racks of ribs, and entire barbecued hams (see the next section on mail-order barbecue). He'll even send you an official $12 Maurice's Piggie Park knit shirt, with collar. In fact, Maurice's Flying Pig delivery service has its own toll-free 800 number, 1-800-MAURICE. The mail-ordering address is Maurice's Gourmet Barbecue, P.O. Box 6847, West Columbia, S.C. 29171. The sauce is available in Regular, Hickory, and Spicy Hot versions, and you can mix and match them. Your authors lean toward the Spicy Hot; it carries all the considerable virtues of the Regular, adding just a discreet crank of the heat meter. In all its variations, Maurice's is a masterly mustard-based sauce, unabashedly yellow and proud of it, but cut with a pleasingly complex mix of all-natural ingredients like apple cider, soy sauce, herbs, spices, and a dollop of ketchup, just to confuse the issue. A 16-ounce bottle costs $6 (including shipping and handling), a three-pack (with the varieties of your choice) is $12, a six-pack $18, and a 12-bottle case $28. Serious junkies also can get a case of four one-gallon jugs for $59.

o **Metro Marketing Sauces and Spices** There are so many items on the Metro Marketing smorgasbord, a person could wreck his diet just reading about them. Take the Kansas City 3-Pack—a nifty, $19.95 set of Kansas City sauces that shows up in a slick "gift box" complete with instruction booklet. Carolyn Wells and the flame-broiled fanatics at MM make the selection of sauces for you from some of K.C.'s finest; you can hardly lose. You can get a similar gift box of Memphis-style stuff, too. There's K.C. Masterpiece "Private Stock" sauce, a $4.95 "gourmet" version of Dr. Rich Davis's mass-marketed sauce. Also on the agenda: Memphis BBQ and Grill Seasoning ($4); K.C. Rib Doctor Blue Ribbon BBQ Seasoning ($6.95); and People's Choice barbecue sauce ($4.95) and barbecue rub ($5.95). We won't even mention the wild game seasoning, the spice samplers, the other gift boxes, and the Al Lawson Custom-Built BBQ Hardware Collection. All the details—and all the seasonings—are available from Metro Marketing, 11514 Hickman Mills Drive, Kansas City, Mo. 64134. All prices are postpaid.

o **Miso Sauce** Made by American Natural Foods, Inc., this may not be barbecue sauce in the classic sense, but we're including it because it's a genuine rarity—a macrobiotic sauce that's billed as downright healthy. The thin, tangy concoction has a "secret ingredi-ent" that could hold its own in the world of barbecue B.S.: fermented soybean paste, called "miso." Developed in Japan centuries ago, it's a mash of soybeans that is sometimes fermented for months, even years, to make a yogurtlike paste claimed to aid digestion and strengthen the heart. This stuff may seem to have all the charm of a spoonful of castor oil, but don't be misled: Its perky fresh-vegetable flavor is balanced with a little garlic juice here and a little toasted sesame oil there for a pleasant, mild mix of nuttiness and tang. And it's filled to its headband with ingredients like apple cider vinegar, barley malt, sea salt, and another ingredient you don't see in a lot of barbecue sauces—natural seaweed extract. It's available in a 10-ounce bottle for $3.99, plus $1.95 shipping for orders under $10. Order it from the Mountain Arc Trading Co., 120 Southeast Ave., Fayetteville, Ark. 72701.

o **Missouri Classic Bar-B-Que Sauce** This rich tomato sauce is subtly smoky and not too sweet, perhaps because it skips cane sugar and makes use of brown sugar and honey instead. It may have a "classic" name, but it comes from plain, ol' Johnny's Smoke Stak in Rolla, Mo. Wendy, who works there and ought to know, said, "We've got kids that put it on everything 'cept cereal." (Actually, it might go rather well with corn flakes.) In a major blow for decisiveness, it comes in only one variety, available in 32-ounce bottles in batches of 6 for $17.10 or 12 for $31.80, plus shipping. Order it from Johnny's Smoke Stak, 201 W. Highway 72, Rolla, Mo. 65401.

o **Moonlite's Bar-B-Que Sauce** If you're planning to have barbecued mutton soon (and who isn't?), this is the place to write for truly authentic barbecue dip. Smack in the middle of muttondom in western Kentucky, the Moonlite is the largest restaurant in Owensboro, a town that wolfs down anywhere from 30,000 to 100,000 pounds of mutton a week. Ken Bosley, who owns the restaurant along with his parents, says, "After the meat is cooked, we serve a combination of three sauces: black dip, a tomato-based sauce that is sweet, and a hot sauce." Actually, there's another available by mail, as well—the Thick & Spicy Bar-B-Que Sauce, sweet, flavorful, and tomatoey ($1.89 per pint). The Barbecue Dip, a watery Worcestershire-and-brown sugar concoction suitable for basting or flavoring mutton or beef, is $1.29 per pint. The Barbecue Sauce, a middle-of-the-roader recommended for pork, costs $1.39 per pint; and the Very Hot Sauce, which is suitable for chemical warfare, costs $3 a pint. This last variety is made of pepper, more pepper, and vodka, and will turn you into a contralto in ten seconds. UPS shipping is extra from the Moonlite Bar-B-Que Inn, 2708 Parrish Ave., Owensboro, Ky. 42301.

o **Ollie's World's Best Barbecue Sauce** Ollie's is a fourth-generation sauce developed by Ollie McClung in 1926 and worked on by his descendants in Birmingham, Ala. It's a vinegar-based sauce with nary a tomato in it, just sugar, spices, salt, and margarine. It'll make your taste buds stand up and say howdy—and in about three seconds yell for help. At Ollie's, they use it as a baste or sauce. A flask would also come in handy for actors who need to shed real tears for the camera. It costs $1.15 per pint, plus shipping and associated charges. A 24-ounce bottle goes for $1.65 plus, a half-gallon for $3.50 plus, and a gallon for $6.50 plus. Order from Ollie's World's Best Barbecue, 515 University Blvd., Birmingham, Ala. 35205.

○ **Rendezvous Barbecue Sauce** The Rendezvous is rightly named for its leagues of Memphis-area fans. It sells sauce in an 8-ounce bottle for $5.95, including shipping—and a 4-ounce jar of dry seasoning for the same price. Garlic and chili powder stand out in the latter, which you can apply to ribs, chicken, or sausage before cooking. The sauce is more flavorful than resolutely hot, thick yet tangy with vinegar. Order from the Rendezvous, 52 S. Second St., Memphis, Tenn. 38103. Or call the toll-free line between 10:30 A.M. and 4 P.M., Tuesday through Friday: 1-800-524-5554 (after the tone, punch in BBCUE).

○ **Rudolph's Barbecue Sauce** A lot of Chicago's ribs never make it into the mouths of Windy City residents, since tons of them are shipped each year to the Minneapolis home of this barbecue chain founded in 1975 by Greek immigrant Jimmy Theros. Rudolph's is named after the silent-movie star, not the reindeer, by the way. Victorious in 1983 and 1985 at Cleveland's National Rib Cook-Off, the restaurant's approved technique is to rub spices onto ribs that have been allowed to marinate for about three days before being cooked. The sauce doesn't go on until the last minute. The sauce also goes out through the mails. What's it like? "It's not tomatoey, there's some vinegar, and it doesn't make you sweat," says Sandra Maxwell, who sells it. You can send Sandy your hard-earned $5 for an 18-ounce bottle (or $6 for a 28-ounce bottle), including shipping, to Rudolph's Bar-B-Que, 2110 Lyndale Ave. South, 2nd fl., Minneapolis, Minn. 55405. Make checks out to Rudolph's.

○ **Santa Cruz Chili Barbecue Sauce** Considering its pedigree, it shouldn't be surprising that this slow-simmered sauce rides in with chilis blazing. Its Mexican heritage should offer an interesting change-of-pace to anyone who grew up with gringoque. Buy a case of twelve 12-ounce bottles for $29.47 (including shipping and handling) from the Santa Cruz Chili & Spice Co., P.O. Box 177, Tumacacori, Ariz. 85640.

○ **Scott's Famous Barbecue Sauce** This is a lively North Carolina–style sauce cooked up originally by the Reverend A. W. Scott and patented in 1946 by his son, Alvin Martell Scott. It features lots of tart vinegar and absolutely no ketchup. It's available by mail from Scott's at 121 Williams St., Goldsboro, N.C. It's available in a six-pack of 6-ounce plastic bottles for $3, plus shipping. It's also available in a case of twelve 10-ounce glass bottles for $9 or a case of twelve 16-ounce bottles for $10.80, plus shipping.

o **Selmon Bros. Fine Bar-B-Q Sauce** This thick sauce will lay a Wichita wallop on you, especially the recommended "Hot" version. For a complete shower of adjectives about this luscious stuff, see the Selmon Bros. capsule in the "Kansas" section. Let's just say that if the garlic and onion don't get you, the smoke or the anchovies will. It's available for $1.40 a pint, plus UPS shipping, from Selmon Bros. Bar-B-Q, 300 S. Greenwich Rd., Wichita, Kan. 67207.

o **Show-Me Liquid Smoke Bar-B-Q Sauce** If you've been looking for a sauce with a pH of 3, here's your baby. It's mixed up in "the only basement approved by the Missouri Department of Public Health" by retired professor and veterinary pathologist Harry H. Berrier. Actually, the pH, like everything else about this dense, smoky sauce, is carefully considered. "Bacteria, including the kind that causes botulism, will not grow in a medium of pH 4.6 or below," he explains, so the sauce needs no refrigeration, even after opening. He is also quick to point out it has no extenders, not even a drop of water. As a result, it's a dusky, ketchupy sauce that's almost a concentrate. Aside from being rich and delicious, it's worth ordering just to read the recipes on the label, which are printed in type that is the size of an atom. You can order it a lot of ways, from a single 21-ounce bottle ($2.75 plus UPS shipping) to a case of four 1-gallon jugs ($37.50 plus shipping). Write to Harry H. Berrier, 1250 Cedar Grove Blvd. South, R. 13, Columbia, Mo. 65201.

o **Smokey's Real Pit Barbecue Sauce** This is a good, old-fashioned, ketchup-based sauce that was good and old-fashioned enough to be one of the winners of the Diddy-Wa-Diddy Barbecue Sauce Contest in Olathe, Kan. It's available in three temperature zones: Mild, which is genuinely temperate; Medium, which is starting to get a bit subtropical; and Outrageously Hot, which is pure jungle sizzle. It's big-city sauce from 230 Ninth Ave., New York, N.Y. 10001, but Josh Lewin prefers for you to call in orders at (201) 861-7213. It's $4 per 12-ounce bottle (minimum of a case), and the different styles can be mixed and matched as requested. Shipping is extra.

o **Wicker's Barbecue Cooking Sauce** We're talking REAL "cooking" here, as in slapping sauce all over a slab of meat while it basks in the inferno of a barbecue grill. Old Peck Wicker's sauce is custommade for that, mixed without a pinch of sugar or a dab of tomatoes, so there's nothing to burn into a coating of cinders on the meat. The recipe for this Missouri boot heel basting favorite takes a vinegar base and adds spices (secret, of course) until arriving at a sharp and sincere medium-hot. Its watery consistency makes it a good choice for marinades, as well as for basting. However, the company doesn't take any chances, also recommending Wicker's for everything from tenderizing meat and making gravy to boiling shrimp and goosing a Bloody Mary. You may do with it what you like; at seventy calories per bottle, you could even drink the stuff straight with a clean conscience. At least you won't be killing your diet. It's available for about $9.25 for a six-pack of 28-ounce bottles (plus shipping) from Wicker, Inc., Box 126, Hornersville, Mo. 63855. Also available are mesquite-flavor and low-sodium versions, and a sauce mixed more for the table, Wicker's Thicker, which is just as devoid of sweetness as the original and just as vinegar-spicy when its afterburners kick in.

○ **Wilber's Barbecue Sauce** The motto on the concoction created in 1962 by Wilber Shirley is "It's Spicy Good," and Wilber is not a man to lie. The sauce is a North Carolina vinegar-based style, so the first impression is a pleasantly sour taste, followed shortly thereafter by a puckery tartness and finally a little fire. The various red and black peppers are used with discretion; this is a well-balanced and reasonably civilized splash of a sauce, suited for basting as well as tasting. In fact, there's a recipe for basting a turkey printed right on the label. It's available in a case of twelve 10-ounce "shaker" bottles for $12, plus shipping, from WWW Associates, Inc., P.O. Box 1155, Goldsboro, N.C. 27530.

○ **Willingham's WHAM Sauce** This sauce can claim back-to-back victories as Grand Champion of the Memphis in May barbecue festival, not to mention a near-sweep and Grand Champion award at the American Royal contest in Kansas City. And anytime you can get judges in Memphis and Kansas City to agree on anything, that's news. The sauces are sold to the public at wholesale prices. "You have to pay those extra shipping costs," explained John Willingham. There are three varieties of sauce, a flavorful Mild, a lively Cajun Hot, and a scalp-tingling Hot Stuff for Big Kids Only. The first two run $31.99, plus shipping, for a case of twelve 20-ounce containers; the Hot Stuff goes for $33.26. Also available are dry-rub seasonings in the same varieties—$39.02 for a case of twelve 14-ounce packages of Mild, $42.12 for Cajun Hot, and $37.07 for a case of itty-bitty 3.5-ounce containers of Hot Stuff for Big Kids Only. "That's small," said Willingham, "but it's dynamite. Believe me, it's big enough." We tried it. We believe. Would-be believers should write to Willingham's World's Champion Bar-B-Que, 2707 S. Perkins, Memphis, Tenn. 38118.

○ **Zarda Bar-B-Q Sauce** Well, you made it to the Zs in this list, and your reward is Zarda sauce. This stuff hails from Blue Springs,

Mo., not far from the barbecue hotbed of Kansas City, and Zarda isn't afraid to take on the big boys. It's a flavor-packed sauce, with tomatoey richness cut with the tang of vinegar and a healthy shot of sweetness from molasses. You can find it sold in supermarkets in the area, so you might conclude that you're looking at another boring, mass-marketed snoozer. You would be quite wrong, of course. This isn't a sauce for fire-breathers; it comes in "original" and "mild," and the original will be mild enough for mom. It's sold in a case of twelve 19-ounce bottles for $24.95, including shipping. If you're planning to fill your hot tub, you might consider ordering the 4½-gallon container ($21, plus shipping) or the 5-gallon "pail" ($26.25, plus shipping). Place your orders with Zarda Bar-B-Q, 214 N. 7 Hiway, Blue Springs, Mo. 64105.

MAIL-ORDER BARBECUE

Mail-order barbecue hasn't been around long enough to have the reputation of, say, mail-order brides or mail-order dentures.

In fact, it doesn't have any reputation.

But several places are starting out to give it a good reputation—including Gridley's, Willingham's, and Charlie Vergos' Rendezvous in Memphis, and Maurice's Piggie Park in West Columbia, S.C. There's even a way to get ready-to-thaw beef brisket from Texas.

Up front, we have to tell you: Mail-order barbecue is not the same as being there. But it is the next best thing to being there. Plus, we must consider our friends in North Dakota and Wisconsin who don't have barbecue to speak of.

To prove they're serious, some of these places even have toll-free 800 numbers. Gridley's spokesman, Randy Nickell, says the company started the toll-free phone service because: "We would get call after call asking if we could ship barbecue. Then we would have to race out to the airport to make a commercial flight. Lots of times they would be late. So we started looking at getting an 800 number. Federal Express being based here, and their reputation for being on time, we decided to go with them for the shipping. Now one call does it all." That one call is 1-800-222-7427. If that's too hard to remember, then remember it this way: 1-800-222-RIBS.

Of course, John Willingham would prefer you to remember it his way: 1-800-227-RIBS. And the Rendezvous is waiting by the phone at 1-800-524-5554 (on this one, you get a computer tone, and then you have to punch in BBCUE).

Maurice's Piggie Park number is easier: It's just 1-800-MAURICE.

The Gridley's 800 number was started in July 1986, and one of the first customers was Memphis native Cybill Shepherd. Nickell says the Christmas season is particularly busy for the 800 line. "We shipped out $2,700 worth in one day right before the holidays. I thought I was going to have to send out a crisis order for dry ice."

Gridley's is pure Memphis-style barbecue: pulled pork topped with a tomato-and-vinegar-based sauce that is tangy without being tart. The sauce was developed in the early seventies by the late Clyde Gridley, his wife, and five daughters. Before opening his own barbecue restaurant, Gridley had worked for Loeb's Barbecue in Memphis.

There are two ways to serve the barbecue. You can dish it out on paper plates or you can serve it on buns. If you want to eat it on a bun, you'll need to buy buns. The bread that Gridley's sends you is a pack of their own Brown 'n' Serve French rolls. French rolls are fine for the French, but they are not for barbecue sandwiches. Take the French rolls and give them to the poor.

Your Gridley's package is also minus two other Memphis barbecue musts: cole slaw and barbecue beans. Cole slaw won't keep. And if you've ever picked up a large can of beans, you know why Gridley's doesn't ship beans. Beans are heavy. It would cost a fortune to ship beans Federal Express. You can buy both at the grocery when you get the buns.

o **Gridley's** 1-800-222-RIBS. For $80 (Mastercard or Visa accepted), Gridley's will ship you five pounds of pork, along with 16 ounces of sauce and a pack of rolls. For $85 you can get three slabs of ribs, plus the bread and sauce. And you'll have it this time tomorrow, courtesy of Federal Express. (Meat to be delivered on Saturday has a $10 delivery surcharge, and no deliveries are made on Sunday.) Orders will arrive frozen and packed in dry ice. Five pounds of barbecue makes about 20 to 25 sandwich-sized servings.

o **Maurice's Flying Pig Barbeque Service** 1-800-MAURICE. Maurice Bessinger suggests hash over rice as the ideal side dish to his South Carolina barbecue. And he even includes it in his dinners for two, along with chopped-ham barbecue and barbecued ribs. An order of eight dinners for two sells for $100, postpaid. There are a multitude of mail-order variations, with a get-acquainted special that includes a little bit of about everything for $79.99. The chopped-ham barbecue sometimes is sold in little eight-ounce supermarket-style packages (suitable for microwaving) at 12 for $76. Or three one-pound packages of the stuff go for $39.50. Before we mention that he also sells sauce, hams, and racks of ribs, it might be good to point out that you can call and ask for a mail-order menu or the delivery details.

○ **Charlie Vergos' Rendezvous** From 10:30 A.M. till 4 P.M., Tuesday through Friday, you can call 1-800-524-5554 (then, after the computer tone, punch in BBCUE). These folks are in the sauce biz (see previous section), but they'll also Federal Express ribs—orders will arrive by 10:30 the next morning. The minimum order is 5 half-slabs of ribs ($85, including shipping, seasoning, and sauce); 10 half-slabs go for $140.

○ **Willingham's** 1-800-227-RIBS. John H. Willingham's place in Memphis sells sauce, smokers, and the Willingham's World Champion Rib Pack, which includes 4 full slabs of ribs, plus hot and mild sauce, for $49.95, shipping included. Call by 8 P.M. and the pack will be sent overnight by Federal Express and delivered by 10 A.M. on any day except Sunday ($10 extra if it arrives on Saturday). All you need is a major charge card; you don't even have to be wearing a bib.

○ **Brazos Beef Emporium** (409) 776-0298. This place doesn't have a toll-free number, but it's in Bryan, in the Brazos Valley area of east-central Texas, so you ought to be glad it even has a phone line. Owner Craig Conlee takes aged choice beef brisket, the mandated meat in Texas, smokes it over mesquite and then ships it off by UPS, vacuum-packed and accompanied by a bottle of the Emporium's 2-Pot Bar-B-Que sauce. The six-pound cuts are sent (when weather dictates, in a cooler, packed in dry ice) for $44.65 delivered. Instructions are included for warming the meat (one way is to boil it for thirty-five

---

PORKLORE ○ Hog Wild

Lexington Senior High (North Carolina), which was the winner of the 1984 Cheer-Off at the Lexington Barbecue Festival, won out over four other squads with this cheer:
"Get pork, big bones and ribs,
"Get extra lean,
"Lexington's home barbecue is really keen.
"So chow down everybody,
"Get in with the best,
"The barbecue from Lexington outshines the rest.
"Hey, outshines the rest.
"Are you ready to chow down?
"Yes, we are."

minutes in the bag it's packed in) and even for carving it. Eating it should be no problem.

MAIL-ORDER WOOD

City dwellers with a taste for wood-smoked cooking had better have their sources for the raw materials. After the bunk beds are burned up and the credenza is gone, it's generally not considered good citizenship to start skulking around likely-looking trees in the park late at night. Look, nobody made these people move to the city, and if they finally have arrived at the point where they have to mail-order wood in order to fuel a halfway decent barbecue, well, that's just too bad, isn't it? You wouldn't believe how inconvenient it is for someone in Lexington, N.C., to see a good opera. It all averages out.

At any rate, mail-order wood for barbecue junkies is definitely available, from these (and similar) places:

o **American Wood Products** A fellow out in Kansas by the name of Duke Wheeler would be happy to pack you off a parcel of chips or chunks. He sells to what he calls "the serious patio chef," as well as to the commercial and restaurant markets. By the way, anyone who has his wood chips sent to him from Kansas is by definition a "serious patio chef." Either that, or he's engaged in some serious one-upsmanship.

The prices, however, are low enough to make ordering pieces of wood through the mail seem almost sensible. As last quoted, a one-pound bag of apple, cherry, grape, or sassafras wood chips costs $3.95 postpaid. A 3½-pound bag of mesquite or hickory chips runs $4.95 postpaid. And a five-pound bag of mesquite or hickory chunks goes for $6.50 postpaid. Send check or money order, plus an address where UPS can deliver, to American Wood Products, 9540 Riggs, Overland Park, Kan. 66212.

o **Char-Broil** Wood also is available from here in mesquite, alder, hickory, sassafras, and grapevine. This place also is a source for Jack Daniel's Barrel Chips, a two-pound bag of 25-year-old bourbon-flavored hardwood used in making the whiskey. Alder (best with fish and poultry), mesquite, and hickory come in two-pound bags of chips for $4.50 or five-pound bags of chunks for $7.50. The bags of grapevine chips and sassafras cost $6.95. Write Char-Broil at 1037 Front Ave., P.O. Box 1300, Columbus, Ga. 31993—or call toll-free at 1-800-241-8981. And until the delivery arrives, one may consider burning one's umbrella stand.

BARBECUE
A Dying Art?

They may cook pork shoulders or beef briskets. They may pull the meat or slice it, drown it in a sweet sauce or serve it unadorned. But one strand unites the Early Scotts of west Tennessee and the Grace Proffitts of east Tennessee, the Sarah Tooleys of south Kentucky and the Wayne Monks of North Carolina, the men and women we told you about in this book. They are practitioners of a dying art: cooking barbecue.

Technology has made the barbecue process easier, but these artists refuse to take the shortcuts. "When you start cutting corners, finding a faster way to do it, you're hurting yourself," says Monk, owner of Lexington Barbecue No. 1 in Lexington, N.C. Monk builds his sauce from scratch, never using a commercial product when he can make it up himself. He shakes his head when told about cooks who use Worcestershire sauce as a base for their barbecue dip. "You don't have to use that stuff. You can make it yourself." Early Scott of Lexington, Tenn., grows all the vegetables for his sauce. And when he is cooking, Scott sleeps in his smokehouse, so he can keep the fire at exactly the right level.

Why do they still cook barbecue the old-fashioned way, the hard way, when it would be much easier to use commercial ingredients and modern conveniences? Simple. As Early Scott told us earlier in this book, it's a matter of pride. "You see that sign out there?" Scott said as he pointed to the marquee over his stand. "That's my name on that sign." That's what this book has been about: the kind of pride that produces a personal art. The teenager who slings hamburgers at the local burger franchise doesn't care if that's the best hamburger he can make. With barbecue people it's different. It's not just cooking barbecue, it's cooking the best barbecue. And that isn't a science. Temperature probes, oven gauges, and heat-flow diagrams can't take the place of a cook who cares.

"It's not something you learn in a day, either," said Hugh Knoth of Knoth's Barbecue in Kuttawa, Ky. The barbecue artists we talked to didn't learn to cook barbecue by reading a book or a manual. They learned by cooking. And they learned to trust themselves more than a gauge. "Most of these boys around here go by how long they can hold their hand on the fire," said Dennis Rogers, columnist for *The News*

& *Observer* in Raleigh. "They know if they can't hold it on more than, say, two seconds, then it's ready."

"We didn't have no thermometers in the old days," recalled Leo Phelps of Oak Ridge, N.C., who has been cooking barbecue for half a century. "We just felt the fire." Phelps and Jack Dempsey of Ty Ty, Ga., and a few others still cook that way. "I open the door and put my hand on the barbecue," said Dempsey. "That's how I can tell if it's ready."

There are gauges to tell when to add one ingredient, electric motors to turn the meat, and automatic brushes to baste it. But they haven't invented a machine yet that can taste. That's where the art comes in. And the only way the art of barbecue will be saved is if it is valued.

Perhaps a growing love of good barbecue can keep the flame burning a while longer.

Index of Restaurants and Towns

ARE WE CRAZY?

The two of us have scoured the country, looking for America's best barbecue, and we think we found it. But maybe you think we're as dumb as two posts, that we missed *your* favorite joint, which just happens to sell the best meat that ever slipped between mortal lips. Maybe you should tell us about it. Maybe we'll go there and see who's crazy—you or us. Maybe it'll make the next edition of this book. Here's a handy form:

Dear Vince and Greg:
    You're crazy. The best barbecue joint I've ever found is

_____

It's the best because _____

_____

_____

Here's the address (phone, owner, etc.) _____

_____

                                        Yours truly,

                        _____

                        (ADDRESS)

                        _____

                        (PHONE)

☐ **P.S.** I'd like a copy of **Real Barbecue News,** a hot update with more inside info. I'm enclosing $2 for postage and stuff and mailing it to P.O. Box 30, Prospect, Ky. 40059, so it'd better be good.